Quotation and Cultural Meaning in Twentieth-Century Music

Throughout the twentieth century, musicians frequently incorporated quotations from works by other musicians into their own compositions and performances. When a musician borrows from a piece, he or she draws not only upon a melody but also upon the cultural associations of the original piece. By working with and altering a melody, a musician also transforms those associations. This book explores that vibrant practice, examining how musicians have used quotation to participate in the cultural dialogues sustained around such areas as race, childhood, madness, and the mass media. The focus of this study is broad, discussing pieces in a spectrum of musical styles (classical, experimental, jazz, and popular) as well as works in the other arts. Part of the young and quickly growing field of study examining musical borrowing, this book takes an important step in discussing the wider cultural ramifications of quotation.

DAVID METZER is Associate Professor at the University of British Columbia, Vancouver. He has published a wide range of articles on twentieth-century music.

New perspectives in music history and criticism

GENERAL EDITORS:
JEFFREY KALLBERG, ANTHONY NEWCOMB AND RUTH SOLIE

This series explores the conceptual frameworks that shape or have shaped the ways in which we understand music and its history, and aims to elaborate structures of explanation, interpretation, commentary, and criticism which make music intelligible and which provide a basis for argument about judgements of value. The intellectual scope of the series is broad. Some investigations will treat, for example, historiographical topics, others will apply cross-disciplinary methods to the criticism of music, and there will also be studies which consider music in its relation to society, culture, and politics. Overall, the series hopes to create a greater presence for music in the ongoing discourse among the human sciences.

PUBLISHED TITLES

Leslie C. Dunn and Nancy A. Jones (eds.), *Embodied Voices: Representing Female Vocality in Western Culture*
Downing A. Thomas, *Music and the Origins of Language: Theories from the French Enlightenment*
Thomas S. Grey, *Wagner's Musical Prose*
Daniel K. L. Chua, *Absolute Music and the Construction of Meaning*
Adam Krims, *Rap Music and the Poetics of Identity*
Annette Richards, *The Free Fantasia and the Musical Picturesque*
Richard Will, *The Characteristic Symphony in the Age of Haydn and Beethoven*
Christopher Morris, *Reading Opera between the Lines: Orchestral Interludes and Cultural Meaning from Wagner to Berg*
Emma Dillon, *Medieval Music-Making and the 'Roman de Fauvel'*
David Yearsley, *Bach and the Meanings of Counterpoint*
Alexander Rehding, *Hugo Riemann and the Birth of Modern Musical Thought*
David Metzer, *Quotation and Cultural Meaning in Twentieth-Century Music*

Quotation and Cultural Meaning in Twentieth-Century Music

DAVID METZER

CAMBRIDGE
UNIVERSITY PRESS

PUBLISHED BY THE PRESS SYNDICATE OF THE UNIVERSITY OF CAMBRIDGE
The Pitt Building, Trumpington Street, Cambridge CB2 1RP, United Kingdom

CAMBRIDGE UNIVERSITY PRESS
The Edinburgh Building, Cambridge CB2 2RU, UK
40 West 20th Street, New York, NY 10011–4211, USA
477 Williamstown Road, Port Melbourne, VIC 3207, Australia
Ruiz de Alarcón 13, 28014 Madrid, Spain
Dock House, The Waterfront, Cape Town 8001, South Africa

http://www.cambridge.org

First published 2003

Printed in the United Kingdom at the University Press, Cambridge

Typeface Palatino 10/12 pt   *System* LATEX 2$_\varepsilon$ [TB]

A catalogue record for this book is available from the British Library

Library of Congress Cataloguing in Publication data

ISBN 0 521 82509 1 hardback

CONTENTS

PLATES

ACKNOWLEDGEMENTS

It is fitting that a book about musical borrowing begin by declaring its debts. As with any such undertaking, they are many and cannot all be mentioned. A large debt is owed to J. Peter Burkholder, who has been a key figure in shaping the growing field of borrowing studies. I have not only benefited from the work that he has done in that field but also from the personal encouragement he has offered. It is one of the great pleasures of academia when two scholars working in the same nook and cranny can so freely discuss and exchange ideas. I am also grateful to Arved Ashby, Matthew Head, Richard Kurth, Vera Micznik, and Gregory Miller for their lively and shrewd comments on chapter drafts. My thanks also to my parents for their undying support. Leora Zimmer provided invaluable assistance with the musical examples. Penny Souster has patiently shepherded me through this new process, answering all my questions, no matter how small, and pointing me in the right directions. I have greatly enjoyed working with Kathryn Puffett and have benefited much from her gimlet eyes and guiding wit.

I would also like to acknowledge the support that this project has received from a grant provided by the Social Sciences and Humanities Research Council of Canada.

Earlier versions of Chapters 1 and 2 appeared in *19th Century Music* (1997) and *Black Music Research Journal* (1997). © 1997 by The Regents of the University of California; reprinted from *19th Century Music* 211 by permission of the University of California Press. I would like to thank BMRJ for giving me permission to include a revised version of my article in this book.

Copyright clearance for musical and literary examples was secured from the following sources

Ives, "Tom Sails Away." © 1935 Merion Music, Inc. Used by
   permission of the publisher
Ives, Fourth Violin Sonata. © 1942 (renewed) by Associated Music
   Publishers, Inc. (BMI); international copyright secured; all rights
   reserved. Reprinted by permission

Ellington and Miley, "Black and Tan Fantasy." © 1927 (renewed 1954) and assigned to Famous Music Corporation and EMI Mills Music Inc. in the USA; rights for the world outside the USA controlled by EMI Mills Music Inc.; international copyright secured; all rights reserved

Schoenberg, "Am Wegrand." Used by permission of Belmont Music Publishers

Schoenberg, *Erwartung*. Used by permission of Belmont Music Publishers

T. S. Eliot, *The Waste Land*. Used by permission of Faber and Faber

Introduction

By the night of 28 April 1964 in Stuttgart, the fables had grown quite long. On this last show of a European tour, Charles Mingus had once again chosen his *Fables of Faubus*. Inspired and driven by Mingus, the bassist's quintet turned the piece into an almost forty-five minute tale, quite a change from the first recorded performance in 1959, which clocked in at around eight minutes.[1] The duration may have changed but the satiric spirit remained the same; it had even deepened over the intervening years. Conceived of in 1957, the piece bit at Governor Orval Faubus of Arkansas for calling in National Guard troops to block the integration of public schools. Seven years later, with Faubus still in office and the Civil Rights struggle having escalated, there were apparently more fables to tell. What Mingus added to the original work and what makes up a large part of that forty-five minutes were bits of American folk songs, many of them celebrating the supposed glory days of the Old South. Mingus especially drew upon those tunes in his solo, distorting them so as to expose the warped recollections in which that glory was enshrined. For instance, after improvising on the main theme with the rhythm section, he launches into a solo with a bit of "Dixie." No sooner has Mingus evoked the "land of cotton" than he quickly and unpredictably cuts off the melody, leaving it like a severed ribbon. What comes next is just as much of a surprise as the appearance of "Dixie." Mingus casts aside the torn tune and plays a brief flourish full of virtuosic figures, timbral shifts, and blue notes. With one phrase, he has created a sound world of his own, one inspired by African-American idioms. That world would be unthinkable in the Old South of "Dixie," as would be all the other fables offered by Mingus.

On the night of 22 April 1969 in London, the songs continued to come one after another. That evening marked the premiere of Peter Maxwell Davies's *Eight Songs for a Mad King*. The work was inspired by a small mechanical organ owned by George III with which the King attempted to teach birds to sing. It was the King's singing that shocked concert-goers that night. Maxwell Davies has the singer playing that part writhe in painful and grotesque sounds. For example, the King begins the

---

[1] The original recording was on the *Mingus Ah Um* LP (reissued on CD as Columbia CK 65512). A CD recording of the Stuttgart performance can be found on *Charlie Mingus, Live in Stuttgart! 1964* (unique jazz RKO 1038).

1

seventh song with the opening phrase of the aria "Comfort Ye" from Handel's *Messiah*. Little comfort is provided as he slides from a spectral falsetto to caterwauling to bass-voice croaking. Even more disturbing is the kitschy foxtrot that follows the crooked Handel. Here is music that evokes madness in the late twentieth century, but that would have certainly been viewed as "mad" – that is, if it could be imagined in the first place – during the time of George III.

Fables of Faubus and *Eight Songs for a Mad King* do not usually brush up against each other in the scholarly literature, or anywhere for that matter. The two seem to have little in common. The above sketches, though, point out a few similarities. Both had important performances or premieres in Europe during the 1960s, and the two also mock men in authority, be it a racist governor or an insane monarch. The most obvious link, as described above, is the use of quotation, but even here the ties appear slight. The two works are in very different idioms and the quoted materials come from even more contrasting repertories: Southern American folk songs and Baroque oratorio. Moreover, they handle those materials in distinct ways. The jazz piece nonchalantly unfurls "Dixie" and then minces it with a bluesy retort. The music theater composition, on the other hand, heavily distorts the Handel aria and then hops into a realm of stylistic perversity.

These differences obscure one substantial similarity. In both works, quotation performs as a cultural agent – that is, it participates in and shapes cultural discourses. That role is intrinsic to the gesture. When a musician borrows from a piece, he or she draws upon not only a melody but also the cultural associations of that piece. Just as with a melody, a musician can work with and transform those associations. Those manipulations provide a means to comment on cultural topics and to reconfigure fundamental cultural relationships. That Mingus's "Dixie" quotation comments on the pressing issues of the day is clear enough; what is less obvious is how the work rises above a protest shout and touches upon cultural relationships, particularly that between whiteness and blackness. Through that borrowing and others, *Fables* presents a specific view of that pair, one in which whiteness, as depicted in the lightly tossed-off "Dixie," appears as a superficial and self-deluded realm. On the other hand, blackness, evoked in the following flourish, has timbral and melodic depths as well as the ability to fight back against whiteness, an ability displayed by the brusque ripping of the quotation.

The Handel borrowing in Maxwell Davies's work reaches into madness, a realm that, as Foucault demonstrated, knots together different cultural strands.[2] *Eight Songs* rips out one particular strand from that

---

[2] Michel Foucault, *Madness and Civilization: A History of Insanity in the Age of Reason*, trans. Richard Howard (New York: Vintage Books, 1988).

knot, remembrance of the past, and displays how excessive reminiscence can be crippling. With that point, the work interacts with another basic cultural relationship, the bond between past and present. Through the spectacle of a mad king, Maxwell Davies comments on the imposing weight that music from previous centuries places on contemporary musical life and how the mass of that tradition can lead to creative anguish, distortions, and even silence.[3] Mingus's work also touches upon the relationship between past and present, although shaping it in very different terms. His quotation of "Dixie" and other tunes rejects the past of the grand Old South, and his own celebratory virtuosic licks proclaim a present free from the violence and pain upon which that era was erected.

This book explores how quotation has served as a cultural agent in twentieth-century music. As the above two examples illustrate, this study looks at the role of quotation in a wide range of styles, including classical, experimental, jazz, and popular idioms. In addition, works from other arts are brought into the discussion. An account of related borrowing practices in painting, film, and poetry enhances the study of musical quotation by showing how those works use borrowing to similar or contrasting effects in engaging cultural discourses. Not only is the stylistic and artistic ground vast but so is the cultural terrain. The interaction between quotation and an array of cultural areas will be discussed, including race, childhood, madness, utopia, the mass media, and the relationship between past and present. Such a broad focus provides many different vantage points from which to view quotation.

With that focus, this study steps into the young and growing field of musical borrowing. Scholars have long explored how musicians incorporate elements of other pieces into new works. That research has traditionally focused on individual composers and repertories, such as Handel's operatic borrowings or the use of chants as tenors in Notre Dame organum. New approaches to borrowing, in contrast, have opened up much wider perspectives.[4] They, for instance, have looked at how borrowing practices extend over different styles and periods. Taking a cue from these approaches, this book considers the uses of quotation in various idioms. Only one period, however, is discussed here, albeit a very diverse one. That diversity in part makes the twentieth century arguably the richest era for a study of quotation. That century had an unprecedented awareness of music from the past and that of other styles and cultures. Not surprisingly, quotation became a

---

[3] The work's relationship to madness and the past is discussed in chapter three.

[4] J. Peter Burkholder has been instrumental in shaping these new approaches to borrowing. See his "The uses of existing music: musical borrowing as a field," *Music Library Association Notes* 50 (1994), 851–70, and "Borrowing," in *The New Grove Dictionary of Music and Musicians*, 2nd edn, ed. Stanley Sadie (London: Macmillan, 2001), vol. 4, 5–8.

prevalent, if not indispensable, gesture for musicians in confronting the spectrum of music surrounding them. As this study explores, the gesture also provided musicians with a means of confronting a range of cultural discourses.

The new approaches to borrowing break additional ground by viewing borrowing not as a single practice, one often indiscriminately referred to as quotation or parody, but rather as a larger mode of music-making comprising different practices, such as quotation and parody, as well as allusion, modeling, and paraphrase, among others.[5] As J. Peter Burkholder makes clear, the lines between these categories are not fixed. Quite the contrary, they frequently "intermingle," a behavior run rampant in the Ives works that he examines.[6] Still, there are some properties that distinguish quotation. That practice, as defined here, refers to the placement of parts of a pre-existent piece in a new composition or performance. The use of actual material from a piece separates quotation from allusion and paraphrase, which broadly evoke works, styles, or textures. Quotation is also set apart by the prominence of the borrowing, which is made to stick out from the surrounding music.[7] That conspicuity contrasts with the unobtrusive, usually background, role played by borrowed elements in parody, cantus firmus, and modeling.

Quotation is also characterized by the use of brief excerpts, like the bits of patriotic songs that shoot through Ives's works. In the first and third movements of George Rochberg's *Music for the Magic Theater*, to give another example, flecks of Mahler, Mozart, and Beethoven glimmer in the dark dissonant music. What then to make of the second movement, which consists of a re-orchestration of almost an entire Mozart Adagio? Does a near fifty-measure block constitute a quotation? In some ways, yes. Like the scraps of Mahler, Mozart, and Beethoven, it stands out as a foreign element from the surrounding music, a patch of tranquil past inserted into the dissonant fracas of the outer movements. Moreover, the Adagio remains a fragment, cut off before it can finish, just like the tattered phrases of Mahler and Beethoven. Finally, a swarm of quotations from Stockhausen, Webern, and Mahler works takes flight after the Adagio suddenly collapses. In that flock of fragments, the Mozart comes across as a quotation itself, a piece of the past that has been recalled and then falls apart.

---

[5] For a breakdown of different practices, see Burkholder, "The uses of existing music," and "Borrowing."

[6] J. Peter Burkholder, *All Made of Tunes: Charles Ives and the Uses of Musical Borrowing* (New Haven and London: Yale University, 1995), 4–5.

[7] Of course, many composers have embedded hidden quotations in their works, using them to make veiled personal or political statements.

Viewing Rochberg's movement as such is not an attempt to lock it in the category of quotation and thereby fasten the lines separating that category from other ones. The above discussion is instead meant to loosen those lines. The Rochberg movement typifies a type of borrowing that became more and more common during the twentieth century. That practice can be seen in pieces that absorb whole or near-whole compositions and rework them to various degrees, often combining them with new materials. As the Rochberg movement shows, this type of borrowing overlaps with quotation. The amount of shared ground between the two varies with each piece, as seen in the following discussions of Luciano Berio's *Sinfonia*, the third movement of which builds upon the Scherzo from Mahler's Second Symphony, and John Oswald's "DAB," which offers a "revised performance" of Michael Jackson's "Bad."

These works and similar ones take elements of quotation far afield into new realms. By following these pieces, this study runs the risk of leaving quotation behind altogether. That point is indeed reached. The last chapter looks at the role of cover songs in Sandra Bernhard's film *Without You I'm Nothing*. Those songs form a distinct borrowing practice – one, which at its best, is characterized by a singer reconceiving in original ways a tune intimately connected with another artist. Bernhard's covers have been welcomed here for they broaden our understanding of quotation. The film, for instance, uses borrowing – the covers – to comment on the act of borrowing, touching upon issues related to quotation and other practices. In addition, Bernhard's songs take on a range of cultural issues, from race to celebrity, and reveal unique ways in which borrowing acts as a cultural agent.

Cover songs also fit into this study, for they exploit the same basic two-part gesture manipulated by quotation and other borrowing approaches. One part of that gesture is what can be called the original, that is, the material taken from an outside source. The original is the fragment as it exists in that source, prior to any alterations made to it. As such, it never sounds in the new work, for there is always some degree of alteration in bringing that fragment into its new surroundings. Nonetheless, the original maintains a strong presence. All transformations are viewed in relation to it, making it a constant point of comparison. In addition, no matter how small or slight, it transports the weighty cultural discourses of the borrowed work into the new one, forcing the borrowing musician and listener to confront those associations. The other part of a borrowing is the transformation, the name given to the fragment as it exists in the new work. As the term states, this side of the gesture involves any alterations made to the original as well as the changed form it assumes in its new context. The transformation is the borrowing as we hear it; however, we hear more than just it, for the original still

5

demands our attention, even if never stated. Borrowing then creates an unceasing interaction between the two sides, between both the original and the altered musical material, and the original and the new cultural associations. That interaction creates the thrill of hearing what happens when music takes on new life within music.

With quotation, this two-part design is heightened. The borrowed material is most often familiar or, if not so, it at least stands apart by virtue of being out of context. Such conspicuity intensifies the engagement between old and new, as we can hear how easily or reluctantly the borrowing settles into its new locale. Once inside, it continually points outside, as the prominence of the borrowing prods us to look back to its origins. At the same time, quotation typically involves a range of transformational techniques. Fragmentation, expansion, rhythmic skewing, stylistic metamorphosis – these are only some of the things that can be done with borrowed elements. This manipulation of pre-existent material adds another dimension to the play between old and new, as we hear what new guises the old can assume. In his discussion of the electronic work *Hymnen*, Stockhausen provided an apt description of the two-sided dynamics of quotation. According to him, the practice involves a rich exchange between the "what" and the "how," that is, the gesture has us hear "what" music has been borrowed and "how" it has been changed. The more familiar and obvious the "what," the more we are drawn into the "how," and the more captivating the "how," the more we can appreciate anew the "what."

It is the ways in which quotation handles the "what" and the "how" that make it so effective a cultural agent. The gesture latches on to a specific work, often a familiar one, and places that work squarely in front of us. The borrowed material is tightly gripped and prominently featured rather than being merely alluded to or buried in the background. This directness calls attention to the cultural associations of the original, for the more discernible and intact the borrowing, the more apparent and whole those associations. In other words, quotation puts a new twist on the maxim that to name something is the most direct way of evoking that object and what it stands for. Here, to state the piece itself is the clearest way of summoning that piece and its cultural dimensions.

Once the borrowing is evoked, the exchange between the original and new work central to cultural agency begins. That exchange, of course, can start only if the listener can recognize the quotation. As described above, quotations are displayed more markedly than other types of borrowing, but that prominence does not ensure that the listener will be able to identify the particular borrowing. The listener has to be able to "name" the quotation in order to understand fully what it stands for. Recognition then forms a crux for quotation, especially in its role as a cultural agent.[8] Simply put, if a borrowing is not detected then it and its cultural resonances go unheard. For example, I initially did not perceive Schoenberg's self-borrowing of an earlier song that dashes through the orchestra in the closing scene of *Erwartung*. However, once discovered, it – a few fragmentary measures – loomed. The quotation demanded my attention, constantly nudging me to ask what it was doing there and what light it shed upon the ambiguous operatic landscape in which Schoenberg had dropped it. My answers can be found in the ruminations on hysteria, memory, and gender found in chapter three.

That some quotations can sneak by without being spotted points to different approaches to the gesture. As with the *Erwartung* fragment, a few borrowings amount to personal asides, and are accordingly shaded if not hidden outright. Others, such as those in Eliot's *The Waste Land* (which is discussed alongside Schoenberg's opera below), are purposely obscure, *recherché* tokens of the creator's elitism. In either case, once revealed – as they almost always are – these borrowings are no longer hushed. Quite the opposite: having remained reticent for so long, they, like the Schoenberg quotation, have much to say and keep saying it to us.

In contrast to the obscure and hidden borrowings are the obvious borrowings. Some composers draw upon materials so well known that they would stand out no matter where they are placed. Prominent and familiar, these borrowings have much to say in a cultural dialogue. They grab the listener's attention right away and have him or her go back and forth between the associations of the known and those of the new work. Oswald's "DAB," for example, draws upon the familiar Jackson hit "Bad," so familiar that many listeners probably would turn off the tune rather than hear it again. They may, though, keep Oswald's version turned on, for not only does he scramble the song in beguiling ways but he also scrambles the cultural associations of the piece, having us discern the studio artificiality of the supposedly real person that we know as Michael Jackson.

With many quotations, it is not a simple matter of being recognized or not. Some can be noticed but not identified. For instance, most listeners will not spot the Ghanaian national anthem in Stockhausen's *Hymnen*; neither will they catch "Ben Bolt" in Ives's *Central Park in the Dark*. They should, however, be able to perceive musical strands that stand apart from the surrounding work. That distinction can be drawn on several different levels, including style (the national anthem or parlor song

---

[8] For a discussion of the various facets of recognition and its implications for the aesthetic effectiveness of the gesture, see Jeanette Bicknell, "The problem of reference in musical quotation: a phenomenological approach," *The Journal of Aesthetics and Art Criticism* 59 (2001), 185–91.

versus the modern idiom), tonal/atonal, and, as with *Hymnen*, acoustic/electronic sound. Such contrast is not possible to anywhere near the same extent in the music of earlier periods, which embeds acoustic, tonal borrowings in acoustic, tonal idioms. Those rich juxtapositions are part of the reason why quotation thrived in twentieth-century music, especially as a cultural agent. Even at this basic level of contrast, the gesture can still play that role. To continue with *Hymnen*, anthems, as a genre, bring to a work a load of associations, including state ceremony, military, and authority. Of course, that load grows larger and more specific when an anthem is linked to a particular country. It is at that stage that this study enters. It identifies the quotations and then quickly turns to the cultural role played by those borrowings. Whether obscure, familiar, or just familiar-sounding, all quotations have broad repercussions in the cultural arena; following those consequences requires keen ears and eyes for they often lead to areas and issues that many listeners would never anticipate.

Other scholars have followed these fanning cultural trails. Of note is Charles Ballantine's study of Ives. Ballantine views quotations as enacting a "dialectic" between "the fragment" and "the new musical context."[9] That dialectic gets at the concept of cultural agency pursued in this study. Ballantine similarly focuses on the play of associations between the original and its transformation. Although he broadly paints those associations as "semantic," he brings out specific cultural topics in his study of Ives, whose quotation works he sees as touching upon notions of community, the relationship between humanity and nature, and "the kaleidoscopic vigor of American life."[10]

How those cultural associations are produced is where this study and Ballantine's part ways. As laid out here, the transformation never assumes "primacy" over the original or provides the exclusive "framework" through which it can be "understood." The original, as stated above, maintains a strong presence in the new work, in terms of both its distinct musical shape and its cultural meanings. The new work, contrary to Ballantine, cannot so easily control, let alone "strip," those associations.[11] What makes the original so obdurate is that it, as exemplified in the pieces discussed here, brings to the new work loaded cultural discourses. They are imposing blocks, comprising a dense web of ideas developed over the course of centuries. Once evoked they can never be dominated; rather, a new piece can only interact with them.

---

[9] Charles Ballantine, *Music and its Social Meanings* (New York: Garden and Breach Science Publication, 1984), 73–74. Ballantine views his model as relevant to a range of other twentieth-century composers, not just Ives.

[10] Ibid., 83, 87–89.

[11] Ibid., 73–74.

Another study to look at the cultural agency of quotation is Glenn Watkins's *Pyramids at the Louvre: Music, Culture, and Collage from Stravinsky to the Postmodernists.*[12] That book astutely examines the role performed by borrowing in a variety of twentieth-century cultural movements, including primitivism and neoclassicism. Watkins treats a group of borrowing practices, all of them lumped under the ambiguous heading of "collage." That practice is made even more ambiguous by the lack of any explanation as to how collage operates as a borrowing strategy. Cultural elements go in and come out, but the inner workings of collage remain a mystery.

This book and Watkins's differ in terms of the range of works and cultural topics discussed. *Pyramids at the Louvre* deals almost exclusively with classical music, making rare and brief excursions into jazz and popular repertories. This book, in contrast, examines the uses of quotation across a spectrum of styles. Watkins's work is also weighted toward the first half of the century, relatively neglecting the role of borrowing in the latter half. This study too is chronologically out of balance, though the scales are tipped in the opposite direction. As explored here, the second half of the century gave rise to a multitude of approaches to quotation, from 1960s collage works to rap sampling. One other difference between this work and Watkins's is the cultural realms covered in each. This book explores several realms – childhood, madness, the mass media, nostalgia, and utopia, among others – that are only touched upon or not mentioned at all by Watkins. By pointing out omissions and thin patches in Watkins's work, I do not mean to slight his accomplishment; rather, a comparison of his book and this one only serves to draw attention to the ample room for research in this expansive topic.

With such a spacious topic, this project makes no attempt to be comprehensive – obviously no single book could encompass the infinite interactions between borrowing and the dense strands of twentieth-century culture. It instead concentrates on a select group of works, treating them as case studies. Each study merits a separate chapter, which discusses how quotation engages a specific cultural discourse. In the order of the presented chapters, those discourses are childhood, race, madness, utopia, theft, and celebrity.

Pursuing such a broad cultural scope, this discussion brings together a diverse collection of topics and works, everything from Ellington's use of spirituals in *Black and Tan Fantasy* to Oswald's dismantling of Jackson's voice in "DAB." Within this diversity, several topics reappear, serving as points of both orientation and elaboration. One such recurring subject is the relationship between past and present. That

---

[12] Glenn Watkins, *Pyramids at the Louvre: Music, Culture, and Collage from Stravinsky to the Postmodernists* (Cambridge, MA: Harvard University Press, 1994).

relationship is crucial to the study of the cultural agency of quotation. On one hand, quotation by nature involves that relationship, as it creates a new (present) take on pre-existent (past) materials, be it the past of centuries ago or a few years back. On the other hand, that relationship forms a significant cultural site in itself. An evocation of the past not only tells us how the present perceives a distant period but also how it views itself in relation to that time. So significant is that pair that other cultural topics group around it. The works to be examined all involve such dense clusters. For example, Ives's evocations of the past tie into both Victorian conceptions of childhood and the contemporary anxiety over new technologies and urbanization. In his songs, nostalgia serves as a way of escaping those concerns and finding refuge in an idealized nineteenth-century small-town childhood. Nostalgia is not restricted to memories of youthful days. Many musicians have fallen under its spell in dealing with the tensions between past and present. Not surprisingly, nostalgia serves as another recurring topic in this book.

One other cultural relationship that appears in different chapters is that between blackness and whiteness. As in Mingus's *Fables of Faubus*, quotation can be used to set the terms of that relationship by offering representations of both racial categories and establishing a dynamic between them. Given the variety of materials that can be drawn upon and the numerous ways in which they can be handled, that relationship can assume innumerable forms. This book looks at how Ellington, Bernhard, and pop and experimental musicians using samplers have approached a racial pairing that continues to shape American culture.

This discussion also keeps coming back to larger questions dealing with the act of quotation, specifically what is the effect of that practice on those who use it and in how many different ways can it be employed? The first query may come as a surprise, for it rarely, if at all, pops up in accounts of musical borrowing. Yet many works featuring quotation directly or indirectly pose that question. We need to hear when a work raises it and then attempt to find an answer. To do so is to open up new perspectives on borrowing, as that inquiry shifts attention from the play of quoted and new materials in a piece to the musician who invents that play. In particular, we can see how the individuality of the musician – how he or she perceives him or herself – is manifested in that play.

Borrowing, in its many forms including quotation, is a creative act that stirs different, often polarized, types of self-perception. On one hand, the act is ridden with fears of creative sterility and desperation, the musician who has nothing original to say and thus feeds upon the works of others. These fears can create paralyzing anxieties, even moments of self-abjection. At the end of *Without You I'm Nothing*, for example, Bernhard breaks down on stage and castigates herself with names like "fraud" and "phony." The collapse appears to stem from doubts rankled by the incessant borrowing that she has done throughout the film, an activity that she has previously linked to "frauds" and "phonies." Her way out of such abjection is ironically through one more cover song. Whereas borrowing can lead to doubts, it can also bestow confidence. The ability to recreate songs in new ways offers an artist an opportunity to magnify his or her talents. Grabbing that chance, Bernhard picks herself up and finishes the show with her most intriguing and audacious cover song.

The "theft" artists in chapter five similarly view borrowing as "empowering." To them, the ability to take elements from a source, usually an off-limits one, and to transform them into something of one's own making amounts to an assertion of individuality. They "steal" materials from the mass media, particularly bits of hit songs and other copyrighted materials, and turn them into media-hostile products. As laid out in their manifestos, these borrowings provide a means of resisting the passivity forced upon us by the media and of reclaiming one's individuality from the pervasive media presence. This declaration of individuality is often achieved by manipulating the individuality of others, particularly the star singers whose voices are "stolen." Through the alteration of those voices, "theft" artists efface the individuality of the people embodied in them. Some works break apart a celebrity identity by undoing the media packaging in which stars exist, leaving them as distorted fragments of their media selves. These works offer a striking example of the degree to which borrowing can center on individuality, both that of the borrower and that of the one borrowed.

Another aspect of quotation explored in this book is the diverse ways in which the gesture can be executed. To recall, quotation is a two-part gesture: the original and its transformation. The inherent simplicity and flexibility of the design combined with the array of materials and transformation techniques create a borrowing practice that can assume countless forms. This study displays a mere handful of those forms and shows the different approaches used to create them. Special attention is paid to what art historian T. J. Clark calls "limit cases," pieces in which a medium or, as in the case of quotation, a practice is pushed to a breaking point, where that practice will either fall apart or take on new forms.[13] The pieces drawing upon whole or almost-whole works discussed above present such cases, as does the opposite example of electronic works that flip through quotations lasting less than a second in length. As the latter pieces make clear, electronic idioms have pushed quotation to extremes. Studio technologies have allowed musicians to

---

[13] T. J. Clark, *Farewell to an Idea: Episodes from a History of Modernism* (New Haven and London: Yale University Press, 1999), 7.

transform borrowed sounds to the brink of unrecognizability. Many musicians have been drawn to that point and some have traveled beyond it. These far-reaching sonic alterations threaten to collapse quotation. For, as asked above, if the original is not recognized at all, is there a quotation?

Quotation also takes different forms when it is pressed into the service of a particular rhetorical or cultural practice. Again the suppleness of the gesture allows it to be adapted to such roles. This study examines the uses made of quotation in a variety of these practices and movements, including signifying, camp, and "culture jamming." As will be discussed, each brings out different sides of the gesture, configuring the relationship between the original and its transformation in distinct ways.

This book is divided into six chapters, each of which presents a study centered around a particular cultural topic. Chapter one begins with arguably the father of twentieth-century quotation, Ives. It discusses the nostalgic childhood scenes that he created through quotations and relates those scenes to contemporary ones by Willa Cather and Mary Pickford. Chapter two focuses on the relationship between whiteness and blackness, looking at the form that relationship takes in Duke Ellington and Bubber Miley's *Black and Tan Fantasy*, the main theme of which, in a unique case of borrowing, is based on a spiritual, itself derived from a white hymn. The racial representations in the work are compared to those shaped by Zora Neale Hurston in a contemporary essay on the spiritual and those found in reviews of the work by white critics and the white director Dudley Murphy's film *Black and Tan*, which features a performance of the title piece by Ellington and his band. Finally, this chapter shows how Ellington and Miley's handling of the spiritual quotation revels in the doubleness and irony typical of the African-American rhetorical practice of signifying.

The following two chapters concentrate on the relationship between past and present. A brief Interlude discusses views of that relationship held by some theorists of postmodernism. Several of these critics, notably Fredric Jameson, have described how postmodern works, especially quotation-based ones, create fragmentary chronological spaces in which the bonds between past and present have been severed, thereby cutting off any engagement between those two periods and limiting, if not outright annulling, the ability of those works to act as cultural agents.[14] This book refutes that view, arguing that recent works, many of them fitting the bill as postmodernist, have opened up temporal worlds in which past and present are very much engaged. Moreover,

[14] Fredric Jameson, *Postmodernism, or, The Cultural Logic of Late Capitalism* (Durham, NC: Duke University, 1991), 25–31.

that engagement has assumed a variety of forms, as have the cultural roles played by those works.

To reveal this diversity, this study puts forth chronological scenes, that is, accounts of the relationship between past and present built around different themes. Two such scenes are staged. The first (chapter three) peers into realms of madness, spheres in which an overwhelming past eclipses both the present and reason. These realms are discussed in works by Schoenberg, T. S. Eliot, Berio, Francis Bacon, and Maxwell Davies. Drawing upon collage compositions by Rochberg, Berio, and Stockhausen, the second type of scene (chapter four) opens up onto idealistic worlds where the combinations of past and present make almost anything seem possible – dreams, though, that are ultimately undone by an unwieldy past.

Chapters five and six both turn to the borrowing of popular culture materials. The former opens with a general discussion of sampling and how it has expanded the scope of quotation. That discussion then narrows in on "theft" artists, who sample, or "steal," copyrighted materials. Their quotation of popular songs is related to borrowing practices brandished in the larger underground artistic movement called "culture jamming." That movement has set its sights on the mass media and aims to expose the artificial and ultimately dehumanizing role the media play in contemporary life.

From the revolutionary underground of the "jammers," chapter six leaps into the extravagantly comic world of Bernhard's film *Without You I'm Nothing*, a work no less sparing of the popular culture materials it extracts from the media. In many ways, the film is a fitting conclusion to this book for it uses borrowing to comment on the act of borrowing. One particular act that it signals out is the appropriation of black songs and styles by white performers, an ongoing practice that Bernhard mocks in her own outrageous, and decidedly not black, performances of songs made famous by African-American singers. Bernhard's handling of race and celebrity are rooted in the practice of camp. As presented here, camp serves as a mode of borrowing, one mercilessly putting on display and altering the out-of-fashion debris of popular culture, as Bernhard does with the bygone Top 40 in her cover songs.

This summary of chapters reveals some surprising omissions. Many musicians who might be expected to appear in a study of quotation are either not discussed or only mentioned in passing. Among the slighted are Stravinsky, Art Tatum, Charlie Parker, Bernd Alois Zimmermann, George Crumb, Lukas Foss, Alfred Schnittke, Public Enemy, and Beck. In defense, it can only be reiterated that this project makes no claims of being comprehensive. It instead has brought together musicians whose use of quotation has created intriguing, and often unique, cultural resonances; that, however, is not to say that works by the above musicians offer any less interesting examples of cultural agency. What may be even more surprising than those neglected are some of those who have been included. Ellington and Schoenberg have never been thought of as quoters, whereas prolific borrowers like Bernhard and the "theft" musicians Negativland and the Tape-beatles have not previously found their way into studies of borrowing, remaining virtual "unknowns" in the field.

These surprise appearances point to one way of appreciating this discussion of quotation. The whole study is in many ways a collage, specifically the form of collage created in the 1960s by such composers as Rochberg, Berio, and Stockhausen (chapter four). The third movement of Berio's *Sinfonia*, the most celebrated collage work of the time, tantalizes us with the "unexpected." The spoken voices repeatedly tell us that the unexpected looms and the orchestra provides it with seemingly random quotations. Nothing so dramatic pops out here, although some of the discussed musicians make surprise entrances. As discussed in chapter four, such compositions adhere to an ideal of expansion and connection, that is, they constantly reach out to apparently unrelated materials and unveil or create linkages between them. This dynamic whirs through both individual chapters and the book as a whole. Chapter one, for example, begins with Ives's nostalgic depictions of childhood and then branches out to similar ones created by Cather and Pickford. On the larger scale, this account of nostalgia feeds into the discussion of works by Janet Jackson and Rochberg, the last of which draws upon Ives's means of conveying nostalgia. With these connections, this book darts in many "unexpected" directions, moves that propel the discussion across the vastness of the twentieth century.

1

Childhood and nostalgia in the works of Charles Ives

Bigelow and Chester mention baseball. Brewster talks of football. Whatever the sport, they all agree that Uncle Charlie played hard – so hard that little Bigelow was "frigthened [*sic*]" by him. Actually, this vivacity amused them, as evident in Bigelow's account of a madcap ride in the "old Model T," during which his uncle stopped at a treacherous spot in the road and "blew the horn real loud," explaining "I was killed here once, and that was enough for me." This same combination of intensity and eccentricity also emerges in the three brothers' discussions of their uncle's musical activities. Brewster remarks that he made them "work at music." Chester relates how Uncle Charlie played the piano "so expressively that any child would respond to it." Poor, always frightened Bigelow, however, describes how his uncle scolded him for not shouting loud enough while performing one of his songs, growling "Can't you shout better than that? That's the trouble with this country – people are afraid to shout!"[1]

Forget about shouting; Bigelow's singing, no matter how frail, was bold enough, giving voice to a significant, yet overlooked and silent, group in the musical world of "Charlie" Ives: children. But even here that group remains silent: we hear not a boy's voice but rather an adult Bigelow along with his brothers sharing their youthful impressions of their uncle. Perhaps this is as close as we will ever get to a child's view of a composer who had so much to say about children in his music and writings. Yet these recollections may be more appropriate than we think, as they parallel the composer's repeated musings on childhood, especially his own. Not surprisingly, Brewster and Bigelow, either as the objects of that nostalgia or later as nostalgic adults themselves, recognized Ives's melancholy. The former commented: "He relived his boyhood in Danbury to a degree that was quite unusual." Bigelow recalled

---

[1] These accounts have been drawn from the recollections of Ives's nephews in Vivian Perlis, *Charles Ives Remembered: an Oral History* (1974; rpr. New York: Da Capo Press, 1994), 72–88.

how during a visit to Danbury the composer was nearly suffocated by childhood memories, leaving him to "moan": "I'm going back. You can't recall the past."[2]

Ives's efforts to "go back" and to "recall the past" have fascinated scholars, who have discussed the composer's nostalgia for a halcyon nineteenth-century small-town America, placing that desire in various contexts, such as the political and psychoanalytical.[3] Often overlooked are the representations of childhood in these nostalgic scenes, as Ives frequently embodied the past in child figures.[4] This study examines the role of childhood in the composer's works, considering how he depicted children in both music and texts and the means by which he cultivated nostalgic desire. Ives's fondness for the past and his portrayals of youth fit within a tradition of childhood nostalgia, part of a larger wave of nostalgia in American culture during the early decades of the twentieth century. Quotation became the means by which the composer participated in that cultural scene. Through that gesture, he could represent the figure of the lost child and the growing gap between past and present in which that figure was caught.

Representing childhood

Around the seventeenth century, generational fission occurred: the child and adult split apart. Before then, historical constructionists argue, the child, as we recognize the concept today, occupied no place in social or artistic spheres, being instead part of an amorphous pan-generational society.[5] After having been "invented" in the seventeenth century, the "child" slowly assumed a place, becoming a new conceptual category, separated from the "adult," itself a new classification. Of course, the

---

[2] Ibid., 72, 82.

[3] Discussions of nostalgia in Ives's works include James Hepokoski, "Temps perdu," *Musical Times* 135 (1994), 746–51, and Leon Botstein, "Innovation and nostalgia: Ives, Mahler, and the origins of twentieth-century modernism," in *Charles Ives and his World*, ed. J. Peter Burkholder (Princeton: Princeton University Press, 1996), 35–74. A political context for Ives's nostalgia is provided in Michael Broyles, "Charles Ives and the American democratic tradition," in *Charles Ives and his World*, 118–60. Stuart Feder discusses its psychoanalytical implications in *Charles Ives "My Father's Song": a Psychoanalytical Biography* (New Haven: Yale University Press, 1992). An account of the debate over nostalgic interpretation in Ives scholarship is provided below.

[4] Feder has examined Ives's "veneration of boyhood," but his discussions have centered on biographical and psychoanalytical issues, not Ives's general representations of childhood. Feder, "Charles and George Ives: the veneration of boyhood," *Annual of Psychoanalysis* 9 (1981), 265–316, and "The nostalgia of Charles Ives: an essay in affects and music," *Annual of Psychoanalysis* 10 (1982), 301–32. Both articles were incorporated into Feder, *Charles Ives "My Father's Song."*

[5] The central text in this approach is Phillipe Ariès, *Centuries of Childhood: a Social History of Family Life*, trans. Robert Baldick (New York: Vintage, 1962).

invention of childhood has by no means been universally embraced by historians. As in the areas of gender, race, and sexuality, the constructionist approach has been challenged on several fronts. Its central point, however, remains convincing: childhood is not an intrinsic state but rather a category defined by various discourses, including education, medicine, and fashion.[6] The constructionist point of view is especially enlightening when it comes to representation of children in the arts, for it reveals not only the degree to which those depictions are culturally conditioned but also how they in turn shape cultural conceptions of childhood.

In his representations, Ives drew upon Victorian notions of childhood, particularly that of innocence.[7] Setting a text by Wordsworth, his song "The Rainbow" presents the child as a pure being from whom the Adam-like adult has strayed, but to whom he or she maintains a spiritual connection.[8] This idea of original childhood innocence emerged during the seventeenth century, was established by Rousseau, embellished by Wordsworth, and ground into clichés by the Victorian middle and upper classes. These commonplaces appear in the texts and programs of Ives's works. The song "Marie" (1898), text by Rudolf Gottshalk, describes a girl – or is it really a "flower," or some sort of sacred object?

> Marie, I see thee, fairest one, as in a garden fair;
> Before thee flowers and blossoms play, tossed by soft evening air.
> The pilgrim passing on his way bows low before thy shrine;
> Thou art, my child, like one sweet prayer: so good, so fair, so pure, almost divine!
> How sweetly now the flowrets raise their eyes to thy dear glance;
> The fairest flower on which I gaze is thy dear countenance.
> The evening bells are greeting thee with sweetest melody;
> O may no storm e'er crush thy flowers, or break thy heart, Marie![9]

---

[6] For a discussion of this approach and responses to it, see James R. Kincaid, *Child-Loving: the Erotic Child in Victorian Culture* (New York: Routledge, 1992), 61–65; and James A. Schultz, *The Knowledge of Childhood in the German Middle Ages, 1100–1350* (Philadelphia: University of Pennsylvania Press, 1995), 2–9.

[7] On Victorian views of childhood, see Kincaid, *Child-Loving*, and Jackie Wullschläger, *Inventing Wonderland: the Lives and Fantasies of Lewis Carroll, Edward Lear, J. M. Barrie, Kenneth Grahame, and A. A. Milne* (London: Methuen, 1995).

[8] The text is Wordsworth's "My heart leaps up." The poet's Prelude significantly shaped such views of childhood innocence. On Wordsworth's views of childhood, see Peter Coveney, *Poor Monkey: the Child in Literature* (London: Rockliff, 1957), 30–31; and Kincaid, *Child-Loving*, 63.

[9] The text was translated from the original German by Elisabeth Rücker. Ives adapted that translation. I have relied on H. Wiley Hitchcock's regularization of the punctuation. I would like to thank Professor Hitchcock for sharing with me his research on Ives's song texts from his forthcoming edition of the *129 Songs*.

How did Marie get to be so innocent? Not by her good deeds, but rather by doing nothing. Instead of being characterized by such praiseworthy traits as honesty, cheerfulness, or diligence, the innocent child was presented as a blank. Only when voided of any agency or uniqueness could a youth be truly pure. Innocence then is a state of vacancy, which, as will be discussed, is left for the adult to fill. "Marie" empties out its title character by first reducing her several times to a flower and then describing her with such hollow adjectives as "good" and "pure." As if that regalia of banality was not enough, the poor girl is raised to the level of the "almost divine." Such heavenly status further nullifies Marie, turning her into a holy relic, one of many stops on the "pilgrim's" tour of girlhood "shrines." Indeed, the protagonist views Marie more as a relic – an object locked in the distant past – than as a child, hoping that she will forever remain in the past of youth, untouched by the "storms" and heartbreaks of adulthood.

Such concepts of purity benefit the adult more than the child, who, if anything, was more burdened than edified by the inculcation of those views in school, home, and church. As Ives mentions in the notes to the "Alcotts" movement of the *Concord Sonata*, innocence formed a necessary ingredient in the American adult's diet.

She [Louisa May Alcott] supported the family, and at the same time enriched the lives of a large part of young America, starting off many little minds with wholesome thoughts and many little hearts with wholesome emotions. She leaves memory–word pictures of healthy New England childhood days – pictures which are turned to with affection by middle-aged children – pictures that bear a sentiment, a leaven, that middle-aged America needs nowadays more than we care to admit.[10]

Ives not only doles out stock phrases of purity – "wholesome" and "healthy" – but also alludes to the construction of childhood innocence. Here, Louisa May Alcott gathers up all those empty "little minds" and fills them up with "wholesome" traits that adults "need." Fortified with such nutrients, childhood becomes something to be consumed by adults – even by the whole nation. Indeed, Ives's statement in some respects offers a more intriguing depiction of adulthood than it does of childhood. In his account, the former emerges as a default, a natural state that is ostensibly beyond construction, but is nevertheless put together just like its youthful antithesis. Placed under similar scrutiny, it also appears as an emptiness, one that fills itself ironically with the purity of childhood, thus feeding off what it originally placed in that category. This consumption both momentarily relieves that hollowness

---

[10] Charles Ives, *Essays before a Sonata: the Majority and Other Writings*, ed. Howard Boatwright (New York: Norton, 1970), 46–47.

and delays decay, that is, the inevitable withdrawal from the "beloved," "healthy" days of youth. As evoked by Ives, childhood and adulthood are two vacuums, the former benign and receding with the gradual ebb of youth, the latter expanding and devouring.

In Ives's works, childhood has receded into the distance. Children almost always populate the distant past, not the near present. In addition, Ives depicts youth as removed from adulthood, both physically and cognitively. Boys and girls, for instance, often meet in special events and places set aside for them, namely the various festivals evoked in many works. These meetings occur in separate realms beyond the reach and comprehension of adults. "The Children's Hour" similarly sets aside an ephemeral period ("between the dark and the daylight") of the day for its tykes, a time that remains mysterious to the musing parent.

Nostalgia

The path that leads to the remote and inscrutable realm of childhood is one of nostalgia. It is a path that Ives frequently travels in his works. Before following him on that route, it is necessary to say a few things about nostalgia in general. First, nostalgia is a concept that took many different forms throughout the twentieth century.[11] Jameson, for instance, has isolated a postmodern stripe, which, as characteristic of such films as *American Graffiti*, evokes the past through remembered styles and looks. Realized in those terms, the period exists only as a simulacrum, having no substance.[12]

Nostalgia may assume different forms but all these forms share a basic outlook on the relationship between past and present. In general, nostalgia places the past at a remove, positioning it, as Susan Stewart says, "impossibly distant in time."[13] Be it a childhood memory or a dress style, the object from the past can never be reclaimed, never experienced as it once was. Nostalgia peers at that remote time from an uncertain and unfulfilling present. The stresses and needs of that period impel a search for stability and fulfillment, which the nostalgic believes can be found in the past. That search leads to a roseate past created in the present, such as Ives's idyllic small-town nineteenth-century America.

If various forms of nostalgia converge around unease with the present and an idealization and distancing of the past, they part ways over the

[11] A similar point is made in Christopher Shaw and Malcolm Chase, "The dimensions of the past," in Shaw and Chase, eds., *The Imagined Past: History and Nostalgia* (Manchester and New York: Manchester University Press, 1989), 2.

[12] Jameson, *Postmodernism*, 18–21.

[13] Susan Stewart, *On Longing: Narratives of the Miniature, the Gigantic, and the Souvenir, the Collection* (Durham, NC, and London: Duke University Press, 1993), 140.

feeling of loss experienced for the latter period. By placing the past at such an unreachable distance, nostalgia recognizes that the past cannot be reclaimed. However, it is the degree to which that loss is felt that separates different strands of the sensation. Jameson's postmodern nostalgia does not lament the irrecoverability of the past. As in a film or magazine spread, it glosses over such feelings by sealing both present and past in the smooth finish of the photographic surface. After all, it is impossible to mourn a simulacrum. Other nostalgic works, especially those tending to childhood, wince at the realization that the past cannot be held. The works by Ives and others discussed in this chapter acutely feel this sense of separation. They not only emerge from the divide between past and present but they also widen it. Each concludes with a gesture that heaves the past further away, leaving us in a present more bereft of the essence we sought to find in the past.

This sense of loss accords with earlier conceptions of nostalgia. Nostalgia first appeared as a physical disease, one codified in 1688 by the Swiss doctor Johannes Hofer. He cobbled together the name for this new ailment from the ancient Greek terms *nostos* (return to home) and *algos* (suffering). As the neologism conveys, nostalgia amounted to a virulent form of homesickness, which resulted in lethargy, wasting, and even suicide.[14] Around the turn of the nineteenth century, nostalgia metamorphosed from a physical condition to the emotional one recognized today.[15] Instead of home, the nostalgic now looked to the past, a realm that swelled well beyond the borders of a village and encompassed broader feelings and states, as seen in the yearning for the lightness of childhood days. Such emotions covered a full range, from dabs of wistfulness to depths of loss.

It is those depths that occupy this discussion. The works of Ives and other artists presented here all cave into loss. The model of nostalgia developed below pertains to such mournful works; however, many of the general points relate to other forms of nostalgia as well, from Hofer's malady to Jameson's postmodern simulacra. One of the first things to remark about nostalgia is that it courts paradox. It sustains itself by suspending opposites, particularly past and present. In this state, the two periods press up so close to each other that they begin to take on characteristics of one another. Nostalgia emerges from a loss of the past – for Ives, of his youth. Triggered by that absence, it seeks to mend the loss by giving the past a sense of immediacy, creating the impression that one

---

[14] On the medical notion of nostalgia, see George Rosen, "Nostalgia: a forgotten psychological disorder," *Clio Medica* 10/1 (1975), 28–51; and Roderick Peters, "Reflections on the origin and aim of nostalgia," *Journal of Analytical Psychology* 30 (1985), 135–48.

[15] For different views of this transformation, see Svetlana Boym, *The Future of Nostalgia* (New York: Basic Books, 2001), 8–18; and Nicholas Dames, "Austen's nostalgics," *Representations* 73 (2001), 117–43.

has recovered it and is living it anew.[16] Such temporal contradictions occur in the programs and texts of Ives's compositions, which often turn back the clock and then relate the past with the spontaneity of the present tense. With the past so lively, the present now appears still and far off – in other words, like the past. That period, however, never disappears, making itself felt in the desires and anxieties of the moment that inspire the backward glance. For instance, Ives's remembrance of "healthy New England childhood days" speaks of both personal and national malaise, which "middle-aged America" does not "care to admit."

These temporal chimeras (past and present appearing simultaneously as themselves and each other) create other paradoxes. Nostalgia, as Stewart argues, gives the impression of the past being at once intimate and distant as well as restored and lost.[17] The illusion of intimacy and restoration allure the nostalgic, pushing him or her further into paradox. As Vladimir Jankélévitch describes, that state can grow so deep as to leave the nostalgic disoriented, being at once here and there, conscious of both past and present.[18] Nostalgia, though, ultimately dissipates such ambiguity. Some works by Ives conclude with a sudden imposition of the present, an appearance that restores the listener to the "here" not to the "there." Nostalgia may float illusions of intimacy but it prefaces and closes them with statements of loss.

While plunged in those fantasies, the nostalgic has seemingly found bliss, believing him- or herself to be reconnected with the past. Those illusions, though, are far from peaceful. Nostalgia, as Jankélévitch argues, is a "restless" state.[19] The nostalgic is a driven figure, driven by the evasiveness of the past. The intimacy that he or she finds quickly fades, prompting yet another reach at that removed period. Recollection begets recollection. Each reminiscence attempts to reach the horizon of the past. Falling so woefully short, the nostalgic pushes on through another memory and gets no closer. Just as quixotic, he or she strives to complete the incomplete past.[20] Memories provide only a residue of the past, an insufficiency that leaves the nostalgic grasping for more in the hope that these traces may stick together and form something substantial. This restlessness can be heard in many Ives pieces. Collage compositions like *The Fourth of July* busily pile quotations on top of each other as if to build a stable shelter for the past. The frenetic construction only creates more instability, which inspires the throwing down of even more quotations and the escalation of chaos, all of which leads to the memory-edifice collapsing in the final measures. The past is more fragmentary at the end of such works than at the beginning.

---

[16] Stewart, *On Longing*, 23–24.   [17] Ibid., 20, 139.

[18] Vladimir Jankélévitch, *L'irréversible et la nostalgie* (Paris: Flammarion, 1974), 281.

[19] Ibid., 281.   [20] Ibid., 302–03.

What makes the nostalgic so restless is that the object of desire is not only out of reach but also vague. Nostalgia strives to return to a point of origins, an amorphous time that is never clearly known and cannot be recalled with any precision, let alone reached. Childhood is such a time, especially as depicted by Ives. In his works and writings, it amounts to either an inaccessible and ultimately unknowable state or a grand emptiness, which we fill with our own thoughts. To return to childhood then would not entail a return to days of picnics – it would instead amount to a fall into ambiguity and nothingness. Some of Ives's compositions sense as much, as they conclude with either open questions (the third movement of the Fourth Violin Sonata) or death ("Tom Sails Away").

If nostalgia does have an object it is not a specific site in the past. As Jankélévitch tells us, "the object of nostalgia is not such and such a place, but rather the reality of the past, in other words, pastness."[21] For pastness to exist, there must be a distance between past and present. Forever caught in paradoxes, the nostalgic wants to close that gap but at the same time he or she realizes that it must remain open. That gap is the space of nostalgia, without which the sensation could never exist. It must always have a far-away point at which to peer and an unsettled present from which to do so. Above all, nostalgia exists as a longing, and, with its object forever unattainable, it becomes in many ways a longing for a longing, a feeling that feeds upon its own desire.[22] Instead of proving embittered, the desire for the past can stir pleasure. To novelist Willa Cather (one of the nostalgics discussed below), nostalgia is a "melancholy pleasure" to be frequently indulged.[23] In yet another blending of opposites, it is a pleasure tinged with remorse, or, seen the other way around, remorse that has forked into pleasure. To preserve that pleasure the gap between past and present must never close.[24] Only when it is open can the nostalgic settle into the illusion of, as Cather put it, the past being brought back "so vividly into the living world for a moment" – but only for a moment.[25]

The music of childhood

Ives employed a range of musical gestures and idioms to evoke childhood. The first to come to mind is the composer's celebrated use of quotation. The compositions containing quotations in many ways

---

[21] Ibid., 290.

[22] Stewart, *On Longing*, 145, and Jankélévitch, *L'irréversible et la nostalgie*, 292.

[23] Willa Cather, *Lucy Gayheart*, in Sharon O'Brien, ed., *Later Novels* (New York: Library of America, 1990), 764.

[24] Stewart, *On Longing*, 145. [25] Cather, *Lucy Gayheart*, 772.

resemble scrapbooks, with the tune fragments as clipped mementos.[26] Ives pressed into his book mostly memories from his youth, many of the quoted melodies bearing childhood associations. This analogy captures the nostalgia surrounding the composer's quotations, as the souvenir collector derives pleasure from relating the surviving object to an original period or event, a connection involving the nostalgic negotiation of past and present.[27]

Quoted melodies invite a similar effort, as the listener links them with the past from which they come. Ever the nostalgic, Ives was not content with that simple affair. He did not merely borrow past tunes but distorted them.[28] Such treatment heightens nostalgia by doubling the distance between a melody and its origins, since to the chronological gap between a quotation and its period of currency there is added a musical one between the transformed and original versions. This expansion suggests something so removed that it cannot be reached, a melancholic assurance to the nostalgic. In Ives's case, that something is the referent of many of his quoted tunes: childhood.

As if distortion did not make the past distant enough, Ives availed himself of other gestures, including his incantational style. That idiom appears in slow passages, usually introductions, and is characterized by metrical stasis, rich dissonant chords, and melodic and harmonic repetition (Ex. 1.1 presents such a passage from "Tom Sails Away"). This feeling of suspension combined with repetition hints at an incantation, a suggestion strengthened by the texts of these passages. The opening of "Old Home Day," for instance, floats the enigmatic spell-like phrase "Go my songs! Draw Daphnis from the city," whereas that in "Down East" conjures "visions of my homeland." The incantations in both songs summon up childhood memories, including boys playing games and "schooldays." As these sections describe, however, such recollections remain elusive, barely coalescing into "scenes" and "visions."[29]

By the end of most childhood pieces, those scenes and visions disperse. These works end with incisive moments of disruption, sudden breaks from the preceding music. The ruptures take various forms, including the sudden harmonic shift in the last measures of "The Things

---

[26] Lloyd Whitesell also uses the scrapbook analogy in his discussion of "The Things our Fathers Loved," in "Reckless form, uncertain audiences: responding to Ives," *American Music* 12 (1994), 308–09.

[27] Stewart, *On Longing*, 145.

[28] For a discussion of this distortion, see Robert P. Morgan, "Ives and Mahler: mutual responses at the end of an era," *19th Century Music* 2 (1978), 72–81; and Lawrence Kramer, *Music and Poetry: the Nineteenth Century and After* (Berkeley and Los Angeles: University of California Press, 1984), 177–78.

[29] Feder has also singled out these passages. In discussions of the two songs, he hints at elements of incantation, referring to the "impressionistic spell-weaving musical texture that whispers, 'Now we are going back.'" Feder, *Charles Ives "My Father's Song,"* 314.

Ex. 1.1 lves, "Tom Sails Away," mm. 1–4

our Fathers Loved," the violent explosion in *The Fourth of July*, and the vague, inconclusive ending of the Fourth Violin Sonata.[30] Whatever the guise assumed, these breaks serve a similar function: they throw us out of a childhood past made to sound revived and intimate and back into an adult present which comes across as cold and hollow.[31] We are left with a feeling of loss, deprived of even the illusion of childhood.[32]

[30] In his discussion of nostalgia, Hepokoski describes a general pattern of "*telos* peaks and decay," in which the work builds up to a "climactic or revelatory *telos*" involving the statement of a quotation and then quickly subsides into a "diminuendo fade-out." Those softer concluding passages, according to him, evoke the loss of childhood. He does not concentrate on the disruptions that precede those passages. Burkholder has questioned Hepokoski's interpretation, pointing out that the "fade-out" is a gesture that occurs in a wide variety of contexts, and not just childhood nostalgia pieces. Hepokoski, "Temps perdu," 746–51; and J. Peter Burkholder, *All Made of Tunes*, 469, n. 70.

[31] This gesture is not limited to nostalgic pieces. It occurs in works focusing on some moments of introspection (like the nostalgic reflection on the past) and serves as a means of breaking the contemplative spell. Such a use of the gesture occurs in *The Housatonic at Stockbridge*.

[32] Not all recollections of childhood end in this fashion. There are exceptions. "Old Home Day" winds up with a rousing march. The second movement of the Third Symphony, entitled "Children's Day," ends conventionally with a gradual diminuendo and *ritard*.

Within these frames of incantation and disruption, boys and girls often appear as sites of boundless energy, a vigor that keeps them one step ahead of adults, thus making them even more removed. Ives captures this dynamism with what can be labeled his rambunctious style. Such early works as "Memories (A)" and "The Circus Band" depicting youthful vitality simply incorporate up-tempo genres like marches. As Ives grew further away from youth, however, children ran faster away from him. The Fourth Violin Sonata, of which the program for the first movement describes children out-maneuvering adults, and other later compositions not only rely on fast tempos but also feature accelerandos, syncopations, metric displacements, and different rhythmic strata, which combine to create a feeling of volatility.[33] Ives underscores these representations of kinetic youth by depicting adulthood as static. In "The Cage," a boy "wonders" if "life" (his adult future) will resemble the pacing trapped tiger, evoked by an aimless ostinato. "The See'r" presents us with a different type of caged animal, the commonplace "old man" sitting on Main Street, whose tedium Ives mocks with the inane repetition of the last line, "a-going by."

Two scenes from childhood

Having discussed childhood and nostalgia in general terms, this chapter will now look at what shapes they take in two works by Ives: "Tom Sails Away" and the Fourth Violin Sonata. The discussion of these pieces examines how the composer's handling of quotation shapes cultural conceptions of childhood. That line of inquiry overlaps with an account of how nostalgia is cultivated in these compositions, particularly the ways in which quotations arrange the relationship between past and present.

Before turning to these compositions, a few more words about nostalgia are in order. That topic has proven to be a disputed one in Ives studies. On one side, Larry Starr has warned against "the widespread misconception of Ives as a nostalgic composer."[34] Concluding his discussion of the song "The Things our Fathers Loved," Burkholder remarks "this is not an exercise in nostalgia for the songs and scenes of the past."[35] Stuart

---

[33] In his discussion of Ives's "up-tempo" movements, Lawrence Kramer also connects the "exuberant, antinomian musical energy" of those sections with "memories of [Ives's] boyhood." Kramer, *Classical Music and Postmodern Knowledge* (Berkeley and Los Angeles: University of California Press, 1995), 188.

[34] Larry Starr, *A Union of Diversities: Style in the Music of Charles Ives* (New York: G. Schirmer, 1992), 58.

[35] Burkholder, *All Made of Tunes*, 311. Burkholder cites Joseph W. Reed's study of Ives, which makes a similar point; Reed, *Three American Originals: John Ford, William Faulkner, and Charles Ives* (Middleton: Wesleyan University Press, 1984), 54–55. In a private

Feder, on the other hand, has called that song "Ives's most concentrated work of nostalgia" and has based much of his psychoanalytical study of the composer on the attempts to reconnect with the past.[36] Along these lines, James Hepokoski has placed Ives in a Proustian light, seeing the New Englander entranced by "temps perdu."[37]

This debate turns on the question of whether Ives's memory pieces extol the past or mourn it.[38] Starr and Burkholder claim that the composer prizes the past as a trove of values that need to be, and can be, reclaimed by listeners.[39] "The Things our Fathers Loved," to go back to that contentious song, are all "things" – the simplicity of small-town life and patriotism – that can still be grasped. This interpretation holds up half of the nostalgic equation, that of a troubled present looking to the past for stability, but rejects the crucial second part, the inaccessibility of that period. Feder and Hepokoski, in contrast, embrace both halves, even going so far as to emphasize the surrender to loss. Both center that loss around childhood. The latter sees Ives seeking the "motive of lost wholeness," the key to putting back together the world of youth, no matter how fleetingly.[40]

Befitting such a paradoxical state, nostalgia can be seen as encompassing, and to a degree reconciling, both interpretations. Hepokoski suggests as much, claiming that the "optimistic reading" and the melancholic one can "co-exist contradictorily" with each other.[41] There, however, may not be such a big contradiction. The works can gratify both interpretations, but only up to a point. Ives's music does rally around the beliefs of the past. But it goes beyond mere campaigning by having us feel the richness of those values. We are led into scenes in which the past and its values seem very much alive, an impression created by the use of the present tense and fast tempos. That illusion can only last so long before the rekindled past gives way to a spent one. The disruption of the fantasy does not completely cut us off from treasured principles of previous times. The sense of loss created at the end of these works

correspondence, Burkholder elaborated upon his position, stating that nostalgia does run through some Ives works but "that not all of Ives's visitations of the past are nostalgic." Private correspondence with author, 24 December 2001.

[36] Feder, *Charles Ives "My Father's Song,"* 253.   [37] Hepokoski, "Temps perdu," 746.

[38] Another important issue surrounding nostalgia is the apparent tension between that sensation and the modernist bearings of Ives's styles. Nostalgia has often been conveyed as a reaction against progress and the march of time. Ives has used it that way, as a protest against developments in modern society. On the other hand, he saw no tension between modernist idioms and the desire for the past. Indeed, the latter served him as a way of evoking the multifaceted scenes of the past and the tensions within his yearning for it. A similar point is made in Hepokoski, "Temps perdu," 751 and Botstein, "Innovation and nostalgia," 35–74.

[39] Starr, *Union of Diversities,* 58–69; and Burkholder, *All Made of Tunes,* 311.

[40] Hepokoski, "Temps perdu," 751.   [41] Ibid.

makes us feel even more urgently the need for those ideals, giving them life through their absence rather than their presence. We are left with the hope that they can be revived, one more shade of nostalgic wistfulness.[42]

The two works discussed below reveal different scenes of nostalgia. Each draws upon some or all of Ives's nostalgia gestures – quotation, disjunction, incantation, the illusion of a revived past – but employs them in distinct ways and to contrasting effects.[43] In a broader scheme, these pieces offer different approaches to memory. For Ives, memory and nostalgia are not one and the same. Not all of the works that turn back to the past get caught up in the paradoxes of nostalgia. Quite the contrary, memory takes a wide range of forms in Ives's music, as reflected in the unprecedented rich repertory of borrowing practices that he cultivated in part to pursue the past.[44] Ives can be seen as participating in a larger modernist fascination with memory, one shaped by such artists and thinkers as Proust, Freud, and Schoenberg, among others.[45] Their probing of reminiscence focuses on such questions as what is memory and how does it work. Each of Ives's memory pieces offers a unique solution to these questions, creating contrasting representations of the act of memory and the sensations it produces.

Some compositions find a solution through nostalgia. Having said that, it would be a mistake to jump to the conclusion that there are a circumscribed group of nostalgia pieces and defined criteria by which to identify them. The richness of Ivesian reminiscence confounds such firm categorization. Moreover, given how Ives's pieces generally position the past as distant (compared to the oppressively near and malignant past in Freudian repression schemes), it could be argued that his recollections (like Proust's) have a nostalgic cast to them. In some works, though, that sensation is especially concentrated. Creating that concentration are a feeling of loss, a wide rift between past and present, and the distance

---

[42] Another view of nostalgia should be mentioned here. Stuart Tannock has described a nostalgia that builds "continuity" with the past, links that can be used to enrich the present. He acknowledges that "discontinuity" is also a key element of nostalgia; however, as he weighs the elements of continuity and discontinuity, it is the former that is "over and above" the latter. That perspective clashes with the model developed here. Tannock, "Nostalgia critique," *Cultural Studies* 9 (1995), 456. Another study to take this position is Nancy Martha West, *Kodak and the Lens of Nostalgia* (Charlottesville, VA, and London: University of Virginia Press, 2000).

[43] These devices of course appear in other contexts than childhood nostalgia; however, Ives most often employed them to convey that desire, using them all together or just a few at a time.

[44] Burkholder, *All Made of Tunes*, 1–7.

[45] For a discussion of approaches to memory that emerged after the French Revolution and developed through the early modernist period (including the works of Proust and Freud), see Richard Terdiman, *Present Past: Modernity and the Memory Crisis* (Ithaca and London: Cornell University Press, 1993).

of the remembered object. When all three of these related elements are combined, the rueful glow of nostalgia is at its richest.[46]

"Tom Sails Away"

The song "Tom Sails Away" (1917) unfolds a triptych of nostalgia: the first panel offers an incantation passage, the second depicts childhood events and characters, and the third reveals a present clouded by war. That closing gloom inspired the work, which Ives placed in a set of three *Songs of the War* written in response to the American entry into World War I.[47] "Tom" ostensibly comments on the sacrifices and patriotism required by the war, yet the song dwells on images of childhood, not battle. Once again nostalgia offers refuge from a troubling present.[48] So in that dark year of 1917, Ives presents us not with trenches but with "lettuce rows" from a childhood garden. War makes one vague appearance, hanging over the day that Tom leaves for "over there."[49]

> Scenes from my childhood are with me,
> I'm in the lot behind our house up on the hill,
> a spring day's sun is setting,
> Mother with Tom in her arms is coming towards the garden;
> The lettuce rows are showing green.
> Thinner grows the smoke o'er the town,
> stronger comes the breeze from the ridge,
> 'Tis after six, the whistles have blown,
> the milk train's gone down the valley.
> Daddy is coming up the hill from the mill,
> We run down the lane to meet him.
> But today! Today Tom sailed away for, for over there, over
>   there, over there!
> Scenes from my childhood are floating before my eyes.[50]

---

[46] It should be mentioned that there are some works depicting childhood that do not embrace this sensation. For example, "Old Home Day," with its driving march, never stops for the melancholic reflection of nostalgia.

[47] For a discussion of how the songs relate to the war, see Alan Houtchens and Janis P. Stout, " 'Scarce heard amidst the guns below': intertextuality and meaning in Charles Ives's war songs," *Journal of Musicology* 15 (1997), 80–84.

[48] Nancy Martha West has discussed how Kodak advertisements emphasized nostalgic scenes during the War; West, *Kodak and the Lens of Nostalgia*, 187–99.

[49] Larry Starr offers an analysis of "Tom Sails Away" in his discussion of Ives's treatment of memory; Starr, *Union of Diversities*, 71–78.

[50] This is the text that appeared in the later *Nineteen Songs* edition (1935). In the original text of the *114 Songs*, the penultimate line reads "But today! In freedom's cause Tom sailed away for over there, over there, over there." The change for the later edition, as mentioned below, serves to call attention to the move from past recollection to the present.

The piece opens with the nostalgic set piece of the protagonist – and the listener – situated in the present and looking back to the past. Typical of Ives, his nostalgia goes beyond convention, as the protagonist does not merely recall the past but attempts to bring it to life through an incantation. A mysterious spell-like atmosphere hangs over the opening two measures, created by the slow tempo, soft dynamics, and, most of all, the use of whole-tone scales (Ex. 1.1). In the first measure, both whole-tone collections appear, but it is collection no. 2 (C♯, D♯, etc.) that stands out, as it sounds in the upper melodic line (d♯–c♯–b–a–g). The bead of that line, the repeated b–a–g figure, reappears in the voice part a measure later (transposed down a minor third), suggesting that it is an important part of the spell. It is.

The melodic phrase comes from "The Old Oaken Bucket," a song that unites Samuel Woodworth's 1817 poem with the air "Araby's Daughter" from the British composer George Kiallmark's adaptation of Thomas Moore's *Lalla Rookh* (1822) (Ex. 1.2).[51] The original text and later vocal setting typify the large body of nineteenth-century verse and songs that indulge in childhood nostalgia, either reflecting on those bygone days or in some cases expressing the wish to turn back into a child.[52] "The Old Oaken Bucket" achieved an unrivaled popularity in this genre. After the first known printing in 1843, it was frequently published, dominating music catalogs during the 1880s, the period of Ives's childhood.[53]

Ives quotes both the melody and text ("scenes [of] my childhood") of the song in the incantation passage.[54] Even with those two elements, "The Old Oaken Bucket" remains shrouded, obscured largely by the harmonic context. In the first measure, the melody hovers above the two whole-tone collections, while in the second, it sits atop a fifths-based chord. A closer look at the latter reveals it to comprise the first six notes of the E major scale, the tonic of "The Old Oaken Bucket" quotation. The slide from a whole-tone to a diatonic area would be expected to distill some clarity to the borrowing, but it does not. The ascending-fifths presentation of the E major pitches clouds the sense of that key, and, with it, the origins of the melody. Here and throughout "Tom," "The Old Oaken Bucket" dangles in the background. Nonetheless, the one-hundred-year vintage of the song and the focus on

---

[51] For a discussion of the sources and publication history of the song, see Josephine L. Hughes and Richard J. Wolfe, "The tunes of 'The Bucket'," *Bulletin of the New York Public Library* 65 (1961), 555–69; and James J. Fuld, *The Book of World-Famous Music: Classical, Popular, and Folk* (3rd edn; New York: Dover, 1985), 413–14.

[52] Kincaid, *Child-Loving*, 67.

[53] Fuld, *The Book of World-Famous Music*, 413; and Hughes and Wolfe, "The tunes of 'The Bucket'," 564.

[54] He quotes the two separately, not the text with the melody that it appears with in the song. This disjunction may suggest the fragmentation of the past.

Ex. 1.2 Woodworth and Kiallmark, "The Old Oaken Bucket"

How dear to this heart are the scenes of my child - hood When
The or - chard, the mea - dow, the deep tang - led wild - wood, And

fond re - col - lec - tion pre - sents them to view. The wide - spread - ing stream, __ the
ev' - ry lov'd spot which my in - fan - cy knew.

mill that stood by it, the bridge and the rock where the cat - a - ract fell, The

cot of my fa - ther, the dai - ry house nigh it, And e'en the rude buck - et that

Chorus

hung in the well, The old oak - en buck - et, the i - ron-bound buck - et, the

moss - cov - ered buck - et that hung in the well.

That moss-covered bucket I hailed as a treasure,
For often at noon, when returned from the field,
I found it a source of an exquisite pleasure,
The purest and sweetest that nature can yield.
How ardent I seized it, with hands that were glowing,
And quick to the white pebbled bottom it fell.
Then soon, with the emblem of truth overflowing,
And dripping with coolness, it rose from the well.
Chorus:

How sweet from the green, mossy brim to receive it,
As poised on the curb it inclined to my lips!
Not a full blushing goblet could tempt me to leave it,
Tho' filled with the nectar that Jupiter sips.
And now, far removed from the loved habitation,
The tear of regret will intrusively swell,
As fancy reverts to my father's plantation,
And sighs for the bucket that hung in the well.
Chorus:

remembering youth combine to make it a potent ingredient in Ives's spell.

The spell works immediately as we find ourselves in a youthful scene brought to life through the use of the present tense ("I'm in the lot behind our house up on the hill"). The movement from present to past eases by, compared to the abrupt disruptions that throw us in the opposite direction at the end of a work. The flow of this transition is enhanced by having elements of the incantation warp and fade away as we slide into the past. The rolled fifth-based chords in the piano lead to a progression of similarly-played dissonant collections, containing no fifths, that ascend by whole and half steps from f♯ to a♮. Apparently, one moves upward to go back in time, at least in Ives's works. Considering that ascending chromatic motion has traditionally created a sense of propulsion, that gesture is appropriate, for it makes the past seem all the more alive. In the vocal part, chips of "The Old Oaken Bucket" dissolve. Brief dotted rhythms lilt in the voice, and the chief melodic phrase splinters, broken apart and now descending chromatically instead of by step (g♯–f♯–e–g♯–f♯–e becomes g–f♯–g–f♯–e♮).

Ex. 1.3 Ives, "Tom Sails Away," mm. 5–8

With the next phrase ("a spring day's sun is setting"), "The Old Oaken Bucket" material has largely disappeared.[55] There is no longer a need for it, as the past has apparently been revived. The text mounts a series of brief individual scenes, each of which receives a distinct setting, distinguished by the use of whole-tone, pentatonic, diatonic, and chromatic collections (or combinations thereof). Within this sequence, the image of "mother" holding the infant Tom in her arms stands out (see Ex. 1.3). The voice cradles this mother–son image with a simple melody appropriate for a nursery-rhyme song. True to character, the melody is tonal, in E major (the key of "The Old Oaken Bucket"); however, the accompaniment, again as in "The Old Oaken Bucket" incantation, dims that key, though not nearly to the same degree. The piano underpins the melody with a dominant-seventh chord, but that chord chromatically wavers, alternating between itself and a diminished triad with a major seventh

---

[55] As pointed out below, fragments of the tune do appear here and there. Wayne Shirley has suggested to me that the opening measures also include a quotation of "Deep River," an appropriate allusion given the equation of death and crossing a body of water in both songs. John Kirkpatrick has also remarked on the possible quotation of "Deep River." Kirkpatrick, *A Temporary Mimeographed Catalogue of the Music Manuscripts and Related Materials of Charles Edward Ives, 1874–1954* (1960; rpr. New Haven: Yale University Press, 1973), 201.

(b–d–f–a). The regular alternation of those two chords is enhanced by the steady swaying of f♯ and b/a pedals. The whole phrase returns in mm. 14–15, this time stated completely in the piano while the voice follows the "milk train" down the hill with a new descending melody.

By this time, we have been caught up in a rush of youthful scenes, which, through the use of accelerandos and an increasingly active accompaniment, have grown "more animated." The song moves from what initially appears to be a narration of the past in present tense to a feeling that the described events are occurring in the present. This increased agitation culminates with the children "running" into the arms of "Daddy." That paternal scene strongly suggests that the protagonist is an Ives surrogate, as the composer often attempted to connect with his father (George) in his childhood narratives. As such the episode makes a fitting climax for the song, in terms of both the musical and the nostalgic dramas at play. The phrase (Ex. 1.4, mm. 15–19) begins with one last accelerando and pushes into the highest and lowest ranges reached by the keyboard. In addition, it concludes with a simultaneous statement of both whole-tone collections, a confluence that gives chromatic completion.

At this point, the nostalgic fantasy nears culmination. No sooner has "Daddy" stepped into the song than the past disappears, eclipsed by the arrival of "today." "But today! Today" the protagonist reiterates so as to make clear the arrival of the present. The accompaniment has already announced that arrival, signaling it with a disruption, the surprise appearance of the fifth-based rolled chord from the incantation (see Ex. 1.4). That chord, though, has sunk down a half step from its first appearance (from an f♯ to an f♮ root). Whereas ascending chromatic motion leads back into the past, descending movement pushes forward into the present.

The gap between past and present has reopened but we have not yet completely crossed over into the latter, instead we are caught between the two periods, part of that limbo – here and there – state that Jankélévitch sees as so characteristic of nostalgia. Ives commemorates the day of Tom's departure with two quotations: one from the past ("Columbia, the Gem of the Ocean" in both piano and voice) and one from 1917 (George M. Cohan's "Over There"). The former may seem at first not to be an object of nostalgia but rather one of the reclaimed past values upheld by some Ives scholars, a patriotic call that is needed in the present. "Columbia" does indeed rouse the present, but it ultimately belongs to the past. Typical of Ives's nostalgia, it remains a fragment. The melodic line in the piano never reaches the final note of the borrowed phrase, left tattered and incomplete like the past. In contrast, the song from the present, "Over There," stays intact (at least the phrase quoted by Ives), being firmly part of "today."

Ex. 1.4 Ives, "Tom Sails Away," mm. 15–26

Another facet of "today" is the return of the opening incantation passage that concludes the song (see Ex. 1.4). That reprise is a unique case in Ives's oeuvre. Once having worked their magic, those spells do not return. Instead of taking us back into the past, the passage now serves to push us further into the present. The conclusion provides a compelling example of how Ives enlarges the gulf between the two periods, as he takes two steps away from the past. The song first moves into a national present, a time when the country must unite in fighting for "freedom's cause." It then strides further ahead into a personal present, the protagonist looking back at the past. That time has moved on, even from the present at the beginning of the piece, is suggested by the transposition of the incantation passage down a half-step, a transposition already heard with the appearance of the rolled chord that proclaimed the arrival of "today." Ives emphasizes the transposition by moving from g♭ to f♮ in the bass (mm. 24–25). Through this second step into the present, the ending deepens what Cather called the "melancholy pleasure" of nostalgia. The protagonist sits in the present mulling over "The Old Oaken Bucket," a treasured tune about childhood memories, and looking back at his own past, which is now even more distant.

The presence of "The Old Oaken Bucket" extends beyond the opening and closing passages, as "Tom" draws additional material from it. Like the older piece, Ives's work moves from the initial instance of recollection to the desired childhood scenes, which in both songs feature outdoor sketches and a father. The two also link childhood with an object that is remembered but cannot be retrieved. In "The Old Oaken Bucket," the "rude bucket" represents youth, whereas, in Ives's piece, Tom, perhaps headed toward his death overseas, embodies the protagonist's vanquished childhood. Both songs muse upon the objects. The chorus of the older one longingly refers over and over to the bucket. In "Tom," the cut-short youth of the title character underlies the melancholic repetition of "over there" with its echoes of "Taps," notably different from the original spirited refrain in Cohan's original, a contrast suggesting Tom's impending death.

The two works conclude by returning to the present. "Far removed from the loved [plantation]," Woodworth's protagonist "sighs" over lost childhood days. The song, however, cushions this blow by concluding with the chorus, which points the listener back to the past and gives the impression that the bucket and the youth it represents are just within reach. Ives, however, is not so comforting. "Tom" ends with a reprise of the opening incantation section, leaving its listener in a troubling present. The abrupt turn from the symbolic childhood object to the adult protagonist and his recollections heightens the sense of distance and loss and, by doing so, surpasses the already high level of nostalgia in "The Old Oaken Bucket."

34

Ives's incorporation of the song illustrates an expanded form of quotation, since, in addition to melodic and textual phrases, the imagery, thematics, mood, and general narrative of the older piece find their way into "Tom." Ives, however, does not so much borrow from "The Old Oaken Bucket" as work within its tradition. As his emulation of that song reveals, cultural objects embodying nineteenth-century childhood nostalgia provided the composer with a means of appreciating youth and of enjoying nostalgic desire. Besides providing a model in how to channel that desire, "The Old Oaken Bucket" becomes the object of it. As if the song's origins in the early decades of the previous century were not enough, Ives buries the piece in "Tom," where it remains a distant and obscured inspiration. Both remote and rooted in the past, "The Old Oaken Bucket" resembles what it longs for: childhood.

Distance is one of the chief means by which Ives depicts youth in "Tom." His childhood scenes occur in a vague past in which characters and object, with the telling exception of "Daddy," fade away: the thinning smoke, the disappearing train, and Tom. In this light, "over there" refers not to far-off European battlefields but to the remembered "lots" and "gardens" of childhood. Only innocent youths play in those areas, and that is the way Ives wants to keep Tom. The possible demise of the characters evokes the dead child, a figure of unequaled purity that appears frequently in representations of youth.[56] Death not only empties those children, including Tom, of any "impurities" but it also keeps them forever in the realm of childhood. Ives's song keeps Tom there. For the portentous line "Today Tom sailed away," Ives turns back to the first and only other line to mention Tom by name: "Mother with Tom in her arms." To recall, the latter line was set with a childlike melody. For the departure of the young soldier, a military melody, "Columbia, the Gem of the Ocean," appropriately sounds. Different in character and circumstance as they may be, the two melodies are linked. They are in close keys – E major for the nursery-rhyme song and B major for "Columbia." Most intriguingly, the accompaniment for "Columbia" draws upon the regular sounding f♯ and a/b pedals that supported the child-like song (see Ex. 1.4). That parallel connects present with past and young adult with child Tom. Above all, it immures Tom in youthful innocence, his death-sleep soothed by the steady rocking of those pedals, a rocking given first and now forever by "Mother."

Desiring such preservation without the cost of early death, Ives joins Tom by jumping into the childhood scenes. "*We* run down the lane to meet [Daddy]," he exclaims, picturing himself and Tom as lads once more. The first-person plural weaves its magic in some of his other works. In "Old Home Day," "we boys," a favorite phrase of the

---

[56] Kincaid, *Child-Loving*, 80–82.

composer, march down "Main Street," whereas in "The Circus Band," they watch the grand entrance of a circus troupe on that same generic street. Such youthful parades and dashes typify regression fantasies, moments in which the adult tries to settle in the removed world of childhood, often by referring to himself as a youth and joining the company of other children.

Even a heart-on-the-sleeve song like "The Old Oaken Bucket" does not go this far, being happy enough to reflect back on youth, not to return to it.[57] Yet the piece teases listeners with the idea of such a return. Woodworth depicts the well in which the bucket is dipped as a fountain of youth, a source that not only replenishes the vigor of the child protagonist but promises to restore that energy to him in later years. Notably, the text does not portray that restoration, or the replenishment for that matter, leaving us with the image of the bucket "poised" on the protagonist's "lips." This lip-hanger preserves the tantalizing possibility that youth cannot be remembered only but perhaps recaptured as well.

Ives, on the other hand, drinks from the bucket, becoming a skipping boy once more. As in the older song, however, he realizes, albeit after the fact, that this fantasy was best left as a tempting dream. This belated awareness leads him to withdraw quickly from that dream. After he and Tom scamper away, the song suddenly turns to the title character's departure. The quotations of "Over There" and "Columbia, the Gem of the Ocean" draw the listener's attention away from the composer's regression into a contemporary patriotic moment. With the following reprise of the incantation passage, Ives takes another step away from that embarrassing moment, much as "The Old Oaken Bucket" cuts to its older protagonist after only toying with the idea of partaking from its fountain of youth. In Ives's concluding passage, an adult speaks to us, recounting a childhood that exists merely in fragmentary scenes, which at the beginning of the song were "with" the protagonist but by the end are, like Tom, "floating" "away."[58]

---

[57] Feder's description of Ives's psychological state at the time of the American entry into the war accords with this interpretation of a regression fantasy. As he points out, "Ives now relived his family's past with a growing inner urgency." Feder, *Charles Ives "My Father's Song,"* 283.

[58] As mentioned previously, the reprise of the incantation passage is a half step lower than its original statement, a transposition suggesting loss and distance. A similar suggestion is made by the last three notes of the piano part (a–d–g) which are a retrograde statement of the preceding three notes (g♯–d♯–a♯) transposed down a half step. The motion down a half step and backwards conveys the idea of moving further away or crossing beyond a certain point, where things are now different (backwards and lower). That idea evokes another Ives song, "Remembrance," which, like "Tom," mixes together images of death, water, and a father. The rhythm of the last three notes in that song (quarter–quarter–half notes) is a retrograde of the dominant rhythm heard throughout the brief song. The two songs also employ harmonies built upon fifths. Moreover, the use of fourths in the final

The Fourth Violin Sonata

The Fourth Violin Sonata, subtitled "Children's Day at the Camp Meeting," stages many of the same representations, characters, and desires active in "Tom."[59] The program of the work features "scenes" from a past childhood; however, unlike those in "Tom," they are specified in terms of place and year: children's church services in rural Connecticut of the 1870–90s.[60] The youths in the two works are similar. Ives once again presents us with boisterous children, who, in the Sonata, repeatedly march or disrupt the ongoing services, an unceasing energy that notably leads them away from the observing adults. Not only do the same types of children pop up in the Sonata, but so does George Ives, evoked by a quotation of his Fugue in B♭ in the first movement, the scenario of which has him "making" his organist son (Charles) play strange dissonances. George and the general memories of youth exert a gravitational pull on Charles, drawing him back into the past. He offers little resistance, as the Sonata presents another regression fantasy, one quite different in both means and outcome from that in "Tom."

Although both "Tom" and the Sonata convey a desire to return to the past, they position that period differently. The song blurs the lines between past and present so as to give the former a sense of immediacy. The Sonata draws a clearer line between the two. The narrated action, unlike that in "Tom," takes place in the past tense. Moreover, these occurrences are described as "actual happenings," placing them in the history books. Whereas the past is rich in details, the present is sparse, almost invisible. No timely event, such as the war, hovers over the work. Nor does a protagonist speak to us from the present and cast spells to call up the past. In lieu of such fantastical incantations, the program

---

pitches of both songs evokes "Taps." These parallels reinforce the idea of impending death in "Tom."

[59] Ives had originally planned for the sonata to be played by a child, his twelve-year-old nephew Moss White; however, the last two movements proved too difficult, not only for Moss but also for his teacher; Ives, *Memos*, ed. John Kirkpatrick (New York: Norton, 1972), 72.

[60] For the program, see Ives, "Notes on Fourth Violin Sonata," in *Sonata No. 4 for Violin and Piano ("Children's Day at the Camp Meeting")* (1942; rpr. New York, n.d.), 21. Pointing out that this program was written after the Sonata, Burkholder argues that it and those for the First and Third Violin Sonatas "should be understood as explaining only the character of the music, not its structure, form, or meaning. What happens in these pieces is based on musical rather than programmatic ideas, and primarily on the formal plan of cumulative setting" (Burkholder, *All Made of Tunes*, 249–50). In contrast to Burkholder, I place much stock in the interpretative value of the program. Whether written before, during, or after composition, a program sheds light on various aspects of a piece. Indeed, a post-compositional program can be regarded as a composer's interpretation of his or her own work and thus provides insights into how he or she understands that work.

of the Sonata monotones: "The subject matter is a kind of reflection, remembrance, expression, etc. of children's services."

By erasing the present, Ives places himself in the past. The first movement finds him already there: Charles playing the organ, George watching over his shoulder, and the boys outside marching. As in "Tom," we encounter a young Charles; however, in the program, that child stands apart from the youths around him. Rather than the inclusive "we," Ives presents himself as removed from the other boys, who become even more distant by tramping away from the central church scene to "their tents," a faraway, undescribed realm of childhood. Regression fantasies serve to close, not to expand, that distance – a contradiction that signals early on that this fantasy will falter.

In the third movement, Ives tries a different approach. Rather than an autobiographical scenario, he presents a universalist tableau played out by boys and "old men."[61] Unlike in other descriptions of childhood, the adults, some of them at least, manage to keep up "(sometimes)" with the marching youths. Their reward for such stamina? In an enigmatic phrase implying some sort of union, the two "Gather at the River."

As the boys get marching again some of the old men would join in and march as fast (sometimes) as the boys and sing what they felt, regardless – and – thanks to Robert Lowry – "Gather at the River."

Ives's quotation of Lowry's hymn "The Beautiful River" (Ex. 1.5), though, suggests that the two will never meet. Before discussing that occlusion, the handling of the quotation needs to be examined. In each of the three movements, Ives employs a quotation technique that Burkholder has called "cumulative form."[62] This design is characterized by a melody slowly taking shape, usually appearing in fragments at the beginning of a piece and, by the end, attaining a near complete form, albeit one with characteristic Ivesian deformations. Following such a pattern, cumulative form lends itself well to the gratification of nostalgic desire. It leaps to the challenge of completing the incomplete past, driven by the promise of clutching a whole melody from childhood, and with it childhood itself. That drive proceeds with the restlessness characteristic of nostalgic recollection. The music constantly picks through, discards, and cobbles together fragments, all the time pushing toward the desired whole statement. That consolidation of memory never comes, as

---

[61] Drawing upon Gayle Sherwood's manuscript research, Burkholder (*All Made of Tunes*, 193) provides a ca. 1914 date for this movement and points out that it is based on a sketch of a work for cornet and strings from 1905. James Sinclair states the work was assembled ca. 1916 from movements composed 1900–16; Sinclair, *A Descriptive Catalogue of the Music of Charles Ives* (New Haven and London: Yale University Press, 1999), 156.

[62] Burkholder, *All Made of Tunes*, 137–266.

Ex. 1.5

the closing statements remain incomplete to different degrees. In some works, the melodies are battered by other tune fragments and the surrounding frenetic activity; in other words, nostalgic restlessness mars the completion that it seeks. Elsewhere, the melodies frequently break down, succumbing to disruptions of various sorts, or they never attain full closure, missing parts of the last phrase or having the final cadence obscured.[63] Cumulative form brings us so close to wholeness yet so far from it. In yet another twinge of nostalgic paradox, such quotations attain the most complete statements of the past – complete in terms of overall melodic and formal structure – but also the most incomplete, in the sense that they, more than fragments, painfully elude our embrace.

That incompleteness wounds particularly in the third movement of the Sonata, as no sooner has the tune formed than it fades into the past. The movement divides into three sections, across which the materialization of the tune takes place. The first part (mm. 1–18) obsessively mills through distorted fragments of individual phrases (those marked a, b, and c in Ex. 1.5) and dissonant accompanimental ostinatos. In the second section (mm. 19–36), the phrase structure – two four-measure units – and the harmony of the tune come initially into view; however, more melodic distortion occurs, especially Ives's play on the opening whole-step descent of the tune (figured as both a whole and a half step in a countermelody).

With the third section (mm. 37–57, Ex. 1.6), Lowry's tune congeals further. The entire melody is stated, with some modifications. The phrase

---

[63] Hepokoski discusses these types of endings; "Temps perdu," 747–51.

Ex. 1.6

format, now two eight-measure units (with extensions), appears, supported by a slight harmonic framework consisting of dominant–tonic definition points. Those tonal touchstones as well as the melody itself, though, are at times overwhelmed and obscured by the rush of nondiatonic triads, triadic extensions, and dissonant collections. The melody makes it through that rush but it never wholly solidifies. At the end of the chief eight-measure phrases, Ives adds on measures (mm. 45 and mm. 54–57) that not only block the continuity of the quotation but also cloud the tonality. The first interruption moves abruptly away from the Eb major tonic and dead-ends into a D major/minor chord, whereas the second leaves the piece suspended on a minor dominant triad in the accompaniment – a tonal phrasing of the unstated textual question "shall we gather at the river?"

Ex. 1.6 (*cont.*)

These interpolations function as nostalgic disruptions.[64] The sense of disruption is especially potent as it is achieved through the kernel of nostalgia, the remembered tune. Both interpolations restate earlier hymn phrases: the first recaptures the just-heard c phrase, while the second elides the c and a units into one phrase. The two are not mere echoes but rather recollections, bearing all the hallmarks of Ivesian memory: a presence in a separate musical dimension (here, softer dynamics and a decrease in tempo), distortion, and melodic and tonal incompleteness. As such, they clash with the cumulative design, which clarifies a melody, having it form in the present, instead of obscuring it in the shadows of the past. This contradiction implies that the union between adulthood and childhood alluded to in the program will not occur. The two reminiscences preserve the distance between past and present,

[64] For Hepokoski's view of this movement, see ibid., 751.

which in Ives's work signifies that between the two generations. At the end of the movement, the listener reflects back on "The Beautiful River" much as the many adults in Ives's pieces muse on the days of their youth. The absence of tonal closure in these passages, and in the movement as a whole, enhances the suggestion that the generation gap has not been sealed. Furthermore, the increase in tempo (Allegro molto) for the second phrase of the hymn, which is notably absent in the related vocal setting ("At the River"), evokes Ives's rambunctious style, hinting that the "marching" "boys" are moving further away from the "old men."

As in "Tom," the attempt to experience childhood – either by returning to it or by fusing together the generations – fails. "Tom" agonizes over that failure, ending with a jerk away from the past and despair over the disintegration of memories. The Sonata, on the other hand, reaches an ambivalent conclusion. The program holds out hope for a union, while the music comments on the futility of that desire. This equivocality checks the despondency voiced in "Tom" and accounts for the restrained, if not enigmatic, ending of the work.

The cultural tradition of childhood nostalgia

With his childhood works, Ives stepped into the shoes of Louisa May Alcott. As he said of her novels, his pieces offer adults "memory pictures of healthy New England childhood days." By dispensing that youthful tonic, the two participated in the cultural discourse of childhood. They both drew upon established conceptions of youth, particularly Victorian ones, shaped those notions in their works, and then released them back into the cultural arena, where they interacted with dominant conceptions. Alcott's novels largely reinforce Victorian views, creating, as Ives recognized, idyllic youthful scenes of purity and innocence. Ives's pieces, on the other hand, uphold such ideals but at the same time work against them by placing those conceptions in ultimately somber, not so idyllic, contexts. His compositions alight upon Victorian notions of childhood – vivacity and innocence – but darken them. Vivacity further drives apart childhood and adulthood; whereas innocence settles in death and mourning. Such "memory pictures" might have unsettled Alcott's readers. In the works discussed above, childhood emerges as a site of loss and emptiness. It has been put asunder by the passing of time. Captured by the distant past, it can never be possessed. "Pictures," or representations of youth, only yield fragments and voids, the emptiness of death and silence. "Memory" proves no more reliable. Its restless energy does not close the gap between past and present but rather broadens it, leaving childhood at an even greater remove.

The cultural role of Ives's childhood works can be better understood by placing them in the context of a larger stream of nostalgia that ran through early-twentieth-century America. That flow has been countered by an equally enduring push for progress. Lawrence Levine describes this conflict as "the central paradox of American history." He cites the 1920s, a decade that billed itself as the "New Era" yet witnessed both a backlash against forces of modernization and a call for the traditional values of small-town America.[65] Similar tensions characterize the previous two decades, the years during which Ives composed the majority of his works. Like the 1920s, this period wrestled with ambivalent attitudes toward new technologies and urbanization, uncertainties that led to a growing idealized vision of the past century.[66]

For his part, Ives repeatedly and bluntly upheld the previous century as an Edenic state, decrying technological developments and the growth of cities. The program of *Central Park in the Dark* curses the "combustion engine and radio" for "monopolizing the earth and air." "The New River" reverberates with "the sounds of man" ("phonographs and gasoline, dancing halls and tambourine") that "kill" those of nature ("rolling water") and the past ("the hunting horn"). As a remedy to such ills, "The Things our Fathers Loved" sets us down on a small-town Main Street decked out in the "red, white and blue" and alive with the very human and traditional sounds of "Aunt Sara humming Gospel" and the "village cornet band."

A child appears behind the scenes of many of these works. "The Things our Fathers Loved" evokes Ives's Danbury boyhood. The ubiquity of children in these and such other memory pieces as "Tom" and the Fourth Violin Sonata places those compositions within a separate tradition in that larger nostalgic current passing through American culture: that of childhood nostalgia. This tradition presents children as symbols of a distant and innocent past. Such depictions crowd early-twentieth-century arts and popular media, emerging from the extensive changes in American life and the increasingly idealized view of the previous century.

Standing out in that nostalgic crowd are the works of Willa Cather and Mary Pickford. Unlike Ives, these two women did not use quotation as a means of channeling nostalgic desire; nonetheless, their works are relevant to this study for they provide a broader context for Ives's

---

[65] Lawrence W. Levine, *The Unpredictable Past: Explorations in American Cultural History* (New York: Oxford University Press, 1993), 190–205. David C. Stinebeck has studied the conflict between modernization and nostalgia in a number of American novels written between 1823 and 1956; Stinebeck, *Shifting World: Social Change and Nostalgia in the American Novel* (Lewisburg, PA: Bucknell University Press, 1976).

[66] On nostalgia during this period, see Peter Conn, *The Divided Mind: Ideology and Imagination in America, 1898–1917* (New York: Cambridge University Press, 1983).

compositions and show that he was involved in a larger evocation of an idyllic nineteenth-century childhood. In such novels as *The Song of the Lark* (1915) and *My Ántonia* (1918), Willa Cather looked back at a disappearing Midwest childhood.[67] Chronicling the life of opera singer Thea Kronborg, the former has more to say about the girl living in Colorado than the Diva's triumphs in New York or Europe. The lengthy opening section entitled "Friends of Childhood" recounts little Thea's adventures in the town of Moonstone, a name begging the nostalgic question: What is more distant – childhood or the moon?[68] Cather's surprising answer is Arizona. Discouraged with her musical studies in Chicago, Thea seeks revitalization by living in the deserted, decaying cliff dwellings of a Southwestern Native American tribe, known only as "the Ancient People." With this Arizona antiquity, Cather suggests a past more remote than that of youth. Yet, like all nostalgics, she realizes that no period is that far away. After a few days in her adobe escape, Thea finds that "everything was simple and definite, as things had been in childhood."[69]

Cather, like many of her contemporaries, intertwines youth and the "primitive" – the label often applied to non-Western or indigenous peoples to convey a perceived "savagery" and chronological remoteness. Besides that distance, both categories share a desired naturalness, purity, and spontaneity, the confluence of which appears in such stereotypes as the childish black featured in nostalgic songs about the South. Ives rejects this association, setting his "scenes of childhood" almost exclusively in New England, a locale that in his works and writings appears to have been always "civilized" and white.[70]

Rather than taking the primitivist route back to childhood, *My Ántonia* pursues a regression fantasy similar to that in "Tom." At the end of the novel, the adult narrator Jim Burden visits his boyhood friend Ántonia Cuzak. He not only reflects back on their youthful activities but also returns to childhood by sleeping in the haystacks with her sons and planning hunting excursions and adventures with them. Not surprisingly, "The Old Oaken Bucket" rolls into the novel; however, unlike in "Tom," it serves not as a means of returning to the past but rather as a

---

[67] On nostalgia in Cather's novels, especially *The Professor's House*, see Stinebeck, *Shifting Worlds*, 101–14.

[68] It should also be noted that Cather presents Moonstone as a place from which her character must "escape," before the tedium of small-town life eventually smothers her talents. The awareness of that potentially dangerous monotony, however, only slightly distracts from Cather's fond recollections of that fading world.

[69] Willa Cather, *Song of the Lark* (Boston: Houghton Mifflin, 1937), 380.

[70] In his discussion of race and gender in Ives's music, Kramer argues that "nostalgia [was] invented in the service of cultural purity"; Kramer, *Classical Music and Postmodern Knowledge*, 198.

symbol of nostalgia gone too far. Ántonia recounts the story of a "tramp" who throws himself into a thresher. One of the few items found on the corpse is a "nearly worn out" copy of Woodworth's poem. Through this satirical suicide, Cather draws a line between unhealthy and healthy nostalgia. Most likely obsessed with and debilitated by that feeling, the tramp fulfills a death wish implicit in the poem: throwing oneself in the well from which the magic water of youth and the past is drawn. Respected attorney Jim Burden (and novelist Cather), on the other hand, merely hop into a haystack.[71]

The most popular child of the 1910s and early 1920s was an adult: Mary Pickford. Throughout her twenties, the actress played a variety of youthful roles, including both girls and boys (the effeminate Little Lord Fauntleroy). With the exception of the occasional spitfire, these parts recycle the cliché of the innocent child, curls and all.[72] Not surprisingly, many of Pickford's child films participate within the tradition of childhood nostalgia, often, as in *Esmeralda* (1915), *The Foundling* (1916), and *M'Liss* (1918), being set in nineteenth-century small-town America. Moreover, several of them derive from either children's literature of that period, including Frances Hodgson Burnett's novel *Little Lord Fauntleroy*, or early-twentieth-century works that shaped this halcyon vision of the preceding era, such as Kate Douglas Wiggin's *Rebecca of Sunnybrook Farm*. Even in films featuring Pickford as an adult, such nostalgia emerges. *Caprice* (1913) has Mary tearfully asking her father to "take me back to the old home."

What made Pickford's brand of childhood nostalgia so popular was her success in conveying regression fantasies. Rather than the allusion of Ives's "Gather[ing] at the River" or Cather's "primitive" sojourns, her films offered audiences elaborate visual realizations of the adult actress as child. This transformation was achieved sometimes through camera angles and oversize props but most often by placing Pickford in the company of real-life children, making her "innocent" by association, much like Ives's magical "we." The actress's publicity team sought to keep the generational lines blurred, forcing her to wear the annoying curls offscreen and forbidding her to smoke. Harry Carr, a columnist for *Motion Pictures Magazine*, suggests how much Pickford's appeal depended on her ability to pull off that fantasy. In his bitchy swipe at the over-the-hill thirty-two-year-old actress, he not only evokes the magic of regression but also repeats the typical nostalgic view of youth as lost and inaccessible.

---

[71] Willa Cather, *My Ántonia* (Boston: Houghton Mifflin, 1949), 118–20.

[72] Pickford also played a variety of adult roles, although many of them hover around the constructed and always shifting border between adolescence and adulthood.

At an age when childhood is almost a sad and forgotten memory with most women, Mary can slip away in her locked garden and be a child again. And Mary Pickford knows that the day is coming when her locked garden will be desolate and empty: when she will call for the little girl among the roses and mignonette; but she will never find her.[73]

That day did come, and, perhaps not coincidentally, Pickford's acting career ended eight years after Carr's prediction. Her films have an ambivalent response to growing up: in some, she plays a girl throughout, whereas, during the course of others, she ages into a young woman. This maturation ironically strengthens the cinematic illusion of regression, allowing the viewer to acknowledge Pickford's adulthood while simultaneously partaking in her childhood world. Moreover, the loss of youth heightens the level of nostalgia. Even films in which the actress plays a child throughout tug at this sentimental cord. *Little Lord Fauntleroy*, featuring a unique case of double casting, contains an embarrassing moment of self-referentiality: Pickford playing mother turns to Pickford playing son and pouts: "Cedric, I cannot bear to have you grow up."

Childhood nostalgia makes for strange bedfellows – or haystack companions. Little else could bring together the trio of Ives, Cather, and Pickford. Even in this company, the three stand apart, each presenting a personal vision of childhood: boys marching in New England, boy and girl best friends scouting the Nebraska plains, and blond-curled cherubs charming small-town adults. No matter what the setting, they each perceive a lost tranquility and innocence. Ruling over these scenes is a child, a figure in which the three adults see so much of themselves, yet at the same time painfully recognize so little.

---

[73] Quoted in Anthony Slide, *The Griffith Actresses* (New York: A. S. Barnes, 1973), 75.

2

Black and white: quotations in Duke Ellington's "Black and Tan Fantasy"

On the Seventh Day, God created the spiritual. The Garden of Eden: a lawn outside of an antebellum Southern white church, where a group of slaves has secretly gathered to hear a Sunday morning church service.

Huddled there, they passed the Word of God around in whispers...Noiselessly...they'd inch a bit closer...When the great white voice inside rang out in Triumph...the blacks outside would grunt subdued approval. When the whites inside lifted voices in joyous song...the blacks outside would hum along, adding their own touches...weaving melodic, harmonic, rhythmic patterns. Thus the spiritual was born. Highly emotional worshipping of God in SONG.

This creation story – spanning seven days from a mythic Monday to Sunday and featuring an Adam and Eve named Boola and Voola – comes from Duke Ellington's scenario for *Black, Brown, and Beige*, his "tone parallel to the history of the Negro in America."[1] As a divinely created song, the spiritual watches over that history. In *Black, Brown, and Beige*, Ellington's spiritual melody – the lucent "Come Sunday" – offers solace, chimes faith, and extols triumphs.

This glorification of the spiritual and the "tone parallel" recounting of African-American history furthered the ideals of the Harlem Renaissance, a cultural movement that aimed to uplift blacks in American society by celebrating their artistic and historical achievements. During the Renaissance, the spiritual was lauded as one of the achievements of the race. In his influential essay "Of the sorrow songs," W. E. B. Du Bois helped crown the genre, presenting it as a noble voice of suffering, raised during slavery, which conveyed the sadness,

---

[1] Duke Ellington, *Black, Brown, and Beige*, typescript (Duke Ellington Collection, Smithsonian Institution, Washington, D.C.). For a discussion of this scenario, see Mark Tucker, "The genesis of *Black, Brown, and Beige*," *Black Music Research Journal* 13 (1993), 67–86. I had the pleasure of working with Mark Tucker on this chapter and am grateful for the stimulating and perspicacious commentary that he gave me, qualities that extend to all things Ellington that he touched.

hope, and faith expressed by its creators to following generations.[2] Du Bois's conception of the "sorrow songs" served as the Renaissance ideal of the genre and was musically realized in the performances of such singers as Paul Robeson and Roland Hayes and in the arrangements of J. Rosamond Johnson, among others. Notably, these versions largely eschewed folk practices, drawing instead upon the vocal and compositional conventions of European concert idioms, an affiliation that enhanced the gravity and classicism that Du Bois ascribed to the genre.[3]

Although incorporating jazz styles, Ellington's evocation of the spiritual still paid homage to the sorrow song ideal with its suggestions of musical and historical transcendence. "Come Sunday," though, came late to the Renaissance veneration of the spiritual. Premiered in 1943, *Black, Brown, and Beige* appeared almost a decade after that movement had died out, a lag resulting from the long gestation of the unprecedented work.[4] Ellington, however, had drawn upon a spiritual during the 1920s, the heyday of the Renaissance.[5] The piece in which that borrowing was made is the celebrated "Black and Tan Fantasy." According to Bubber Miley, co-composer and a cornetist in Ellington's band, the

---

[2] W. E. B. Du Bois, *The Souls of Black Folks* (Chicago: A. C. McClurg, 1903), 250–64. The focus on Du Bois is not intended to diminish other writers on and performers of the spiritual. The emphasis arises from the fact that Du Bois's essay solidified much of the earlier celebrations of the genres, including performances of the Fisk Jubilee Singers and writings of Frederick Douglass (*The Narrative of the Life of Frederick Douglass*). It also influenced such subsequent authors as Alain Locke and James Weldon Johnson, who are discussed below.

[3] Ronald Radano, "Soul texts and the blackness of folk," *Modernism/Modernity* 2 (1995), 71–95; Eric J. Sundquist, *To Make the Nation: Race in the Making of American Literature* (Cambridge, MA: Harvard University Press, 1993), 525–39.

[4] On the long history of the work and Ellington's relationship to the Harlem Renaissance, see Tucker, "The genesis of *Black, Brown, and Beige*," and "The Renaissance education of Duke Ellington," in *Black Music in the Harlem Renaissance: a Collection of Essays*, ed. Samuel A. Floyd, Jr. (Westport, CT: Greenwood Press, 1990), 111–27.

[5] Between "Black and Tan Fantasy" and *Black, Brown, and Beige*, Ellington performed another work featuring spirituals. In 1933, he and his orchestra recorded "Dear Old Southland," a 1921 song by the African-American composer/lyricist pair Turner Layton and Henry Creamer. This piece stitches together the melodies of "Deep River" and "Sometimes I Feel Like a Motherless Child." The added text features such vaudeville-minstrel touches as "my old Kentucky home," "the Swanee shore," "Mammy Jimmy," and "pickaninnies." Ellington and his band discarded the minstrel hokum (in his brief solo, Louis Bacon avoids these phrases, settling instead for such untainted ones as "I want to be" and "I love to see") and turned the song into an essentially jazzed-up version of spirituals. That combination of idioms comes across as rather superficial compared with the thick stylistic mix in "Black and Tan Fantasy." "Dear Old Southland" also lacks the ironic tone created by the friction of sacred and secular elements in the earlier piece, nor does it engage in the same level of "distortion" or suggest shadowy musical realms.

main theme of the work quotes a spiritual. As discussed below, that spiritual was not one of the treasured sorrow songs but rather a hybrid tune derived from a sacred song by a white composer.

That hybridity suits such a highly variegated piece, one that mixes together sacred and secular idioms, including the spiritual, blues, contemporary urban jazz, call-and-response patterns, and a Chopin quotation. This amalgam creates a variety of moods and sensations, a beguiling mixture that fascinated listeners, as seen in the reviews, commentaries, and even motion-picture adaptation that tried to decipher the work. The fascination with the piece also stemmed from the ways in which the spiritual quotation culturally provokes. As discussed here, Ellington and Miley's handling of that melody shapes conceptions of race, specifically the relationship between whiteness and blackness. "Black and Tan Fantasy" presents different views of that relationship, ones that turn on how the listener approaches the spiritual, as originally a white or black song. In addition, the quotation places the work in a contemporary debate over the nature of the spiritual. Is the genre the sacred and refined voice of sorrow upheld by Du Bois or is it a volatile voice, one that glows with sanctity but at any moment could break into raucous sounds and even dip into the blues?

The cultural provocation of the spiritual borrowing in "Black and Tan Fantasy" can be better appreciated by discussing how the piece employs the African-American rhetorical practice of signifying.[6] Flourishing in both oral and written traditions, signifying takes many different forms and pursues a range of strategies. Henry Louis Gates Jr. describes signifying as "the trope of tropes," meaning that it hosts a group of other tropes, from the classical oratorical modes of metaphor and irony to the black practices of testifying and rapping.[7] In its myriad forms, signifying outlines the basic strategy of "repetition and revision."[8] Practitioners draw upon existing formal structures and concepts and continually rework them to create new versions that break away, often ironically, from the originals.

That impulse, as Gates points out, shapes many African-American musical idioms, especially jazz. He describes black musicians reconceiving tunes by other black musicians (Jelly Roll Morton's take on Scott Joplin's *Maple Leaf Rag*) and those by white composers (John Coltrane's time-defying elaborations on Rodgers and Hammerstein's "My Favorite

---

[6] The now classic account of this practice is Henry Louis Gates Jr., *The Signifying Monkey: a Theory of African-American Literary Criticism* (New York: Oxford University Press, 1988). Other scholars, of course, have discussed signifying. An account of these efforts can be found in Gates's book (pp. 64–88).

[7] Ibid., 52.   [8] Ibid., 60.

Things").[9] The same fundamental impulse, of course, drives quotation. As used in jazz, that practice would seem to be a lodestone for signifying. "Black and Tan Fantasy" and performances by Art Tatum and Charlie Parker among others reveal how well quotation lends itself to that practice.[10] Focusing on the Ellington–Miley work, this study will look at what makes that combination so potent. Put differently, it explains how signifying "signifies" on the act of quotation, that is, what sides of the gesture it brings out and how it stimulates the ways in which quotation acts as a cultural agent.[11]

Before marveling at the rich signifying in "Black and Tan Fantasy," we should discuss the form of the work (see Fig. 2.1).[12] Shadowed by Joe "Tricky Sam" Nanton on trombone, Miley opens the piece with his spiritual theme, presented as a dark minor twelve-bar blues chorus (Ex. 2.1). Ellington immediately contrasts that melody with a second theme, a sixteen-bar (two eight-bar units) non-blues melody set in the major mode. Polished by Otto Hardwick's alto saxophone gloss and featuring smooth harmonic progressions, this theme has been dismissed by

[9] Ibid., 63–64. Several scholars have applied theories of signifying to jazz, including John P. Murphy, "Jazz improvisation: the joy of influence," *The Black Perspective in Music* 18 (1990), 7–19; Samuel A. Floyd Jr., "Ring shout: literary studies, historical studies, and black music inquiry," *Black Music Research Journal* 11 (1991), 265–87; Gary Tomlinson, "Cultural dialogics of jazz: a white historian signifies," *Black Music Research Journal* 11 (1991), 229–64; Robert Walser, "Out of notes: signification, interpretation, and the problem of Miles Davis," *Musical Quarterly* 77 (1993), 343–65; and Ingrid Monson, "Doubleness and jazz improvisation: irony, parody, and ethnomusicology," *Critical Inquiry* 20 (1994), 283–313.

[10] Quotation in jazz has received little attention. Two notable studies include Krin Gabbard, "The quoter and his culture," in *Jazz in Mind: Essays on the History and Meanings of Jazz*, ed. Reginald T. Buckner and Steven Weitland (Detroit: Wayne State University Press, 1991), 92–111; and Katharine Cartwright, "Quotation and reference in jazz performance: Ella Fitzgerald's 'St. Louis Blues,' 1957–59" (Ph.D. diss., City University of New York, 1998), 16–77.

[11] Samuel A. Floyd Jr. has commented on the relationship between signifying and quotation:

Musical Signifyin(g) is not the same, simply, as the borrowing and restating of pre-existent material, or the performing of variations on pre-existing material, or even the simple reworking of pre-existing material. While it is all of these, what makes it different from simple borrowing, varying, or reworking is its transformation of such material by using it rhetorically or figuratively – through troping, in other words – by trifling with, teasing, or censuring it in some way.

Floyd, "Ring shout," 271. For another discussion of that relationship, see Cartwright, "Quotation and reference in jazz performance," 202–08.

[12] This chapter focuses on the Victor recording (21137, 26 October 1927) featuring Miley as soloist. The Ellington band recorded the piece several more times in the next few years. "Black and Tan Fantasy" actually remained in the band's repertory and later appeared in new arrangements.

Chorus 1	Chorus 2	Choruses 3–4	Chorus 5	Chorus 6
spiritual theme	second theme	Miley solo	Ellington solo	Nanton solo
twelve-bar blues	sixteen bars	twelve-bar blues	twelve-bar blues	twelve-bar blues

Chorus 7

"call and response"
Chopin Funeral March quotation in last four measures
twelve-bar blues with two-measure extension

Fig. 2.1 Formal diagram of *Black and Tan Fantasy*

Ex. 2.1 Ellington and Miley, "Black and Tan Fantasy" (1927 Published Stock), trumpet, mm. 1–12

Gunther Schuller as "slick trying-to-be-modern show music."[13] Schuller, though, fails to appreciate how the second theme ironically rubs against the first, adding to the play of opposites – sacred/secular and urban/rural (blues) – that so characterizes the varied piece. This taste of "sweet jazz" is only fleeting as the blues idiom returns, heard in four successive choruses: two by Miley, one by Ellington, and one by Nanton. Whereas Ellington alludes to the harmony and character (smooth ragtime) of the second theme, Miley and Nanton evoke the spiritual of the first.[14] The two performers, however, switch to the major mode and, as typical of blues improvisation, rarely touch down on that melody, instead indulging in a series of timbral twists and turns around common pitches. Both horn players lard their solos with trademark growling and ya-ya sounds, tones that later became part of the primitivist fantasy of "jungle music" heard in the Cotton Club. The closing chorus, a call-and-response section, enhances the sacred display of the work. The passage winds down with the celebrated quotation of Chopin's Funeral March in the final measures.

Miley based the opening theme on a spiritual entitled "Hosanna," which, extending the moment of mother–child transmission that appears often in the spiritual tradition, he remembered his mother

---

[13] Gunther Schuller, *Early Jazz: its Roots and Musical Development* (New York: Oxford University Press, 1968), 330.

[14] Mark Tucker, *Ellington: the Early Years* (Urbana: University of Illinois Press, 1991), 245–46.

Ex. 2.2 Quoted melody from "The Holy City"

singing.[15] Yet as Roger Pryor Dodge, a friend and chronicler of the cornetist, pointed out, the theme and its parent spiritual derive from "The Holy City," a sacred song by the white composer Stephen Adams.[16] This popular song not only appeared in religious services but was also frequently performed in secular contexts. W. C. Handy, for instance, recalled playing the piece as a cornet solo in various traveling shows.[17] In the opening theme, Miley quotes the melody of the chorus, which repeats cries of "Hosanna" (see Ex. 2.2). He, perhaps drawing upon some of the changes made by his mother, strikingly transforms "The Holy City": darkening the melody by shifting to the minor mode, adding syncopations, and, most conspicuously, changing its character from an ebullient sacred song to a somber blues (Ex. 2.1).

A 1934 essay by Zora Neale Hurston sheds light on Miley and his mother's alchemization of "The Holy City." Hurston described the role of "negroidised" white hymns in Southern black church services, particularly Baptist churches in New Orleans.[18] For her, these mutations belonged to a larger family of spirituals that she broadly defined as "Negro religious songs, sung by a group, and a group bent on expression of feelings and not on sound effects." In her account, African-American congregations did not merely import these hymns intact. Instead, they made them their own by severely altering them, both musically and liturgically. The words were "liquified" and the melodies "converted into a barbaric chant that is not a chant." This metamorphosis occurred most often during funerals, occasions for which, she argued, appropriate white hymns were used because blacks had no suitable songs of their own, all African-American songs being "based on a dance possible rhythm."[19]

The idea of "negroidisation" (to expand upon Hurston's term) was not unknown to Ellington, who claimed that the spiritual emerged from that act. The *Black, Brown, and Beige* scenario, to recall, describes the genesis

---

[15] For another instance of such transmission, see Du Bois, *The Souls of Black Folk*, 254.

[16] Roger Pryor Dodge, "Harpsichords and jazz trumpets," in *The Duke Ellington Reader*, ed. Mark Tucker (New York: Oxford University Press, 1993), 108. Stephen Adams was the pseudonym adopted by the British composer and singer Michael Maybrick (1844–1913).

[17] W. C. Handy, *The Father of the Blues* (New York: Macmillan, 1941), 63.

[18] In her essay, Hurston only twice identifies the services that she is describing, referring once to an anonymous "Baptist church in New Orleans" and then more specifically to the Second Zion Baptist Church in that city. It is unclear whether all the activities in her account occurred in those churches or elsewhere.

[19] Zora Neale Hurston, "Spirituals and neo-spirituals," in *Negro: an Anthology*, ed. Nancy Cunard (1934; repr. New York: Frederick Ungar, 1970), 223–25.

of the genre in slaves "adding their own touches... weaving melodic, harmonic, rhythmic patterns" around white hymns. From a mythic antebellum Southern past to 1920s Harlem, "Black and Tan Fantasy" does not weave patterns around "The Holy City" as much as transform it, recasting it into a twelve-bar blues. This blues "negroidisation" may also appear far removed from Hurston's Baptist services, but her essay and "Black and Tan Fantasy" place their metamorphosed hymns in similar settings. The jazz work elaborates upon the funerals that are briefly mentioned by Hurston, evoking those ceremonies with the dark appropriation of "The Holy City" and a Chopin eulogy.

Ellington and Miley's funeral, though, has a satiric bent that would be out of place in Hurston's ethnographic study. With its bluesy spiritual, "Black and Tan Fantasy" extends a black entertainment tradition of satirizing religious display. Such parodies typically targeted the figure of the preacher. For instance, Louis Armstrong occasionally played the part of a minister. In "The Lonesome Road" (1931), "Reverend" Armstrong introduced the members of his flock, or band, and passed around the collection plate.[20] Nearly a decade later, Armstrong as the selfless "Elder Eatmore" offered inspirational sermons on the evils of gossip and the virtues of generosity.[21] Elsewhere, in a recording of "In dat Mornin'" by Jimmie Lunceford and his Chickasaw Syncopators, Moses Allen took his gospel reading from "the books of Matthew, Mark, Luke, or John" and described the Angel Gabriel blowing his trumpet, evoked by Sy Oliver's plunger-mute cries.[22]

Miley also donned the preacher's robe. Frank M. Davis, a syndicated columnist for the Associated Press, described to Marshall Stearns a show by Ellington's band at the Lafayette Theater in Harlem during the mid-1920s. Davis acknowledged that the incident may be apocryphal but claimed that it was told to him as "the gospel truth."[23] Although "Black and Tan Fantasy" is not mentioned, it was most likely the performed piece, especially considering the use of sacred elements, the slow tempo, and "weird" sounds. The show was part of a cutting contest between Miley, the new kid in town, and Johnny Dunn, a leading New York player. Wearing a white silk tuxedo and blowing "hot jazz," Dunn was all class, but Miley offered a different look and sound:

So just as the audience got back to their seats, the curtain rolls up revealing the inside of a beat-up church. There was Duke leading the band in one of those weird slow jobs. And off-stage, Bubber was cutting loose with his jungle-iron,

---

[20] "The Lonesome Road" (1931, Okeh 41538).
[21] "Elder Eatmore's Sermon on Throwing Stones" (1938, Decca 15043) and "Elder Eatmore's Sermon on Generosity" (1938, Decca 15043).
[22] "In dat Mornin'," (1930, Victor 38141).
[23] Quoted in Tucker, *Ellington: the Early Years*, 247.

choking and wailing like a lost soul. He walked on dressed like a preacher and let them have it. New York had never heard anything like it, the result was terrific. People stood on their seats and yelled. The music went over the top, and stopped while Miley bowed. It was the biggest thing that theatre had for years. Somewhere in the back rows, Johnny Dunn walked quietly out, completely unnoticed. He never quite lived it down.[24]

If that floor show did feature "Black and Tan Fantasy," it would have served as a theatrical realization of the ironic play in the work. Much of that activity centered around Miley's spiritual quotation. In consciously drawing upon what he called a spiritual, the cornetist evoked different forms of the genre, setting up an intra-genre dialogue between them and "Black and Tan Fantasy." Such dialogue typifies signifying, which operates in a larger field of related genres, works, and ideas.[25] To achieve its play of repetition-with-difference, it must interact with the familiar and pre-existing. It transforms those elements but never to the point where they disappear, for the practice must always stay involved in a larger conversation; only then can it gain material with which to work and a forum in which to display the wit with which it can manipulate those materials. This inherent dialogism enhances the cultural role played by quotation, as signifying keeps the borrowing front and center in the cultural arena.

The dialogue in "Black and Tan Fantasy" is especially rich with the Du Boisian sorrow songs, which held sway in several areas of African-American culture, including literary and cultural writings, the concert stage, and the church. The signifying in the work takes the form of an ironic reversal of the sorrow songs. "Black and Tan Fantasy" rejects the restraint and musical decorum of the spiritual arrangements, which were largely modeled upon European concert idioms. In lieu of such refinement, it charges its spiritual with a blues intensity that yields a series of bizarre sounds – Miley's "choking and wailing" and Nanton's ya-yas and horse whinny – unheard in either the church or concert hall. The sounds of the contorted spiritual were also unheard in the nightclub, as the story of Miley's Harlem performance makes clear. The emphasis on timbre, not to mention Miley's showmanship, reveals how much performance shapes the signifying of the work. Delivery – from the verbal duels of playing the dozens to the heat of testifying – is crucial to the act. As Gates emphasizes, "one does not signify on something; one signifies in *some way*."[26] The same could be said for quotation as used in jazz and other African-American traditions. In those idioms, the style of performing the borrowing, particularly the timbral transformations of

---

[24] Marshall Stearns, "Bubber Miley's jungle iron, choking and sobbing fades Dunn," *Downbeat* 4 (June 1937), 10.
[25] Gates, *The Signifying Monkey*, 60–64.   [26] Ibid., 54.

the original, are central to the gesture, making us experience the original in strikingly new ways. Most striking are the ways offered by players like Miley with one-of-a-kind sounds, for they take the original into a unique sound world, where it, like the borrowed spiritual, can assume whole new guises and meanings.

"Black and Tan Fantasy" also violates the religious and musical "purity" claimed by the sorrow songs. As described by Alain Locke, the spiritual had "completely sublimated" any secular influences that may have shaped its origins, becoming "indelibly" of an "intense religious" and Christian "character." He decried the "crude and refined secularization" of the genre, proclaiming that "to call them Spirituals and to treat them otherwise is a travesty."[27] "Black and Tan Fantasy" may have earned such rebuke, so freely does it mix sacred and secular idioms. Instead of sullying the spiritual, however, the work weaves together sacred and secular to create new stylistic blends, wrapping its spiritual in those vibrant patterns rather than in the austere ones of the sorrow songs.

Understanding "Black and Tan Fantasy" as an ironic upending of the sorrow songs reveals more affinities between it and Hurston's essay. The latter also challenged Du Bois's ideal, making some of the same basic points as the jazz work. Hurston cut to the heart of the matter by questioning what she believed to be Du Bois's skewed views of the genre. First, she disputed "the idea that the whole body of spirituals are 'sorrow songs'," pointing out that the genre addresses a variety of subjects, ranging from "a peeve at gossipers to Death and Judgement." Hurston next separated the "spirituals," those songs documented in her research, from the "neo-spirituals," the arrangements for "glee clubs and concert singers" favored by Du Bois. The latter, she conceded, were "a valuable contribution to the music and literature of the world" but were not "the songs of the people as sung by them." Far from being a relic of the slave past, the spiritual was part of a living tradition in which songs "are being made and forgotten every day."[28]

Removed from that tradition, Hurston believed that the sorrow songs had little life in them, lacking the sonic vitality and emotionality heard in the church services that she discussed. For Hurston, the spiritual thrived in "crude" sounds, not in the smooth harmonies and mellifluous singing of the concert arrangements. "The real Negro singer," she

---

[27] Alain Locke, "The Negro spirituals," in *The New Negro: an Interpretation*, ed. Alain Locke (New York: A. and C. Boni, 1925), 201.

[28] Hurston, "Spirituals and neo-spirituals," 223–24. Hurston's corrective was accepted by some Renaissance writers. Alain Locke, for instance, found the division between spirituals and neo-spirituals to be "helpful." Locke, *The Negro and his Music* (Washington, DC: Associates of Negro Education, 1936), 21.

asserted, "cares nothing about pitch," each member of the congregation chiefly aiming "to express himself through song." The result of this "every man for himself" approach was a song of "jagged harmony," "dissonances," "shifting keys," and "broken time." Hurston also described how the singers' bodies became part of the musical wreckage. Instead of concealing breathing and other means of vocal production, African Americans, according to her, exaggerated those sounds and worked them into spiritual performances, adding "explosive exhalations" and vocal "straining" to the already raging "harmony and disharmony."[29]

"Black and Tan Fantasy" also places its spiritual in a sonic storm produced by intense musical and emotional expression. Although the sounds produced by Ellington's band and Hurston's congregation cannot be directly equated, the "jagged" musicality that she described accords with "Black and Tan Fantasy": bent and smeared pitches, "strained" tones, clashing, vibrant timbre, and, as with the growling and vocal ya-yas, corporeal resonances as well. Again, the tone of the two could not be more different – a satirical smack of blues versus passionate religious fervor – yet both display the spiritual as a site of sonic and timbral extravagance.

The connection between "Black and Tan Fantasy" and Hurston's article may be broad, but still a connection can be drawn. Both present spirituals, or "negroidised" white hymns, and do so in ways that are at odds with one of the dominant views of the genre. In that way, the two raised complementary voices in the cultural arena of 1920s to early 1930s Harlem. Hurston's voice was part of a countermovement in the Harlem Renaissance led by her and such other young writers as Langston Hughes, Wallace Thurman, and Claude McKay. The youthful vanguard contested many of the ideas espoused by Du Bois and other elder figures.[30] As with Hurston and her praise of the "living" spiritual, this group celebrated the folk and popular styles, especially jazz and blues, that had been largely dismissed by Du Bois.[31] Those idioms, in their opinion, served as a cultural foundation upon which young artists should build.

Ellington and Miley were not part of this group – or of any organized cultural movement, for that matter. The nightclub and literary salons were distant worlds. Still, from these different fronts the musicians and writers could make cultural commentary that shared similar ideas, like the undermining of the sorrow song ideal. For his part, Hughes believed that common ground existed between them. He described "the blare

---

[29] Hurston, "Spirituals and neo-spirituals," 224.

[30] David Levering Lewis, ed. *The Portable Harlem Renaissance Reader* (New York: Viking, 1994), xxxi–xl.

[31] Kathy J. Ogren, *The Jazz Revolution: Twenties America and the Meaning of Jazz* (New York: Oxford University Press, 1989), 117–19.

of Negro jazz bands and the bellowing voice of Bessie Smith" as rich sources that had much to say and urged young artists to listen and to learn from them.[32]

The view of "Black and Tan Fantasy" as an ironic take on the sorrow songs is one way of appreciating Miley's borrowing of a spiritual. That there are other ways of interpreting his quotation goes without saying, especially considering that there is some ambiguity in what the cornetist is quoting in the first place. "Black and Tan Fantasy" is a rare work in the studies of borrowing. It presents two quotations in one: the opening chorus can be heard as incorporating either a spiritual (and a largely unknown one, at that) or a transformed version of "The Holy City."[33] Such doubleness, though, is not rare in signifying. Quite the opposite, that practice forms a "double-voiced discourse," which draws upon different traditions, such as black oral and written idioms or black and white novels. Instead of having one term dominate or cancel out the other, signifying keeps both in play, with the two appearing simultaneously.[34] Gates traces this discourse back to the Yoruba mythological character Esu-Elegbara, who is depicted in sculptures with two mouths, an attribute that allows him to say two things at once.[35]

In "Black and Tan Fantasy," Miley's cornet seems to possess two different bells. Through his signifying on the spiritual borrowing (whatever it may be), the piece draws upon both black and white elements, and sacred and secular idioms. It sustains these opposites, having us hear the two at all times. So deep is this play of opposites that one term cannot exist without the other. The sacred is impoverished without the secular, blackness hollow without whiteness. This double-voicing enhances the play between the original and its new surroundings created by quotation. In most uses of the gesture, we are encouraged to hear a tension between the two, tensions that have us either downplay one at the expense of the other or perceive a contrast between them. The signified quotation, on the other hand, makes the two more than equals or opposites, but part of a larger whole, in which they are constantly interacting with each other. The spiritual, for instance, can never be separated from the blues idiom, nor can the latter exist without the borrowing. The two instead have been amalgamated into some new musical essence.

With its double voice, "Black and Tan Fantasy" challenges interpretation. Signifying, in general, poses such challenges, as it resists being

---

[32] Langston Hughes, "The Negro artist and the racial mountain," *The Nation* 122 (23 June 1926), 693–94.

[33] A third possibility is that the listener will not recognize a quotation but will still sense some sort of sacred quality. For instance, in the review discussed below, R. D. Darrell mentions a vague connection between "Black and Tan Fantasy" and the "spiritual tradition."

[34] Gates, *The Signifying Monkey*, xxv–xxviii.   [35] Ibid., 3–43.

trapped by any one view. It courts an "indeterminacy of interpretation" through an abundance of meaning.[36] Such ambiguity suits the trickster Esu. Contemporary audiences found "Black and Tan Fantasy" to be quite tricky. Compared to most jazz pieces of the day, it elicited considerable commentary, ranging from extended reviews to a film inspired by it. Such a reception testifies to the puzzle created by the different styles and borrowings in the work, as each interpretation tried to put these pieces together in some way.

One of the most compelling attempts is Dodge's 1934 essay. As mentioned earlier, Dodge related Miley's claim of using a spiritual and pointed out "The Holy City" connection. Having brought up the sacred work, he could not let it go, spending much of his review trying to reveal its presence in the piece. Surprisingly, Dodge did not focus on the opening chorus but rather on Miley's solo sections, which he admitted were far removed melodically from "The Holy City" but which he still believed preserved Adams's melody, even if it could not be heard.

For Dodge, "Black and Tan Fantasy" cast a shadow: a split between the heard and unheard, between the solo choruses and "The Holy City" melody that he sensed was there. With a change of light and hymn, that shadow could be cast in the opposite direction. Dodge recalled Miley's funeral (the cornetist died at the age of 29) and how "the congregation sang 'Rock of Ages,' and all through it [he and his wife] heard the 'Black and Tan Fantasy.' "[37] Either heard or unheard, that piece captivated Dodge with its suggestion of some other music existing beyond its periphery.

Not content with merely suggesting that Adams's melody was present in Miley's solo choruses, Dodge tried to expose it. He notated solos from four performances of the piece and compared his transcriptions with "The Holy City" melody, hoping that the notes would reveal what the ear could only sense.[38] Not surprisingly, few correspondences emerged. The gap between the two, however, did not convince Dodge that the song was completely absent; rather, he explained the gap as resulting in part from the limitations of notation to capture improvisation. That caveat echoed similar statements regarding the inadequacies of notation made by transcribers of spirituals who, along with Dodge, found the incompleteness of notation fascinating. For spiritual scholars, those inadequacies suggested "primitive" sounds tantalizingly beyond Western comprehension and script.[39] Similarly, for Dodge, his incomplete transcriptions suggested that "The Holy City" was more "removed" than he

---

[36] Ibid., 22.   [37] Roger Pryor Dodge, "Bubber," in *The Duke Ellington Reader*, 455.

[38] Dodge includes in his transcriptions solos by Nanton and Jabbo Smith. The latter he mistakenly took for Miley, an error that he later acknowledged.

[39] Ronald Radano, "Denoting difference: the writing of slave spirituals," *Critical Inquiry* 22 (1996), 524–44.

thought, perhaps part of some "primitive" cry, thus making it even more alluring. The "vague resemblance" that he found confirmed that "The Holy City" melody was indeed there but was just beyond his reach.

What especially fascinated Dodge about "Black and Tan Fantasy" was that the melody could be so transformed as to appear simultaneously present and not present. Hurston might have referred to such a metamorphosis as an instance of "negroidisation." Her phrase is again apt not for the musical insights it offers but rather because the neologism itself captures what it describes: the bringing together of fragments – words or music of white origin – to create new compounds that declare black creativity. For Hurston, "negroidisation" yielded the new and was not beholden to the old, establishing the relationship between blackness and whiteness as one of creativity and raw material. Immediately discarded in her essay are the original white hymns, dismissed as resources and never heard from again. "Black and Tan Fantasy" similarly leaves behind "The Holy City." The melody of the song is pushed aside by the soloists' flights of creativity, which unleash sonic swells that would have been unthinkable in the restrained world of the church anthem. The melody of the song may be gone but the traces of whiteness and sacredness that it imparted in the first chorus continue to drift through the rest of the jazz work.

Dodge attempted to hold on to those traces, doing so by gathering as many notated scraps of "The Holy City" melody as he could. Those efforts to preserve Adams's melody reveal an underlying racial dynamic in Dodge's interpretation. Referring to clubs where blacks and whites mixed, the title "Black and Tan Fantasy" invites listeners to hear the work along racial lines, but, typical of the elusive piece, it never clarifies where those lines are to be drawn or how the two races interact. Dodge drew his own line, defining the relationship between blackness and whiteness as one between distortion and purity, quite different terms from those put forth by Hurston's examples of "negroidisation." He described the distortion of Adams's melody as an act of theft – stealing time from some notes – and devilish tricks, including the alteration of one of Adams's b♭s to an e♮ (invoking the dreaded interval of the tritone, the *diabolus in musica*).

So thorough was this deformation that there was little of "The Holy City" to hold on to, and Dodge, despite finding some of these changes "wonderful," needed to hold on to some "pure" music. Looking well beyond Adams, he found that purer and more resilient music in compositions of Bach and Palestrina. In a strange move, Dodge used their works to reveal the "purity" of jazz, not an original purity but one only achieved through "resemblance" to these classics. Calling a phrase by Miley "the purest I have ever heard in jazz," Dodge immediately qualified: "I speak of purity in its resemblance to the opening of the Credo for soprano voices in Palestrina's 'Missa Papae Marcelli.' "[40] By making Miley a copy of Palestrina, the reviewer outmaneuvered the cornetist, who may have been able to distort "The Holy City" but presumably could not transform Palestrina or Bach. At best, he could only resemble them. Although several centuries removed, purity was found, and along with it the creativity of whiteness confirmed.

Whereas Dodge may have been the only listener of "Black and Tan Fantasy" to look over his shoulder to the distant past, he was not alone in being spellbound by the "distortion" in the work. The critic R. D. Darrell confessed to not being able to "shake off" its "twisted beauty," a phrase suggesting some mixture of distortion and purity. Describing the piece, he recited a litany of deformation: "oddity," "tortured," "agonizing," "distorted," and "perverse." Unlike Dodge, Darrell did not wrap these phrases around a borrowed hymn, though he did sense a connection to the spiritual, claiming that "Black and Tan Fantasy" "sounded an equal depth of poignance" as "the heavily worked 'spiritual' tradition."[41] As with Dodge, however, those distortions belonged to another dimension of the piece, a space not audible to the average listener, like that unheard realm in which Dodge sensed "The Holy City." For Darrell, the distortion only became apparent after he crossed over the boundary separating the "hot" and "funny" music from the "twisted beauty," a crossing his friends could not make.

With the majority I did not recognize it when it first came to my ears in the form of the "hottest, funniest record you ever heard." It was a Brunswick disc by a dance band named the Washingtonians, and I laughed like everyone else over its instrumental wa-waing and gargling and gobbling, the piteous whinnying of a very ancient horse, the lugubrious reminiscence of the Chopin funeral march. But as I continued to play the record for the amusement of my friends I laughed less heartily and with less zest. In my ears the whinnies and wa-was began to resolve into new tone colors, distorted and tortured, but agonizingly expressive. The piece took on a surprising individuality and entity as well as an intensity of feeling that was totally incongruous in popular dance music. Beneath all its oddity and perverseness there was a twisted beauty that grew on me more and more and could not be shaken off.[42]

That both critics focused on elements of distortion is not surprising. Miley's presentation of "The Holy City" indulges in a variety of melodic and timbral opposites that can be heard as an evocation of the opposition between purity and distortion. Indeed, any musician incorporating a spiritual (or "negroidised" white hymn) into a jazz or blues piece would have to confront that pair, either attempting to minimize the tension between the two, or, as in Miley's case, exploiting it. Miley's exploitation

---

[40] Dodge, "Harpsichords and jazz trumpets," 108–09.
[41] R. D. Darrell, "Black beauty," in *The Duke Ellington Reader*, 59.   [42] Ibid., 58.

Ex. 2.3 "Black and Tan Fantasy," Miley solo; Gunther Schuller transcription from *Early Jazz* (Oxford University Press, 1968, 331)

Ex. 2.4 "Black and Tan Fantasy," Miley solo; Gunther Schuller transcription from *Early Jazz*

is especially apparent in his solo choruses, the sections that captivated Dodge and Darrell.

With so few solid traces of "The Holy City," Miley's solo appears to be all distortion, but even here he evokes purity – his own, not Adams's. The high b♭ with which he begins his solo is a unique sound in the piece (see Ex. 2.3). Floating above the rhythm section, it has an "intense stillness" and an unalloyed timbre removed from the surrounding growling and "slick" music; in other words, it is the purest sound in the piece.[43] It may not be a stretch to suggest that the heavenly register and sweetness of the pitch are timbral allusions to the borrowed spiritual.

The purity of the note especially comes across when comparing "Black and Tan Fantasy" with Louis Armstrong's celebrated 1928 recording of "West End Blues." Armstrong similarly begins the final chorus with a sustained high b♭, but that pitch swells, a crescendo and timbral effusion leading directly to a spray of quickly descending four-note patterns beginning on that note. Despite a small crescendo, Miley's b♭ stays relatively peaceful, a sensation blotted out by the following ripping figure full of growls and blue notes. This "extraordinary contrast" pushes the dichotomy of purity and distortion to a level beyond the benign deformation of "The Holy City" in the opening theme statement.[44]

The b♭ is not heard again; nothing so pure is heard again in the piece. Miley, however, continues to play with the idea of distortion, no longer twisting the pure but contorting the already contorted. Throughout the rest of his solo, he frequently states a brief idea, usually heavily colored by pitch and tonal inflections, and then immediately repeats it, coloring and warping it further. For instance, the blue-note streaked idea that opens his second chorus is followed by an even more daubed variant that is growled instead of wah-wahed as in the first statement (see Ex. 2.4). Whereas such immediate variation is common to blues performance, the technique stands out in a piece preoccupied with the transformation

---

[43] Schuller, *Early Jazz*, 330.   [44] Ibid., 330–31.

of melodic material and the related idea of purity and distortion. In particular, these repetitions can be heard as ripples emerging from the original distortion of the spiritual or "The Holy City."

With these broadening deformations, Miley gradually erases any suggestion of purity in the piece. The cornetist first supplants the purity of the sacred melody with his own, the high b♭, and then dismisses the notion of purity altogether by forging a chain of distortions that connect only to each other and not to some pure original. This rejection also affects the racial interplay of the work. For Dodge and others aware of the white origins of the transformed "The Holy City" melody, that repudiation possibly struck at the larger cultural connection between whiteness and purity, a link evident in the attitudes toward miscegenation. The gradual nullification of purity ("The Holy City") and its related racial privileges may have threatened Dodge and led him to retain as much of the song as he could and, when that failed, to turn back to Bach and Palestrina.

"Black and Tan Fantasy" was not the only contemporary jazz work to draw upon "The Holy City." It was, however, the only piece to make so much of the borrowing, both rhetorically and timbrally. Engaging in the one-upmanship typical of signifying, Ellington and Miley distanced themselves from these and other works by showing that they could use similar materials in much more imaginative, and often critical, ways. Recorded in 1923 by King Oliver and his Creole Jazz Band, "Chimes Blues" also incorporates the refrain from the church anthem, similarly transforming it into a twelve-bar blues. Oliver, however, maintains the major mode of the original (C major in this recording) and presents the melody as a contrasting idea within the piece rather than as an opening theme. Appearing a year after the first recording of "Black and Tan Fantasy," Johnny Dodd's "Weary City" turns the tables on the popular piece and responds to it. The title makes clear that some jazz musicians were familiar with Adams's melody and thus perhaps recognized its appearance in "Black and Tan Fantasy." In his work, Dodds opens and closes with brief C major quotations of "The Holy City," bookends to a succession of melodically unrelated blues choruses.

These are slight differences compared with those in overall sound and expression between the two works and "Black and Tan Fantasy." Relying on a superficial contrast between sacred and secular, Oliver's and Dodd's straightforward quotations snicker "look what tune popped up here." "Black and Tan Fantasy," on the other hand, boasts "look what's happened to that tune," fascinating listeners, like Dodge, with its distortions and play of opposites. Neither "Chimes Blues" nor "Weary City" steps into that timbral hall of mirrors, satisfied instead with conventional yet involving blues and group improvisation. The two also do not indulge in the sacred elements heard in "Black and Tan Fantasy," be it the impassioned call-and-response chorus or the funereal atmosphere. With peals of C major bells, "Chimes Blues" gets closer to the church than "Weary City," but both still remain outside. "Black and Tan Fantasy," though, is inside, using a rhetorical command of sacred and secular elements not possessed by the other two works to engage in ironic play and alluring distortions.

Just as with "The Holy City," "Black and Tan Fantasy" was not the only contemporary work to quote Chopin's Funeral March.[45] Felix Arndt's *Desecration Rag* (1914) also uses strains of the march in a closing tag.[46] Once again, though, the jazz work stands apart, creating rhetorical depths that the ragtime piece cannot equal. Like the "Holy City" borrowing, this one turns back and forth between two seemingly opposite sides, humor and sorrow. As "Black and Tan Fantasy" and *Desecration Rag* make clear, the Chopin Funeral March had developed that second side by the early twentieth century. It had become a cliché, a familiar and bombastic portent of death.[47] The Ellington band plays up that quality by performing the quotation in an overblown style. The fat tones are about ready to burst into the freakish ya-ya and neighing sounds heard earlier. At the same time, sadness resonates in these bars. They absorb the passion from the preceding call and response. That passion brings out the sorrow that inheres in the Chopin original and by doing so it reinforces the sorrow that underlies both the religious and blues fervor that have shaped the work as a whole.

Many listeners have remarked upon the equivocality of the quotation. Darrell, to recall, laughed at the "lugubrious reminiscence" of the march but then realized that it along with the bizarre sounds in the work spawned "an intensity of feeling that was totally incongruous in popular dance music."[48] Writing several decades later, Ralph Ellison praised the "mockery" of the Chopin bit, which he found "most Negro American."

---

[45] Elements of the Funeral March appear in other works. The second movement of Satie's *Embryons desséchés* draws upon the Trio theme. Jelly Roll Morton's "Dead Man Blues" opens with a fragment similar to the Chopin, but is most likely part of the hymn "Flee as a Bird."

[46] In the recording of the work by Arndt, the Chopin quotation comes at the very end of the work, serving as the big finale; however, in the sheet music (New York: G. Ricordi, 1914) the quotation is followed by a return of the opening quotation of Dvořák's *Humoresque* and a brief tag. The discrepancy may be the result of the time limits of the recording (the end does sound rushed) or Arndt's preferred way of performing the piece.

[47] The Funeral March continued to have its tragic associations throughout the century. For instance, it was played at the funeral of John F. Kennedy. The two sides of the Funeral March in the twentieth century – that of "public mourning" and "mock solemnity" – are discussed by Lawrence Kramer in his article on the Funeral March and the evocation of death. Kramer, "Chopin and the funeral: episodes in the history of modern death," *Journal of the American Musicological Society* 54 (2001), 97–98.

[48] Darrell, "Black beauty," 58.

Yet within that mockery, he perceived a touching reminder of "how fleeting *all* human life must be."[49] Finally, Ellington in his typically evasive manner commented on the evasiveness of the quotation. In a 1944 *New Yorker* article, he recalled the performance of the "Black and Tan Fantasy" solos by Arthur Whetsol, a replacement for Miley, who had left the band in February 1929. As the reporter put it, Ellington "chuckled": "When he played the funeral march in 'Black and Tan Fantasy,' I used to see great big ole tears running down people's faces."[50] For Ellington, "chuckles" and "tears" mix, the two cannot be separated. Even the tears themselves splash with laughter. They are not small precious drops but rather "great big ole" ones. Still, there were tears. Listeners did cry.

Arndt's *Desecration Rag* contains not only a quotation of the Funeral March but also a string of ones by Chopin, Liszt, Dvořák, and Sinding (*The Rustle of Spring*). Placing these classical works in the syncopated gait of ragtime amounts to "desecration," so the title tells us. That word evokes the opposition between purity and distortion, but the rag cannot manipulate that opposition to the same beguiling effect as "Black and Tan Fantasy." It treats the borrowed material in a superficial manner, giving the classical melodies a trivial ragtime makeover. They have not been distorted, or "desecrated," as much as lightly spoofed. The Funeral March quotation does no better at handling the opposition of sorrow and humor. There is plenty of humor. Played in a low, rattling minor, the march balloons to tragic pomposity. Breaking away from the slow, steady tread of the original, it even adopts a syncopated strut every few measures (Ex. 2.5). There is, though, not a trace of sorrow. At the end of the work, there are no tears, only "great big ole" laughs.

The fluid play of doubles in "Black and Tan Fantasy" captivated many listeners. Among them was Dudley Murphy, who directed the 1929 short film *Black and Tan*. Released by the white-run studio RKO Productions, the film starred Ellington and his Cotton Club Orchestra and the actress-dancer Fredi Washington.[51] The closing scene is of particular interest to this study, for it contrasts a performance of "Black and Tan Fantasy" with a concert-version spiritual, thereby allowing us to hear Miley and Ellington's version of the genre back to back with the Du Boisian form.

---

[49] Ralph Ellison, "Homage to Duke Ellington on his birthday," in Tucker, ed., *The Duke Ellington Reader*, 395–96.

[50] Quoted in Richard O. Boyer, "The hot Bach," in Tucker, ed., *The Duke Ellington Reader*, 230.

[51] For background and discussion of the film, see Thomas Cripps, *Slow Fade to Black: the Negro in American Film, 1900–1942* (New York: Oxford University Press, 1977); Klaus Stratemann, *Duke Ellington: Day by Day and Film by Film* (Copenhagen: Jazz Media ApS, 1992); and Krin Gabbard, *Jammin' at the Margins: Jazz and the American Cinema* (Chicago: University of Chicago Press, 1996).

Ex. 2.5 Felix Arndt, *Desecration Rag*, mm. 156–72

The final scene takes place at the deathbed of Washington, who has collapsed while dancing at a swank nightclub (see Plate 2.1). Aware of her bad heart, she nonetheless took the job so that her boyfriend Ellington and his band could perform there. As the scene opens, we see a chorus gathered around Washington singing the spiritual "Same Train." She turns to Ellington and whispers, "Play me the 'Black and Tan Fantasy.' " Joined by the chorus, Ellington and his band oblige. The work entrances Washington, pulling her heavenward. With the quotation of the Funeral March, she takes her last breath, but not before turning for one final look at Ellington. A tear winds down his face as the camera fades out.

With an illustrious pedigree, the cinematic version of "Same Train" exemplifies the elite Harlem Renaissance ideal of that genre. First, it clearly derives from the arrangement of the spiritual by J. Rosamond Johnson in James Weldon Johnson's *Second Book of Negro Spirituals*, one of the most significant collections in the Renaissance.[52] Furthering Du Bois's efforts to enshrine the genre, that work defined the spiritual as "the finest distinctive artistic contribution [America] has to offer the world."[53] Although no arranger is credited in the film, Johnson most likely adapted his own arrangement for the film. A month earlier, he

[52] James Weldon Johnson, ed., *The Book of American Negro Spirituals* (New York: Viking, 1962), 60–62.
[53] Ibid., 13.

Plate 2.1 Still photograph from the film *Black and Tan*. Frank Driggs
Collection, Archives Center, National Museum of American History,
Smithsonian Institution

had worked on Murphy's *St. Louis Blues,* which incorporated the same
choir and many of the same actors, and he probably followed that troupe
to the new project. As with other spiritual arrangements, this one avoids
the "barbarisms" that thrilled Hurston, cultivating instead a timbral and
harmonic smoothness.

By juxtaposing the blue-blood "Same Train" with "Black and Tan
Fantasy," the film places the two different presentations of a spiritual in a
dialogue. Whether either Murphy or Ellington planned this intra-genre
commentary is doubtful, yet the fortuitous union offered something for
each of them. For Murphy, following a spiritual with an intense piece
that mixes sacred and secular elements and is full of evocative sounds
only served to enhance the "primitivist" spectacle of African-American
folk life and worship.[54] That spectacle is enhanced by the primeval sil-
houettes of the musicians projected against the back wall. With this exaggerated shadow play, Murphy visually captures the distortions heard by
Darrell and Dodge. In the director's realization, these "twisted" sounds
are beyond the capabilities of human musicians, emanating instead from

[54] This primitivism is especially brought out by the "jungle jazz" show put on during the
nightclub scene.

66

looming shadows. As with the possible earlier Harlem performance featuring Miley, the cinematic pairing allowed Ellington to bring out the spiritual roots of "Black and Tan Fantasy."[55] That connection made, the work proceeds to separate itself from and eclipse "Same Train," claiming its own sonic and emotional realms. As discussed above, the distorted timbres, precarious pitches, and blues intensity of the piece conform more to Hurston's heretical views of the spiritual than to the established ones of Du Bois or J. Rosamond Johnson.

Inspired by either Ellington or Miley's ironic reversal of the sorrow songs or Murphy's primitivist notions, the film, not surprisingly, favors Hurston's view.[56] So does Washington. She cuts off "Same Train" to make her last request, feeling the need for something more fervent than the spiritual's doleful locomotive to carry her into the next world. Banished by her, "Same Train" is not heard from again, but, perhaps in an attempt to preserve its presence, Johnson, or possibly even Ellington, has the choirs sing during the performance of "Black and Tan Fantasy." The group, for instance, doubles the altered melody of "The Holy City" in the opening chorus. This gesture evokes the church origins of that melody, but, at the same time, it reveals how far "Black and Tan Fantasy" has distanced itself from both "The Holy City" and the just-heard "Same Train." The choir cannot match the growling timbre of the cornet melody. Indeed, the choir's lustrous sound comes across as a distraction that threatens to drown out the more colorful instrumental line. Equally intrusive is the added text, which has been rendered largely incomprehensible on the soundtrack. Clear or not, the text would be irrelevant because it most likely could not create as strong an impression on the listener as Miley's (Whetsol's) snarling minor-mode transformation of the original melody.[57]

The disparity between the jazz work and the spiritual grows larger with the second theme. In this most secular and urban patch of the Ellington piece, the chorus continues with its evocation of the spiritual, overlaying a new melody and sacred text on that theme. This

[55] Miley and Ellington's backwoods scene, or, more accurately, Stearns's account of it, obviously comes close to the folk backdrop in the primitivist *mise-en-scène* of the film. This affinity demonstrates how the lines between black self-representations and white racial fantasies were not always that clear, as, in this case, the satirical excess of the Harlem performance could spill over into the latter.

[56] Hurston's emphasis on "crude" sounds makes her essay a target for primitivist fantasies, like those in Murphy's final scene. Not surprisingly, her essay was grouped in the Cunard *Negro* collection with George Antheil's article "The Negro on the spiral or a method of Negro music," a primitivist account of black styles. These affiliations reveal how difficult it was for black self-representations, no matter how assertive and "authentic," to avoid being entangled in such fantasies.

[57] Miley had so imprinted his interpretation of the solo on the piece that almost all soloists after him, including Whetsol, imitated his style.

interpolation sounds like an attempt to convert the "sweet" jazz melody or, at least, to cover it up. Such proselytizing fails, and the choir remains silent during the solo choruses; no arranger would dare encroach on the horn players' timbral displays. When the choir does return, it is no longer in the mode of "Same Train" but rather on the terms of "Black and Tan Fantasy." The voices, for instance, fill out the call-and-response chorus, making it even more evocative of an impassioned church service, rather than a polished concert version. Finally, the added choral part for the Chopin tag enhances the mockery of that quotation. The interpolated text – it sounds like the old "Pray for the Dead and the Dead will pray for you" – conveys that "gallows humor" that Ellison so loved in that line.[58]

That mockery is mixed with melodrama. A young woman has sacrificed her life so that her boyfriend can get his big break. He repays her with a deathbed performance and tears. As Whetsol plays the Funeral March, it is now Ellington who has "great big ole tears" streaming down his face. With that crying and the fade-out shot, the film recognizes the sorrowful side of the borrowing. It does not recognize the comic underside, or, at least, it does not appear to do so. This is not to say that the ending is not humorous. The overdrawn melodrama is amusing, especially to present-day audiences. Perceived as such, the melodrama mocks the tragic Funeral March. Inadvertently or not, the doubleness of the quotation emerges.

Whereas the film clumsily handles the Chopin quotation, it does a much more interesting and assured job of dealing with the spiritual. The last scene stages a dialogue between the spiritual in "Black and Tan Fantasy" and the sorrow songs, one in which the former has the last word. That exchange can be heard as complementing a larger debate within the Harlem Renaissance over the nature and performance of spirituals and other African-American idioms. The quotation of the spiritual also provides a means to shape the relationship between blackness and whiteness, a relationship that constantly changes depending on how the listener approaches the borrowing. Shedding light on how "Black and Tan Fantasy" comments on the spiritual and race not only provides a cultural context for the piece but also reveals the work's rhetorical virtuosity, the ability to create a variety of effects and sensations, many of which – irony, fervent blues, and "twisted beauty" – are as beguiling now as then.

[58] Ellison, "Homage to Duke Ellington," 395–96.

Interlude: chronological scenes

According to Umberto Eco, we find ourselves in

...a universe...where it is hard to say that the Beatles are alien to the great musical tradition of the West, where comic strips enter the museums via pop art but museums' art enters comic strips via the far from ingenuous culture of men like Crepax, Pratt, Moebius, and Drouillet. And for two evenings in a row the kids pack into a Palasport, but on the first night it's the Bee Gees and the next it's John Cage or a performer of Satie; and the third evening they would go (and, alas, can go no more) to hear Cathy Berberian singing a program of Monteverdi, Offenbach, and – in fact – the Beatles, but sung like Purcell. And Berberian added to the Beatles' music nothing that it was not already quoting, and only in part without knowing, without wanting to.[1]

In other words, we find ourselves in a universe shaped by – if not ultimately becoming one with – the mass media. As Eco argues, the mass media have erased the lines between high and low art, lines not even seen by the media-age "kids" driving from the Bee Gees to John Cage to Satie to Cathy Berberian. Those "kids" also drive right over the lines separating the past and present, the media having removed those divisions as well. Like many writers, Eco describes how the mass media have created an eternal present, a realm with "no memory."[2] In this world of uniform time, the past has been absorbed by the present, it being immediately evoked through the television, radio, and other conduits. So thin is this time world that not only has the past slid into the present but the present has also sunk into the past. With the instantaneity of the media, any present moment is at once displaced by the next effervescent moment, settling into that broad realm of the already said and done, which the media keep preserved in the present, the always available said and done. The climax of this media joyride by the "kids" is surprisingly not a television show or a radio program but a live recital (which will most likely end up on the television or radio). The Berberian concert, however, has also attained a timeless present. It not only skips from Monteverdi to Offenbach to the Beatles, but also

---

[1] Umberto Eco, *Travels in Hyperreality*, trans. William Weaver (New York: Harvest Books, 1986), 146–47.
[2] Ibid., 146.

reveals how the Beatles' songs enfold Purcell, the twentieth-century popular hits mingled with the seventeenth-century courtly airs.[3]

Fredric Jameson also claims that we find ourselves in a timeless present, a state that he considers endemic to postmodernism. Indeed, for Jameson, there is no past. The past, as captured in "the survival, the residue, the holdover, the archaic," has "disappeared," to be replaced by simulations of the past, such as restored buildings and the revivals of earlier styles.[4] The past has become a creation of the present, never knowing the distant decades and centuries that it supposedly inhabits. With the past severed from itself, the linear flow of time, the pathway between past, present, and future, has been blocked. There are no longer any connections between the facets of time, all of them cut off from each other. Time, as Jameson describes, succumbs to schizophrenia. In making that diagnosis, he draws upon the Lacanian account of that state, which describes how the signifying chain fractures, creating "a rubble of distinct and unrelated signifiers."[5] According to Jameson, the links of time have similarly shattered, leaving us in "a series of pure and unrelated presents."[6]

The evocation of schizophrenia brings us back to a Cathy Berberian recital, not the one recalled by Eco but one staged by Berio, a friend of Eco and a former husband of Berberian. That concert is the theatrical work *Recital I (for Cathy)*, which dates from the late 1960s. During this dramatized recital, Berberian does sing bits of arias by Monteverdi and Purcell, but that is all we ever get, just bits. Having suffered a nervous collapse, she breaks away from her program and rambles through a monologue, which she haphazardly interrupts with quotations from works in her repertory. These fragments amass and eventually overcrowd the present. Buried under that debris, Berberian finishes her show with a desperate prayer for liberation, liberation from the past.

Jameson's theory of temporal schizophrenia may appear to be the apposite means by which to analyze Berberian's chronological ravings. As used by Jameson, though, that theory has been stripped of any clinical associations. Never once is it applied to mad scenes, characters, or artists. His account of schizophrenia deals only in time, and as such it still promises to shed light on the fragmentary temporal world in which Berberian is trapped. Even here, though, the theory is of limited use, for it and the musical work construct those spheres in very different ways, especially in regard to what the fragments represent and how they relate to each other. In *Recital I*, the past is the past and not a simulation created in the present, even if it appears in a simulated concert. It comes

---

[3] Eco is most likely referring to Berio's Beatles arrangements, some of which have Baroque affectations.

[4] Fredric Jameson, *Postmodernism*, 18 and 309.   [5] Ibid., 26.   [6] Ibid., 27.

across as a force emerging from elsewhere, a realm as distant as the seventeenth and eighteenth centuries. That realm, however, grows less and less distant as the past bears down upon the present, eventually crushing Berberian. Not only is the past the past, but it interacts with the present. Far from "a series of pure and unrelated presents," *Recital I* reveals a present and past very much related, locked in a frightening scenario of clashes and disintegration.

That a work bearing so many Jamesonian standards of postmodernism – quotation, pastiche, and simulation – should contradict his conception of time is worth noting. This dissent does not topple Jameson's vast conception of postmodernism (which remains a very sturdy and impressive theoretical edifice); rather, it prods us not to take his depiction of time as the inevitable and encompassing vision that he holds it up to be. We should instead consider what Mieke Bal has called different "kind[s] of temporality," meaning the various ways in which the past and present interact.[7] In her study of how contemporary artists have engaged the imagery and aesthetics of Caravaggio's paintings, Bal conveys the rich give and take between the present and the Baroque. Her account encourages us to explore the infinite forms that such temporal relationships can assume. One such form is Jameson's schizophrenic present. That view keenly describes the temporal worlds of the works he discusses. It also captures the seemingly random play of photographs and paint in the still-unrolling collage scroll of Robert Rauschenberg's *The 1/4 Mile or 2 Furlong Piece* (1981–present) and the aleatoric fracas of eighteenth-century and electronic scraps in Cage's *HPSCHD* (1969).

Other types of temporal relationships, ones equally indicative of postmodernism, can be found in both *Recital I* and the works covered by Bal. What sets these works apart from those above is an engagement between the past and present. Much of the founding theoretical literature on postmodernism rules out the possibility of such an encounter, either rejecting it outright, as Jameson does, or simply disregarding it.[8] These

---

[7] Mieke Bal, *Quoting Caravaggio: Contemporary Art, Preposterous History* (Chicago and London: University of Chicago Press, 1999), 64–65.

[8] The theoretical accounts of postmodernism by Charles Jencks and Andreas Huyssen do not describe tensions and interactions between the two periods. See Jencks, *What is Postmodernism?* (New York and London: St. Martin's Press, 1986) and Huyssen, "Mapping the postmodern," in *After the Great Divide: Modernism, Mass Culture, Postmodernism* (Bloomington: Indiana University Press, 1986), 178–221. Some critics have discussed the relationship between the two periods. Eco, for instance, mentions how postmodern works may evoke the past but keep a distance from it through the use of irony. Eco, *Postscript to The Name of the Rose*, trans. William Weaver (New York: Harcourt Brace Jovanovich, 1984), 65–72. Hal Foster has viewed postmodernism in a modernist light, describing how the movement reacts against the past and seeks to repudiate it. He focuses on two veins of postmodernism. The postmodernism of reaction challenges the tenets of modernism and attempts to displace that movement. The postmodernism of

71

studies, as Andreas Huyssen points out, emphasized "issues of space" over "thematics of time and temporality."[9] In this spatial view, pieces of past and present float beside each other without any sort of interaction or tension. To claim engagement between the two periods, these accounts seem to say, is to return to modernism, a period born from the clash between old and new.[10] In modernism, the relationship between the two took many different forms, including the Futurist efforts to raze the past, Ives's nostalgic fantasies of reclaiming the small-town idyll of the previous century, and the neoclassical refashioning of eighteenth-century idioms.

It could be argued that postmodern works contain just as many different types of temporal engagements. This assertion opens up the problematic relationship between modernism and postmodernism. Theorists have continually picked at the prefix, arguing over the ways in which the latter either breaks from or extends modernism. This is not the place to enter into that larger debate; rather, this study will stake out a particular corner of the discussion, that of temporal relationships. As maintained here, many postmodern works, a general label for works from the 1960s to the present based on quotation and/or the use of reproduction techniques, continue the engagement between past and present undertaken in modernism.[11] Chapter three makes such a case as it creates an intriguing din by bringing together the mad railings against the past in *Recital I* and Peter Maxwell Davies's *Eight Songs for a Mad King* with those in such arch-modernist works as Schoenberg's *Erwartung* and T. S. Eliot's *The Waste Land*.

resistance, on the other hand, concentrates on the larger past by questioning basic cultural codes. Foster, "Preface," in *The Anti-Aesthetic*, ed. Hal Foster (Seattle: Bay Press, 1983). In her discussion of postmodernism in contemporary musical works, Jann Pasler makes creative use of Foster's views and offers her own intriguing perspective on the relationship between past and present in both modernist and postmodernist compositions. Pasler, "Postmodernism, narrativity, and the art of memory," *Contemporary Music Review* 7 (1993), 3–32.

[9] Huyssen, *Twilight Memories: Marking Time in a Culture of Amnesia* (New York and London; Routledge, 1995), 3. As Huyssen admits, an interest in "time and temporality" led him to take a new direction in his work, one that focuses on "issues of time and memory as they keep haunting our present." This new direction shapes the essays that make up the above collection.

[10] As Huyssen points out, spatially focused theories of postmodernism "relegated the thematics of time and temporality to an earlier cultural moment of high modernism"; Huyssen, *Twilight Memories*, 3.

[11] The postmodern label is used loosely here. This study will not define a set group of characteristics of musical postmodernism. The concept is used primarily to engage theoretical writings that have concentrated on prominent trends in the arts in the latter decades of the century. Having said that, most of the works discussed in the following chapters do adhere to conceptions of postmodernism presented in those writings, particularly in the use of quotation, stylistic pluralism, and self-reflexivity.

As demonstrated by these works, madness is one "kind of temporality." Expanding upon Bal's phrase, this study stages chronological scenes, that is, accounts of the relationship between past and present built around different themes, like madness. This descriptive approach highlights the dynamics between the two periods and offers distinct ways of viewing that interaction.[12] The following two chapters unveil such scenes. The first deals with madness, in which, as in *Recital I*, the past overwhelms the present, driving both characters and time itself into delirium. The second scene looks at compositions built upon the promise that engagement with the past can enrich the present, even help attain utopian designs. Both scenes feature compositions by Berio, a linkage that testifies to the various forms the relationship between past and present has taken in recent pieces by revealing the different ways in which one composer has conceived of that relationship.[13]

Whatever the setting, these scenes take place on a cultural stage. Treading that stage, the past and present are two actors who command our attention. To depict the past is an act of cultural agency, one that shapes perceptions of that time as well as those of the present. The works discussed in the following two chapters set the past and present in ways that make forceful cultural pronouncements. The madness pieces warn that the past, specifically that of the centuries of artistic works that surround us, is a crushing burden, a weight that the present does not have a strong enough creative buttress to withstand. The utopian compositions view the past not as pressing down upon the present but rather as dovetailing with it, the two being interconnected. For the composers of these pieces, a musical work should reveal those connections, an act that can broaden our perceptions of the present. Some of those composers notably viewed that act as having social ramifications, as the forging of musical/temporal linkages could encourage listeners to see the common ground between different social elements or, as with Stockhausen, even provide the foundation for a utopian nation. Both scenes reveal the past and present engaging each other in surprising ways, intricate bonds where some scholars have seen shredded ties. Mounted on a cultural stage, these quick and constant scene changes are part of one of the most fascinating dramas of the twentieth century: the relationship between past and present.

---

[12] In his discussion of evocations of the past, David Lowenthal describes the different forms the relationship between the two periods has taken. Lowenthal, *The Past is a Foreign Country* (Cambridge: Cambridge University Press, 1985).

[13] Another scene featuring a work by Berio can be found in Metzer, "Musical decay: Luciano Berio's *Rendering* and John Cage's *Europera 5*," *Journal of the Royal Musical Association* 125 (2000), 93–124.

3

Madness

Three portraits of madness:

Lucia di Lammermoor: Entering after murder, Lucia hears not the gasps of gathered guests but only memories. The orchestra entrances her with reminiscences of ghostly cavatinas, wedding marches, and love duets – brief fragments of her operatic life.

Erwartung: Another murder, another woman. She too clutches the past, repeating memories of her lover, his infidelity, and death. The orchestra reminisces along with her, recalling memories not from her life but from one she has never known. It murmurs a song written several years before the opera, a mysterious memory, which, unlike the woman's obsessive thoughts of perfidy, appears briefly and then evanesces.

Recital I (for Cathy): Not murder, but self-destruction. A woman on the recital stage perseveres to get through the evening, yet all the time falling into memory and falling into madness. She spits out scraps from works spanning centuries – remnants of history that will eventually bury her. At the end of the evening, all that can be heard are cries and a disjointed prayer.

In these sketches, a story repeats itself: women driven mad by memory. It is an old story, one going back centuries before *Lucia*. What is new is that the memories themselves have begun to stretch back centuries, taking us into remote and sometimes unknown pasts. *Lucia*, though, leads us into no such places. Donizetti's mad scene recalls a time within the opera, that is, one that both the heroine and we have experienced. The orchestra quotes only numbers (Act I cavatina and love duet; Act II Wedding March) related to events that have occurred on stage. Schoenberg's *Erwartung* and Berio's *Recital I*, on the other hand, evoke pasts beyond their dramatic boundaries. The former briefly reflects on a song never heard on the stage: Schoenberg's "Am Wegrand," written four years earlier and far removed from the atonal wanderings of the monodrama. In *Recital I*, the anonymous singer reaches back centuries, joining her voice with those of such characters as Monteverdi's Nymph and Lucia.

From the perspective of the twenty-first century, these recollections of a distant past are nothing new, being part of what is by now an old story. So much art from the twentieth century has pushed back into previous periods that traditional chronological and stylistic walls have collapsed. The results are works in which Mozart meets the present day, with neither being surprised to encounter the other, nor we to hear them together. Such meetings result from the extraordinary presence of earlier art in the twentieth century, a presence so strong that many artists have not been able to resist recalling and incorporating it into their works. *Recital I* and *Erwartung* view those recollections in the context of madness. They are not alone in drawing that connection, as can be seen in three other works discussed here: T. S. Eliot's *The Waste Land*, Francis Bacon's *Study after Velázquez's Portrait of Pope Innocent X*, and Peter Maxwell Davies's *Eight Songs for a Mad King*.

In these works, the evocation of madness makes a blunt point: such excessive artistic and historical reminiscences are not "normal." More than that, they are debilitating. Only the mad obsessively return to memories of operas and poems written centuries ago, fragments of which cram their thoughts and speech. Those recollections ravage them and eventually rob them of their own private pasts. These scenes of madness contrast strongly with the works of Rochberg, Berio, and Stockhausen discussed in chapter four, which views the use of past materials as promising. The works discussed here suggest that there was an underside to that optimism, an anxiety that the constant recollection of the past came at a cost, the union of old and new leading to disintegration and possibly even madness.

Despite these different outlooks, these two groups of works share a fascination with the ways of using borrowed materials – how they can be transformed and transplanted into new surroundings. Madness provides a realm in which to indulge that fascination. In many ways, quotation is the apposite technique for such works. Besides channeling memories, it produces many other effects evocative of madness, including fragmentation, distortion, discontinuity, incoherence, and the use of multiple languages. Madness in turn heightens these effects. It is a state of excess in which gestures are taken to an extreme; witness Lucia's roulades and Salome's chromatic splurges.[1] In the hands of the mad, quotation too becomes exaggerated: the borrowed melodies more distorted, the juxtaposition of different phrases more random, and the mix of languages more confusing. Excessive too are the memories crowding

---

[1] Susan McClary, *Feminine Endings: Music, Gender, and Sexuality* (Minneapolis: University of Minnesota Press, 1991), 80–101.

these works. Those recollections dwell upon artworks and figures from the past, a past that during the course of the five works expands until it claims both the present and the future.

Erwartung and *The Waste Land*

The excesses of madness strongly appealed to many early modernist artists who were themselves seeking to move, like the mad, beyond convention and to step into realms of apparent irrationality and disorder.[2] Insanity often provided a context for iconoclastic departures, the *modus operandi*, as it were, for such radical steps as severely distorting the human figure or writhing melodies into shrieks. Several works from the period, not surprisingly, delve into madness, including two standard-bearers of innovation: *Erwartung* and *The Waste Land*. At first glance, madness is about all that the two have in common, and even that is not a strong connection. The depictions of mad characters in both works could not be more different, but those representations do share one feature: the use of quotation. Again, though, there are crucial differences. *Erwartung* includes only one quotation, whereas *The Waste Land* overflows with a countless number of them. However, that one, like the multitude, is a reminiscence born out of madness, a memory that travels back into far away pasts.

In approaching *Erwartung*, scholars have been quick to reach for their Freud, particularly Freud and Josef Breuer's *Studies on Hysteria* (1895). Various attempts have been made to link the monodrama with Breuer's case study of Anna O., a connection prompted by the belief that Bertha Pappenheim, the real Anna O., and Marie Pappenheim, Schoenberg's librettist, were related.[3] Moreover, the latter's medical training raises the possibility that if not personally familiar with the case, she would have at least been *au courant* with it and other developments in the emerging field of psychoanalysis. However, just as it has been argued that the two women were not related and had no sort of personal connection, so too it can be suggested that the monodrama and case study are not directly

---

[2] For a discussion of the prominent role played by evocations of madness in modernist arts, see Louis A. Sass, *Madness and Modernism: Insanity in the Light of Modern Art, Literature, and Thought* (New York: Basic Books, 1992).

[3] There have been various suggestions as to how the two women were related. Discussions of that relationship can be found in Eva Weissweiler, "'Schrieben Sie mir doch einen Operntext, Fraülein!', Marie Pappenheim's Text zu Arnold Schönberg's *Erwartung*," *Neue Zeitschrift für Musik* 14 (1984), 4–8, and José Maria Garcia Laborda, *Studien zu Schönbergs Monodram "Erwartung" (Op. 17)* (Laaber: Laaber-Verlag, 1981), 18. Based on an interview with Pappenheim's son, Diane Holloway Penney claims that the two women were cousins. Penney, "Schoenberg's Janus-work *Erwartung*: its musico-dramatic structure and relationship to the melodrama and lied tradition" (Ph.D. diss., University of North Texas, 1989), 61.

related either, in the sense of the former being an operatic transcription of the latter.[4] Rather than such an explicit connection, *Erwartung* and *Studies on Hysteria* can be viewed as united by a loose cultural bond, the two being among the numerous and often overlapping representations of madness scurrying around fin-de-siècle Vienna.[5]

Freud and Breuer's work, though, still has much to say about the opera. A rare combination of theoretical tract and literary short story, it perhaps best illuminates the various artistic works emerging from that cultural fascination with madness. One terse diagnosis particularly applies to *Erwartung*: "Hysterics suffer mainly from reminiscences."[6] The opera too suffers from reminiscences. It springs from an act of memory: a return to the scene of the crime. Pushing through a nocturnal forest (her psyche), the clinically anonymous Woman finds her way to the dead body of her lover and to the home they once shared.[7] Her route, though, is not so clear or direct. Along the way, she strays into various hallucinations, including "a hundred hands" thrashing in the bushes and crawling shadows. Even the corpse may not be real, as it is never seen by the audience.

What the audience does encounter is a contemporary understanding of hysteria as a morass of reminiscence and delusion. *Erwartung* builds its case study around these two elements. The beginning of the opera alternates almost regularly between fragmentary recollections and hallucinatory paroxysms. The line separating the two quickly blurs. As the possibly imaginary corpse suggests, the Woman's recollections

---

[4] A refutation of the possibility of a familial relationship between the two women can be found in Lewis Wickes, "Schoenberg, *Erwartung*, and the reception of psychoanalysis in musical circles in Vienna until 1910/11," *Studies in Music* 23 (1989), 96. For interpretations of the opera in light of the Anna O. case study, see Weissweiler, "'Schrieben Sie mir doch einen Operntext, Fraülein!'," 4–8, and Robert Falck, "Marie Pappenheim, Schoenberg, and the *Studien über Hysterie*," in *German Literature and Music, An Aesthetic Function: 1890–1989*, ed. Claus Reschke and Howard Pollack (Munich: Wilhelm Fink, 1992), 131–44. A critical view of the use of psychoanalytical theory in reference to the work can be found in Alan Street, "'The ear of the other': style and identity in Schoenberg's Eight Songs, op. 6," in Charlotte Cross and Russell A. Berman, eds., *Schoenberg and Words: the Modernist Years* (New York and London: Garland Publishing, 2000), 120–27.

[5] For a contrasting interpretation of the work as a feminist statement (a "feminist *Bildungsroman*"), see Elizabeth L. Keathley, "'Die Frauenfrage' in *Erwartung*: Schoenberg's collaboration with Marie Pappenheim," in *Schoenberg and Words*, 139–77.

[6] Josef Breuer and Sigmund Freud, *Studies on Hysteria*, trans. and ed. James Strachey as vol. 2 of *The Standard Edition of the Complete Psychological Works of Sigmund Freud* (London: Hogarth Press, 1955), 7.

[7] Pappenheim's opening scenic description and dialogue equate the forest and the Woman through various pairings: moonlight/white dress, jewelry/silver trees, and flower gardens/flowers on her dress. These parallels suggest that the Woman is entering her own psyche.

themselves may be delusions – there may have been no murder, perhaps even no love affair. These ambiguities fascinated Schoenberg, who went so far as to enhance them. In setting the libretto, he deleted several lines, including a passage that pointed, albeit diffusely, to an actual murder.[8] Where Pappenheim offered the Woman a brief moment of awareness, Schoenberg pushes her further into madness, denying her the certainty of memory.

Schoenberg's score goes a step beyond that by denying even the act of memory. The opera establishes a tension between music and text that centers around reminiscence. On one hand, the music refuses to remember, while, on the other, the libretto cannot stop doing so. This refusal has much to do with the lack of repetition. At the risk of overstatement, the score avoids any sort of regular thematic restatement or recapitulation, moving restively from one short motive to another, with little or no connection between them.[9] In other words, *Erwartung* recalls nothing from its musical past; it refuses to reminisce. The flow of constantly changing music takes us into the sound world of hysteria, often depicted as an unpredictable outpouring of speech, cries, and singing, among other noises.[10]

The libretto, on the other hand, constantly peers back at the past and itself. "Ah, now I remember . . . it's so long since . . ." and similar phrases unfurl the Woman's frayed memory episodes. Pappenheim's text also repeats over and over key phrases and images, notably the moon. Ripe for leitmotif treatment, these elements go unexploited by the score, so

---

[8] On these deletions, see Bryan R. Simms, "Whose idea was *Erwartung?*," in *Constructive Dissonance: Arnold Schoenberg and the Transformations of Twentieth-Century Culture*, ed. Juliane Brand and Christopher Hailey (Berkeley and Los Angeles: University of California, 1997), 104–5.

[9] Attempts have been made to find some sort of governing motive or theme. H. H. Stuckenschmidt pointed to the regular appearance of a three-note collection (d–f–c♯) throughout the work. Herbert H. Buchanan has also pointed to other units (some derived from the "Am Wegrand" quotation) playing similar roles. Penney similarly focuses on that quotation as serving as a *Grundgestalt* for the monodrama. Instead of looking for a unifying element, most analyses have described the work as concentrating on select ideas for short sections and then moving on to other ideas. Stuckenschmidt, *Arnold Schoenberg*, trans. Edith Temple Roberts and Humphrey Searle (London: John Calder, 1959), 54, and Buchanan, "A key to Schoenberg's *Erwartung* (Op. 17)," *Journal of the American Musicological Society* 20 (1967), 434–49; Penney, "Schoenberg's Janus-work *Erwartung*," 250. An example of the more local motivic approach can be found in Carl Dahlhaus, *Schoenberg and the New Music*, trans. Derrick Puffett and Alfred Clayton (Cambridge: Cambridge University Press, 1987), 151–53. For a discussion of how the avoidance of repetition in the work reacts against Wagnerian ideals and responds to the text, see Daniel Albright, *Untwisting the Serpent: Modernism in Music, Literature, and Other Arts* (Chicago and London: University of Chicago Press, 2000), 148–57.

[10] Janet Beizer, *Ventriloquized Bodies: Narratives of Hysteria in Nineteenth-Century France* (Ithaca and London: Cornell University Press, 1994), 43.

preoccupied with avoiding any sense of repetition and recollection of its own past. The score even appears to have cut itself loose from the operatic past, its radical harmonic and thematic language seeming to be without a precedent. However, the libretto has a past – that is, a precedent. Despite its modern fragmentary style, it scours earlier operas, including Strauss's *Salome*. Far from ancient Judea, an aloof moon still watches over an embraced corpse and a kiss.[11]

A libretto repeating dramatic and genre memories, a score sounding like tonal logorrhea in which little is ever repeated: two representations of madness, each taken to an extreme. With these contrasting depictions keeping abreast of each other throughout the opera, a tension slowly builds. Something has to give: either the libretto becomes amnesiac or the music suddenly remembers a melody. The latter occurs, but quite unpredictably. Near the end of the monodrama – the climax of this representational tension – a quotation of Schoenberg's earlier song "Am Wegrand" emerges.[12] It is triggered by a line that appears to be Pappenheim's own: "Tausend menschen ziehen vorüber" (Thousands of people pass by), the exact words that begin the John Henry Mackay poem set in "Am Wegrand."[13] The line points to the feelings of alienation and longing pervading both works.[14] Mackay's poem narrows in on an anonymous woman, one not so different from Schoenberg's character. Stranded in a crowd, she is as alone as the woman in the forest.

---

[11] The monodrama also alludes to *Tristan und Isolde* (an ecstatic, drawn-out lovedeath) and *Pelléas et Mélisande* (the distraught, confused woman wandering through a forest).

[12] Robert Falck has proposed that Schoenberg also quotes "Traumleben," another song from the op. 6 collection. He points to textual and motivic parallels between the two works. Although plausible, the case for this second quotation is not wholly convincing; neither of the two parallels is as direct as those in the "Am Wegrand" quotation. Alan Street has found another example of what he views to be a quotation of "Traumleben" in the work. Again, the connection between opera and song is not as strong as that with "Am Wegrand." Still, as Falck suggests, it cannot be ruled out that there are other instances of self-quotation in the monodrama, all of which could be seen as resulting from the pressure of reminiscence discussed below. Falck, "Marie Pappenheim, Schoenberg, and the *Studien über Hysterie*," 140–42; Street, " 'The ear of the other'," 122–26.

[13] It appears that the line was originally written by Pappenheim and not inserted later by Schoenberg in order to provide an opportunity for the quotation. In his study of the opera, Garcia Laborda provides a transcription of Pappenheim's handwritten text with the later annotations made by Schoenberg. There are no changes by the composer to the line in question; Garcia Laborda, *Studien zu Schönbergs Monodram "Erwartung" op. 17*, 141.

[14] It may be this shared mood between the two works that Schoenberg referred to in a discussion with the psychologist Julius Bahle. When asked about using previous material in song composition, the composer responded: "I can remember only one single instance when for a new work I took over a theme invented in some other context. Principally because musically speaking I was very fond of it, and it had a related mood." Quoted in Willi Reich, *Schoenberg: a Critical Biography*, trans. Leo Black (New York and Washington: Praeger, 1971), 240.

Ex. 3.1 Schoenberg, "Am Wegrand," mm. 18–23

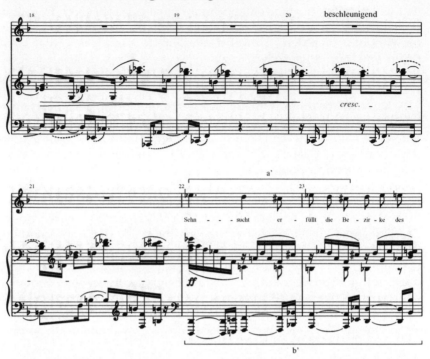

People "flow" by her, but they never reach her, nor she them. From her solitude, she too waits for a man who will never come. Expectation rules both women, possesses them, and becomes their essence. As Mackay's woman bewails: "Longing fills the realm of life" ("Sehnsucht erfüllt die Bezirke des Lebens").[15]

So intertwined are the two women's fates that this line passes from the song character to the operatic Woman. The vocal and piano lines supporting the exclamation in Schoenberg's song (Ex. 3.1) are quoted in mm. 410–11 of the opera (Ex. 3.2). These phrases are not the first bits of the song to find their way into the stage work. Snipped and distorted fragments of the opening vocal line from the song scamper through the orchestral underbrush in mm. 401–02 (cellos, violas, and clarinets). As typical of the episodic motivic development discussed by Carl Dahlhaus, these bits foreshadow the more extended and intricate statement that follows.[16] Here that motivic play focuses on a quotation,

---

[15] The translation is taken from Adorno's *Philosophy of Modern Music*. Adorno views the character in the poem as a symbol of modern urban alienation – "that of city dwellers who are totally unaware of each other." Theodor W. Adorno, *Philosophy of Modern Music*, trans. Anne G. Mitchell and Wesley V. Blomster (New York: Seabury Press, 1973), 47.

[16] Dahlhaus, *Schoenberg and the New Music*, 151–53.

Ex. 3.2 Schoenberg, *Erwartung*, mm. 410–11

as Schoenberg first offers traces of the borrowed materials and then a more complete presentation.

The presentation is not so complete, for once again we have just fragments. Schoenberg begins the quotation with slivers of an accompanimental figure used to introduce the setting of the vocal phrase (mm. 19–20 in "Am Wegrand," m. 410 violas and bassoons; Exx. 3.1 and 3.2). The two quoted measures that follow (mm. 22–23 in m. 411) come from the second stanza of the song, where they form an emotional peak. In that work, Schoenberg conveys how claustrophobic the woman's ruminations are through his incessant and distorted repetition of melodic ideas. At this point, the voice and piano return to phrases stated at the beginning of the song (Ex. 3.3, marked a and b). It is the piano left hand (b′), though, that now states the opening vocal phrase, albeit in an altered form that breaks off in new directions, whereas the voice circles around pitches from the opening left-hand ostinato (a′). The range and roles may change, but the same thoughts reappear over and over again.

Those musical ideas also reappear in *Erwartung*, though in a characteristically fractured and scattered form. Schoenberg jumbles fragments

Ex. 3.3 Schoenberg, "Am Wegrand," mm. 1–5

from the openings of the first and second stanzas of the song, thickening the mix of those same two sections that he already churned in that work. Here the voice sings the text of the opening line ("thousands of people march by") to a new melody. The woodwinds, on the other hand, turn to the beginning of the second stanza (mm. 21–22). High clarinets (D, B♭, and A) play the vocal line (a'), whereas the bass clarinet, bassoons, and contrabassoon bellow what appears to be the piano left-hand part (b'). To recall, in the song, that left-hand line presents an altered version of the opening vocal phrase. Instead of giving us that transformed version (b), Schoenberg states the original vocal phrase in the bass instruments, thereby having the text (soprano) and melody (low woodwinds) of that phrase sound apart. The handling of the quotation effectively underscores the feeling of loneliness common to both song and opera. Schoenberg scores the borrowing of the left-hand line in the original low register (D1 and D) but places the vocal line up an octave (e♭'''). Played by shrieking clarinets in that upper register, the borrowed vocal line is surely isolated; however, it is the woman who is most alone. She sings midway between these extremes, unable to reach out to the melodies from the song to which she has turned. Traversing almost two octaves herself, she still cannot grasp those lines. Most tormenting is the remote bass line, the line that bears the melody to the words that she sings. She is separated from the melody, and the melody from the words. All are alone.

In such detached and brief shreds, the "Am Wegrand" quotation proves just as fleeting as the other melodic strands in *Erwartung*. Indeed, without prior knowledge, it remains inconspicuous; however, once exposed, it stands out, primarily for being an anomaly that demands an explanation. One explanation for its appearance is the pressure of reminiscence building up throughout the opera, a pressure that is finally released in that brief passage. The textual parallel provides a convenient occasion for the release of a musical memory. But why is an outside work evoked? In reminiscing, the monodrama perhaps could draw only upon such a work; no earlier theme or motive is prominent or substantial enough to serve as a recollection. Besides, to restate a previous melody would obstruct the non-repetitive flow of the music. The "Am Wegrand" quotation has it both ways. It is a memory (albeit an outside one) and a new element in the score, a previously unheard melodic idea which, like those stated before it, is introduced, momentarily elaborated upon, and then forgotten.[17]

The reference to "Am Wegrand" may be a musical memory, but whose? It is most likely not the Woman's. She has never heard the song before, at least not during her moonlit rovings. The memory may very well belong to Schoenberg, who, as Eliot described in his 1917 poem "Hysteria," has been "drawn in" by the spectacle of the illness. Whereas Eliot's protagonist becomes "involved in" the convulsive laughter and gasps of a female companion at tea, Schoenberg appears captivated by the incessant memories of his character. Having entered the realm of excessive reminiscence, he too looks back at his past, one that in some ways is not unlike the Woman's.

In composing the opera, her story must have drawn Schoenberg in, himself having just experienced the psychic anguish of infidelity. *Erwartung* emerged in the aftermath of an affair between his wife, Mathilde, and his friend Richard Gerstl, which ended with Gerstl's suicide and Mathilde's mental and physical collapse. Watching those days again through the Woman's monologue, Schoenberg, like her, may have reached for a past before the beloved's infidelity. Composed a year before he met Gerstl, "Am Wegrand" stems from such a lost time. However, like many of the Woman's recollections, it is not a look back to a blissful time. No halcyon reminiscences surface, only the dark

---

[17] Forgotten in the sense that it is never heard in its original form again. As Buchanan and Penney have discussed, many of the motives in the opera bear some intervallic relationship to the quotation. Buchanan, "A key to Schoenberg's *Erwartung* (Op. 17)," 134–43; Penney, "Schoenberg's Janus-work *Erwartung*," 341.

"Am Wegrand," which, four years later, must have appeared as a storm cloud bringing the anguish and loneliness that would soon envelop the composer.

The intermingling of memories suggests some sort of identification of Schoenberg with the Woman. Such involvement is rare in male depictions of female madness. The protagonist in Eliot's "Hysteria," for instance, may be fascinated by his companion, but he keeps his distance, acting as some sort of psychological archeologist who will collect the "fragments" of that character and peruse them later. Schoenberg, on the other hand, not only shares a reminiscence of infidelity with his character but also presents it in a similar fashion. Scattered and lacking any visible proof, the Woman's memories of her love affair may be delusions. Equally scattered and barely recognizable, the "Am Wegrand" quotation too comes across as a hallucination. It is not only the ephemerality of the borrowing but also the way the orchestra presents it that creates that impression. Throughout the opera, the orchestra often produces the sounds that the Woman claims to hear, sounds that may or may not be real. One noise that is not real is that of the weeping mentioned in scene 2 (unless the Woman hears herself). No other crying character is lost in the forest that night, but the orchestra evokes one. In m. 70, the first oboe plays a brief descending half-step phrase marked *klagend*. That sigh figure – an aural realization of a delusion – prods the woman to ask: "Who is that weeping?" – a question to which there is no response by either her or the orchestra.

The woman may also remark upon the shadowy "Am Wegrand" fragment. After the orchestra has laced threads of the song around her line "Thousands of people pass by," she comments "I don't recognize you." That "you" may be the unknown and out-of-place "Am Wegrand," and not just the beloved amid the "thousands of people passing by." If so, she has heard another barely perceptible melody from the orchestra, one which, like the weeping, comes from a person not on stage – in this case, Schoenberg. For him, the melody is no delusion, but, by presenting it in that guise, he reveals how caught up he is in the hysterical display, his recollections taking the form of hers.

The "Am Wegrand" borrowing is not just an autobiographical aside, a commentary on Schoenberg's torment and anxieties. It also has much to say about the Woman. Quotation can be used to striking effect in depicting madness. For instance, the fragmentation of "Am Wegrand" heightens that of the protagonist. Just as the song sounds only in disconnected scraps, the Woman slips between flickering hallucinations and memories, never being able to extend a thought, to settle one, or to find some comfort within it. Schoenberg also distorts the song. As heard in the altered reminiscences in *Lucia*, depictions of madness often employ that gesture, the transformations suggesting the awry perspectives of the insane and that things are no longer as they once were. "Am Wegrand" is no longer lyrical or tonal: its arching melodic lines are shattered and its D minor bearings lost in the new atonal surroundings. In this form, the song embodies the disintegration and disorientation of madness.

The fact that "Am Wegrand" is foreign to the musical world of the monodrama also adds to the portrait of hysteria. By bringing outside elements into a work, quotation conveys a loss of autonomy, or self. Writing on this passage and instances of borrowing in pieces by Berg, Adorno described how quotations undermine the "autonomy of form" and reveal the "monadological depth" of a composition to be "illusory."[18] Phrased differently, a quotation breaches a work, opening it up to outside elements and showing it no longer to be a self-contained musical world. In depictions of madness, this breaching extends to the troubled psyche, which, like the musical work, is no longer whole and impermeable. If a foreign melody can find its way into such a stylistically unique and self-defined composition as *Erwartung*, then a host of recollections and delusions have little trouble crawling into the Woman's mind, no longer able to hold up the wall between reality and hallucination, itself and the outside world.

That psychic wall is not the only fortification to tumble. As Susan McClary has discussed, *Erwartung* breaks the representational frames, plot and tonal devices traditionally used to contain madness.[19] The opera marks the culmination of a nineteenth-century fascination with madness in which the imposition of order was increasingly delayed so as to draw out the spectacle of insane characters.[20] For instance, in *Salome*, the last-minute crushing shields and C minor tonic abruptly end the title character's sexual and chromatic rampages. In *Erwartung*, though, there are no shields, nor is there a tonic. The Woman, unlike her Straussian predecessor, is not killed; rather, as suggested by the open ending, she lives to ramble through another day, and perhaps many more after that one, a torturous cycle that nonetheless punishes her.[21] The closing diaphanous chromatic ascent that sends her out into that infinite series of mornings also leaves the opera tonally open-ended, washing away the hints of D minor evoked earlier. One of those hints is the "Am Wegrand" quotation. Splintered and obscured, it no longer has any tonal strength to contain the Woman's madness; it has instead become one of the many

---

[18] Adorno, *Philosophy of Modern Music*, 48, n. 14.
[19] McClary , *Feminine Endings*, 84–85.   [20] Ibid., 104.
[21] Keathley also sees the conclusion of the work as "open" but interprets that openness in very different terms. She sees it as a sign of the woman rejecting her "passive role" and of the "holding out the possibility – but no guarantee – of the Woman's self-realization." Keathley, " 'Die Frauenfrage' in *Erwartung*," 161–62.

elements suspended in that madness, or as she tellingly describes her state, a "dream without limits."

That evocative phrase, one of the many to pour out of the mouths of hysterics, also applies to *The Waste Land*, a poem that appears to be free of physical or chronological boundaries. Floating around that space are a host of borrowings. Those quotations give voice to madness, quite literally. Many of them were originally spoken by mad characters, including Ophelia and Hieronymo from Thomas Kyd's *The Spanish Tragedy*. Such literary figures need not speak to suggest madness. The flow of different voices and languages formed by the series of borrowings also creates that impression, what an original reviewer dismissed as a "mad medley."[22] Babel has long been considered a symptom of insanity, appearing in Hieronymo's macaronic machinations and the case study of Anna O., who, in her most distraught states, attempted to talk by stringing words together from "four or five languages."[23]

Quotation in *The Waste Land* also plays into another traditional conception of madness codified by Freud and Breuer: excessive reminiscence. At the heart of the poem's shifting scenes and voices is a male protagonist haunted by "memory and desire," the same two elements that crippled Schoenberg's Woman. As with her, both erotic fulfillment and the past remain elusive. His numerous recollections reveal a past that exists only in hazy scenes and offers little to reassure him. Such frustrations lead him to push further back, not into his personal life but into literary history – the plays, poems, and religious writings that he compulsively gathers around him. Instead of finding in those works a foundation upon which to build, he encounters only "a heap of broken images."

In the epigraph, Eliot offers a cautionary tale about living in the distant past (done not so ironically with a quotation). He selects a brief excerpt from Petronius's *Satyricon* (first century AD) that tells of the Sibyl of Cumae. Granted anything she desired by Apollo, she wished to live for as many years as grains of sand that could be held in her hand. Having forgotten to ask for eternal youth, she shriveled into a creature tiny and helpless enough to be kept in a small cage. It is in that state, nothing more than an exhibit in a Greek freak show, that Petronius's character sees her:

For once I saw with my very own eyes the Sibyl of Cumae hanging in a cage, and when the boys said to her, "Sibyl, what do you want?" she answered, "I want to die."[24]

---

[22] Quoted in Nancy K. Gish, *The Waste Land: a Poem of Memory and Desire* (Boston: Twayne Publishers, 1988), 10.

[23] Freud and Breuer, *Studies on Hysteria*, 25.

[24] Translation from Gish, *The Waste Land*, 41. Eliot's quotation is in the original Latin and Greek.

Table 3.1 *Final paragraph from* The Waste Land

I sat upon the shore
Fishing, with the arid plain behind me
Shall I at least set my lands in order?
London Bridge is falling down falling down falling down
Poi s'ascose nel foco che gli affina[a]
Quando fiam uti chelidon–O swallow swallow[b]
Le Prince d'Aquitaine à la tour abolie[c]
These fragments I have shored against my ruins
Why then Ile fit you. Hieronymo's mad againe.[d]
Datta. Dayadhvam. Damyata.[e]
Shantih shantih shantih[f]
[Then dived he back into that fire that refines them
When shall I be like the swallow
The prince of Aquitaine, of the ruined tower][g]

[a] Dante, *Purgatorio*
[b] Anonymous, *Pervigilium Veneris*
[c] Gérard de Nerval, Sonnet *El Desdichado*
[d] Kyd, *The Spanish Tragedy*
[e] *Brihadadranyaka-Upanishad*
[f] Formal ending to an *Upanishad*
[g] Translations from Gish, *The Waste Land*, 101.

As with all things Sibylline, this tale portends. It warns readers that the past may endure but that it is always crumbling. The epigraph also reveals the creative depletion to be suffered by those who cannot let go of the past. Having seen and heard so much over thousands of years, the Sibyl can say little herself. As with her sisters she once spoke in bewitching enigmas, now she is pleadingly and crudely direct. Unlike her past oracles, "I want to die" is not heeded; rather, the wish is denied by the poem's opening rueful evocation of spring: "April is the cruelest month."

From the opening line to the final ones, the last paragraph of *The Waste Land* offers its own version of Sibylline fragments, the leaves imprinted with individual letters that the Sibyl scattered before supplicants, challenging them to arrange the pieces in the correct order to spell out her prophecy. The protagonist has thrown before us literary scraps drawn from different languages. We are to make some sense of them; however, translating and tracking down the provenance of these lines does not make things immediately clearer (see Table 3.1).

Each one of these quotations has a story to tell, and much has been written about how they relate to each other and to the poem as a whole.[25] Not having time to examine the individual pieces of the puzzle, let's look at the larger picture and ask to what kind of conclusion this passage brings the work. As with many earlier sections, this one produces an equivocal effect. On one hand, it suggests that the protagonist has at last attained some degree of stability – the "arid plains" are behind him, his quotations buttress him against "ruins," and a blessing of peace is repeated. On the other hand, anxieties over disintegration persist: both a larger cultural collapse – the ever falling London Bridge – and a personal one – the individual sitting in the crumbling tower.

It appears that the psychic wall has completely collapsed. The paragraph presents the rubble and confusion of madness, an effect largely achieved through quotation. In discussing this paragraph, it is important to remember that much of "What the thunder said," the fifth and last section of the work, is void of quotations (but not allusions, as Eliot's notes make clear). The first seventy-nine lines contain none and then only three brief ones appear: "Datta," "Dayadhvam," and "Damyata," the conflicting human translations of the noise of thunder recorded in Indian sacred writings. After the last of those claps, the downpour of borrowings opens up in the closing paragraph. Withheld for so long and finally released, those quotations produce a powerful effect. They throw the reader suddenly into a world where fragments never yield a whole and numerous voices clamor in different languages. As if the picture were not clear enough, "mad" Hieronymo briefly steps to the center of the stage and adds his voice to the din.

The Hieronymo lines also become the center of another aspect of madness at work in this passage: excess. Besides drawing two lines from Kyd's drama, the last paragraph exaggerates the work's representation of insanity. In *The Spanish Tragedy* (subtitled *Hieronymo's Mad Againe* in a later 1615 folio), Hieronymo plots revenge for the murder of his son, a crime which has apparently driven him insane. Asked to write a play for court, he responds, "Why then Ile fit you." He "fits" his audience with a drama written in Latin, Greek, Italian, and French, which leads one character to object: "But this will be a mere confusion / And hardly shall we all be understood." Hieronymo reassures him: "It must be so, for the conclusion / Shall prove the invention and all was good." The result is a drama thinly based on the treacheries leading to his son's murder and performed by those involved in the crime. Hieronymo's "good" "conclusion" entails killing the actors during the play.

---

[25] For different interpretations of this passage, see Hugh Kenner, *The Invisible Poet: T. S. Eliot* (New York: Ivan Obolensky, 1959), 177–81; Calvin Bedient, *He Do the Police in Different Voices: The Waste Land and its Protagonist* (Chicago and London: University of Chicago Press, 1986), 205–21; Robert L. Schwarz, *Broken Images: a Study of The Waste Land* (Lewisburg, PA: Bucknell University Press, 1988), 233–41; and Elizabeth Gregory, *Quotation and Modern American Poetry* (Houston: Rice University Press, 1996), 55–72.

Eliot's protagonist also "fits" his readers with a macaronic episode, employing three of Hieronymo's languages – the fourth, Greek, can be found in the Sibyl epigraph. Always anxious about his own creative powers, he is not to be outdone in "invention" and throws in Sanskrit, a language well beyond Kyd's Elizabethan world, and even reaches for the voice of the Divine with the three human approximations of the noise of thunder. This passage also goes well beyond the "confusion" of Hieronymo's play, as no revenge plot girds together the different languages. Nor is there any sort of "conclusion" to dispel that confusion. The protagonist leaves us with enigmatic liturgical blessings, whereas Hieronymo left his audience with dead bodies on stage, props that expose his grisly designs.

Adding to the excess is the surfeit of literary reminiscences. Those memories, including that of *The Spanish Tragedy*, have some connection to the protagonist's life, commenting obliquely on his past as well as his desires and fears. The quotations cloak these memories so as to obscure what is too painful to recollect. Those personal reminiscences, though, are not merely covered but gradually effaced, rubbed away until the protagonist appears to have no past of his own.

The play of quotation and memory is part of "A game of chess," the title of the second section of the poem. The first half of this section depicts an evening at home with a carping wife and a stolid husband, clearly based on Vivien and Tom Eliot, who knew these scenes of domestic torment all too well. "My nerves are bad to-night. Yes, bad. Stay with me. Speak to me. Why do you never speak? Speak" begins "Vivien's" inquisition of the protagonist (111–12). She wants to know what is in his mind because there appears to be so little in hers, just thoughts about her "nerves" and about noises that the wind may or may not be making.

That delusional rapping is more noise than she gets out of the protagonist. Not until her last question does he respond directly to her. Before then, he answers only with inner reflections, thoughts that to her are "nothing." These musings skip from Biblical times to the present-day, landing in between on Shakespeare, a line from *The Tempest*.

> You know nothing? Do you see nothing? Do you remember
>   "Nothing?"
> I remember
> Those are pearls that were his eyes.

Such ambiguous responses have us side with "Vivien," wanting to know even more what he is thinking and remembering. What she and we really want is some sort of personal memory, not a literary scrap. Such recollections, though, have never flown freely from the protagonist – witness the enigmatic reminiscence about the "hyacinth girl," an affair that ended in some sort of collapse, the protagonist's voice and eyes "failing" (35–38). As fleeting and vague as that memory is, it hovers over the rest of the poem, never named directly but somehow always felt. In the original version of the above passage, though, that recollection appears unobscured: "I remember / The hyacinth garden. Those are pearls that were his eyes, yes!"[26]

"The hyacinth garden" was one of many lines excised by Ezra Pound's editorial scalpel. Besides testifying to his neat surgical work, the omission of the line suggests that the memory was ultimately too painful to recall. Pruned of the protagonist's phrases, the Shakespeare line appears free of personal torment. Like other quotations, though, it alludes to the protagonist's past, allowing him to conceal such troubling thoughts in other people's words. The loss of eyes, for instance, may refer to the failure of sight after the encounter with the "hyacinth girl." The quotation may also evoke the memory of a dead young man.[27] That's how the same line is used earlier in the opening "The burial of the dead," where the protagonist first utters it to himself after Madame Sosotris shows him the tarot card with "the drowned Phoenician Sailor," a figure that recalls someone in the protagonist's past (47–48). Whatever the object of memory, "A game of chess" reveals how dependent the protagonist has become on this evasive strategy. Each one of "Vivien's" aggressive moves prompts this maneuver, one resulting from an unwillingness or an inability to remember his own life.

The protagonist continues to rely on this strategy until the end of the poem, making his last desperate move in the final paragraph. The mass of quotation in that passage responds to sketchy reminiscences of both the hyacinth garden (400–09) and the dead sailor (418–22). Anxious to evade these memories, he again relies on quotation, not just the mere one that was necessary to fend off "Vivien's" demand to remember but a cluster of them. The borrowings of the last paragraph cannot erase those reminiscences, but they can draw attention away from them, disorienting the reader, and the protagonist, in a flurry of literary scraps.

Surrounded by centuries of writings, the protagonist calls to mind the Sibyl of Cumae. Going back to the beginning of the poem, the epigraph offered an omen about the weight of the past. It is a warning that the protagonist did not heed. Whereas the Sibyl has lived over expanses of

[26] Valerie Eliot, ed. *The Waste Land: a Facsimile and Transcript of the Original Drafts Including the Annotations of Ezra Pound* (New York: Harcourt Brace Jovanovich, 1971).

[27] James E. Miller Jr. has argued that the Phoenician sailor mentioned throughout the poem refers to a young man that the protagonist loved. He suggests that this conceit was Eliot's means of mourning Jean Verdenal, a young French medical student who died in battle in the Dardanelles during World War I. It has been proposed that Eliot may have had a homosexual relationship with Verdenal. Miller, *T. S. Eliot's Personal Waste Land: Exorcism of the Demons* (University Park, PA, and London: Pennsylvania State University Press, 1977).

the past, the protagonist has recalled fragments from it. Such exposure proves debilitating. It shrivels the Sibyl as well as the protagonist, not his body but his past. By seeking refuge from memory in the literary past, the protagonist has lost his own history. The final paragraph reveals a character with an "arid" life behind him, the recollections of anguished love banished. All that he has is a vast store of literary memories. Like the Sibyl, he is trapped, his prison being not a tiny cage but the limitless reaches of the past, in which he is just as small and helpless.

The weight of the past also squelches the Sibyl's creative eloquence. The protagonist is well aware of that threat. Two of his quotations refer to characters who had their tongues ripped out. After his theatrical murders have been exposed, Hieronymo mutilates himself in order to prevent his enemies from getting any explanation for his crimes out of him. "O swallow swallow" alludes to the tale of Philomel, who had her tongue removed so she could not tell anyone that her sister's husband had raped her. During her escape, she was turned into a nightingale and her sister a swallow.[28] For the protagonist, the threat is metaphoric. He is in danger of losing his creative expression. One of the costs of using quotations to conceal memory is that of being dependent on other people's words, a loss of voice for such a poetic character. In the final paragraph, the protagonist does speak, a few words assuring us of his having attained some stability, but he mostly recites others, reduced to a mouthpiece for the past.

He can still, though, arrange his literary fragments into captivating and enigmatic patterns, forcing the reader to decipher them. That's more than can be said for the Sibyl, who instead pules a stark death wish. This role reversal points to a distinction between male and female madness, a difference based partly on quotation. In discussing Eliot's female representations, it is important to remember his remark in the accompanying notes that "all the women are one woman." That "one woman" encompasses many troubled characters who are presented as hysterics, including "Vivien," Ophelia, the Sibyl, Philomel, and – from "The Burial of the Dead" – Marie, whose memories of sledding ring of childhood trauma.[29] Together they form a chorus of hysterics that confront the protagonist throughout his journey. In their taunting, the hysterics do not quote, either because they are quotations themselves, like Ophelia and the Sibyl, or because they are unaware of the past, dwelling instead on their own memories and problems. "Vivien," for instance, remains oblivious to the paintings of mythological scenes, the "withered stumps of time,"

[28] Philomel is mentioned earlier in "A game of chess" (99).

[29] For a discussion of the evocation of hysteria in the poem, see Wayne Koestenbaum, *Double Talk: the Erotics of Male Literary Collaboration* (New York and London: Routledge, 1989), 112–39.

on her walls, all the time fretting about her bad nerves. Moreover, even if these women could draw from the past they would be incapable of transforming those borrowings into new poetic strands. They instead chat in banal phrases, like Marie: "I read, much of the night, and go south in the winter."

The protagonist also obviously reads much, as evident in his extensive literary knowledge and profuse quotations. In addition, he can work Sibylline magic on those borrowings, transforming them into evocative lines. That literary alchemy and arcana allow him to keep a distance from the hysterics. They haunt him not only because of his experiences of sexual inadequacy with women (again the hyacinth garden) but also because of the threat of madness that they embody. Besides this personal struggle, the protagonist's stylistic evasion of the hysterics can be seen as part of a larger male modernist abjection of female creativity.[30] Unlike the protagonist, the women in the poem exhibit no poetic talent, not even in the heightened state of madness.

Whereas quotation helps Eliot's protagonist keep away from the hysterical "ladies," it brings Schoenberg closer to his operatic madwoman, his memories of adultery nudging hers. Moreover, the composer bestows – or projects – upon her the tonal innovations that he so prized, making her extravagantly, if not dangerously, eloquent, unlike Eliot's women.[31] The borrowings in the two works differ in many other respects. *Erwartung* draws upon a work from the composer's own past to convey a personal reminiscence. In contrast, *The Waste Land* draws upon works by others to obscure the protagonist's recollections, and eventually to eclipse them. Moreover, the poem has a much longer chronological reach. The monodrama goes back only four years, touching a still tender wound. The quoted works in *The Waste Land*, on the other hand, are dusty and have never been directly experienced by the protagonist, being at least decades and at most centuries before his time. Despite these differences, both works are paralyzed by memory. They push to remember the past, but the act of recollection goes nowhere in each, as characters cannot recall the immediate past, the time experienced within the dramatic confines of the work. Not only is that past a void, but the works obstruct reminiscence, either shunning the act, as in *Erwartung*, or evading it, as in *The Waste Land*. The desire to remember cannot be held off forever. Unable to be fulfilled within the two works, it is ultimately diverted, pointed to a remote and outside past – a time that can be reached only through, and perhaps because of, madness.

---

[30] This abjection of female creativity is also discussed in Sandra M. Gilbert and Susan Gubar, *No Man's Land: the Place of the Woman Writer in the Twentieth Century*, vol. 1: *The War of the Words* (New Haven and London: Yale University Press, 1988), 155–56.

[31] On this projection, see McClary, *Feminine Endings*, 104–09.

Recital I (for Cathy)

Like *The Waste Land*, the works by Berio, Bacon, and Maxwell Davies also stretch across centuries. They, however, not only recall the distant past but also become part of that time, either by extending it or by returning to it. *Recital I* (first conceived in 1966 but not fully composed until 1972), for instance, extends the rituals of the past, the means by which that period endures. That ritual is the concert, which, typical of postmodern irony, *Recital I* presents in the context of staging a concert.[32] The soloist for this performance is a female singer, who, like Schoenberg's Woman, is left anonymous. The parenthetical "Cathy" is Cathy Berberian, the creator of the part whose repertory inspired the choice of quotations. In this monodrama, as in *Erwartung*, the singer undertakes a psychological journey, feeling her way through a "mondo interiore," represented by a recital evening instead of a nocturnal forest. During that journey, she too waits for a male figure: her accompanist, who shows up alive but very late.

His absence causes a stir at the outset of the concert. The singer begins her evening with Monteverdi's *Lettere amorose*; however, she is accompanied only by an offstage harpsichord and abruptly cuts the piece off to look for the pianist. He eventually arrives, but his absence sets off a meandering monologue that takes over the recital.[33] That speech consists of clichés ("it's important to be in the right place at the right time"), vague phrases ("that's why we are cautious and innocent"), bits of foreign languages ("eco di un mondo interiore"), and quotations (from Keats and Shakespeare, among others). To this mix is added a barrage of musical quotations, brief excerpts from her repertoire.[34] At the end of the show, the last few borrowings, excerpts from the mad scenes of *Lucia* and Meyerbeer's *Dinorah*, make clear how much she has crumbled during the evening. After those fragments, all she can do is whimper a setting of the text "Libera nos," praying for liberation from both the recital and the past.

This scene of psychological disintegration was scripted by Berio, who wrote the monologue and selected the quotations.[35] He has the singer lurch back and forth between speech and song, caught between those two different worlds. At times those realms are distant, there being no

[32] The only extended discussion of the work is Susan Youens, "Memory, identity, and the uses of the past: Schubert and Luciano Berio's *Recital I (for Cathy),*" in *Franz Schubert – Der Fortschrittliche?*, ed. Erich Wolfgang Partsch (Tutzing: Hans Schneider, 1989), 231–47.

[33] The work is scored for vocalist, three keyboards (pianos and harpsichord), and chamber orchestra.

[34] See Appendix 1 for a list of quotations in the work.

[35] For her recording, Berberian translated the text into English.

apparent connection between the surrounding spoken lines and the quotations; in other words, juxtapositions that only the mad could create. For instance, the singer spouts the line "You know what, luv?" in a Cockney accent, switches immediately to the *Sprechstimme* of *Pierrot lunaire*, and then formally addresses the audience: "Ladies and gentlemen." Elsewhere the links are clearer. For instance, the singer remarks that nobody "lead[s] the life of courtier," which latches onto the borrowing from Rigoletto's aria "Cortigiani, vil razza dannata" (Courtiers, vile accursed race). Others partake in those recondite ties of which Berio is so fond. The singer contrasts a rant about a man watching "half-naked" "girls" in a strip club with an excerpt from Berio's *Epifanie*, which sets a passage from Joyce's *A Portrait of the Artist as a Young Man* describing young Stephen Dedalus's erotic stirrings upon watching a girl at the seashore.[36]

The musical quotations connect not only with lines from the monologue but also with each other, binding together to form both tonal and topical clusters. Adjacent borrowings often create pockets of one key or of related ones. The opening three quotations (from Monteverdi, Bach, and Armenian liturgy), for instance, are in A minor. In addition to these tonal bonds, many of the quotations are united by similar topics. Some originate from works dealing with madness, including *Lucia, Dinorah, Pierrot lunaire, Lamento della Ninfa*, Ravel's *Don Quichotte à Dulcinée*, and Shakespeare's *Hamlet*.

These quotations are not just symbols of the singer's madness but also the source of that agony. The singer is oppressed by her repertory, the body of music that she has amassed and from which she borrows. She refers repeatedly to her hoarding of the past, once through the anecdote: "on the way to the theatre tonight an old banker told me that life is only accumulation." That adage has proven frightfully true for her. She recognizes herself only as a repository of music, her own identity having disappeared. About all that she can tell us about herself is "I can remember everything," "I've seen everything," and "I've heard everything."

For a character who "can remember everything," the singer tells us little about her own past, seemingly unwilling to confront it. The same could be said about Eliot's protagonist, whose private recollections similarly disappear in the welter of his literary memories. Unlike him, the singer promises that she will share with us "innermost thoughts," a declaration made in the opening *Lettere amorose*. All we ever hear are hints of a lover having deserted her, a torment relived by the late pianist, who could well be the missing lover. What cannot be said directly can be alluded to through quotations. The singer refers to her despair by placing herself in a line of abandoned women, many of whom either went

[36] James Joyce, *A Portrait of the Artist as a Young Man* (New York: Viking Press, 1964), 171.

mad or killed themselves, including Purcell's Dido, Wolf's "verlassene Mägdlein," Monteverdi's Nymph, Shakespeare's Ophelia, and Meyerbeer's Dinorah. In contrast to Eliot's protagonist, she gathers this chorus of hysterics around her, making their voices her own.

Or, viewed from a different angle, her psyche has crumbled into a quarrel of voices. Each one of the quotations is, as she puts it, a "piece out of [her] life," pieces that are now scattered all over the stage floor. This disintegration sends her in a desperate search for wholeness. Looking for it, she begins to talk about "rituals," which she defines as a "form where gesture, sound, and meaning coincide." In that light, a recital is a ritual. By presenting itself as such, *Recital I* puts all the pieces of the ritual together and then proceeds to take them apart. Using the singer's own definition, sound, meaning, and gesture no longer coincide, or not as they are expected to. The musical borrowings constantly block off the stream of sound. Moreover, the meaning of the quotations – how they relate to their surroundings – is not always clear. Nor do some of the theatrical gestures, such as the comic "exercises" of the orchestral musicians that at one point disrupt the performance, fit within the context of the recital.

The ritual of the recital may have failed, but the singer has not given up on rituals as a means of attaining stability, turning her attention away from concerts to religious ceremonies. That's where her attention was when she first mentioned the idea of rituals at the beginning of the concert. "Their eyes are expecting an official ritual," she commented about the audience and then provided them with three quotations from a Bach cantata and one of an Armenian liturgical chant. Four sequential quotations centered around a single idea is as focused as the singer ever gets, but, as usual, she cannot sustain that thought, moving abruptly to her story about the banker and accumulation.

Near the end of the concert, her thoughts return to sacred ceremonies – first only in allusions and finally, and desperately, in an attempt to create her own ritual. Instead of Lutheran and Armenian liturgies, the singer now dreams of weddings. Three of her final borrowings come from works – *Lucia, Dinorah,* and *Alexander Nevsky* – that feature or refer to marriages, all of which have far from blissful outcomes. Lucia is forced to wed a man she does not love and whom she later kills, whereas Dinorah is left at the altar. These calamitous ceremonies cause both characters to go mad, just as the collapsing recital does to the singer. In *Alexander Nevsky*, a young woman sings of the brave man she will marry, a deluded hope for a character walking through a battlefield covered with the bodies of soldiers. The singer also finds herself in desolate surroundings, the elements of a recital – words, music, and gestures – scattered around her. Unlike the Russian girl, she is not hopeful, her pessimistic allusions to marriage expressing a dwindling faith in the power of rituals as well as the despair over her own abandonment.

For her last quotation, the singer returns to the *Dinorah* fragment, now presented in a "grotesque" and "exaggerated" cry. From that wail, it is not much further to the ultimate debasement for a musician: begging the audience to clap. "Why don't you applaud?" she pleads. The desired ovation is not to commend her on the performance but to bring an end to the tormenting recital. No applause emerges. Even that part of the ritual fails. With no end in sight, she begins a prayer, singing the phrase "Libera nos." Liberation from the recital and from the burden of the past is what she seeks. The prayer may also be a final attempt to find liberation in ritual, to enter a realm of wholeness. The text alludes to the Requiem Mass, a service in which gesture, sound, and meaning do coincide and one that provides a conclusion, death instead of applause.[37]

Being out of context in a concert, that ritual is doomed to fail, offering neither the unity nor the closure the singer desires. Her prayer, though, does provide some stability. The "Libera nos" is an extended self-contained piece, one that offers refuge from the fragmentary quotations. Some degree of wholeness is also attained. No longer in separate spheres, she and the orchestra join forces, the latter providing a restless background for her prayer. Language also begins to cohere. At the beginning of the prayer, the singer can enunciate only a few vowel sounds and "desperately" attempts to place them in order, which is achieved when she finally sings the complete Latin text, stating it, though, only three times.[38] She similarly struggles to shape a melodic line, working with even fewer resources, two pitches (C and C♯) compared to a handful of phonemes.[39] Alternating back and forth between those notes (either a half step or a major seventh apart), it is unclear what type of melodic line she is trying to construct. The melismas of the Bach cantata and Armenian liturgy appear now out of reach, so much has she deteriorated during the concert. Perhaps she has in mind a very modest, and liturgical-sounding, single-pitch recitation. Even this, though, fails, as she cannot stay on one pitch, always sliding back and forth between the chromatic pair.

Besides being a last attempt to secure wholeness, the "Libera nos" can be seen as a further descent into madness. As many case studies have observed, hysterics often unexpectedly slip into states of religious ecstasy, falling on their knees in prayer and staring toward heaven.[40] The

---

[37] The text for the Requiem Mass contains the phrase "libera me."

[38] Berio's marking in the score.   [39] The pitch A is stated once in the vocal part.

[40] Elaine Showalter, *The Female Malady: Women, Madness, and English Culture, 1830–1980* (New York: Pantheon, 1985),150–54.

singer similarly makes a sudden conversion, at one moment a frenetic figure begging the audience for applause, the next a penitent asking for liberation. Not just hysterics experience these religious fits. At the end of *The Waste Land*, the protagonist also chants liturgical phrases, which abruptly emerge from a din of quotations dealing with madness, decay, and mutilation.[41] Those voices appear stilled by the liturgical close. However, given the equivocality of the final paragraph, it is unclear whether the "Shantih" evocation expresses the peace finally attained by the protagonist or whether it is just another quotation, the spillings of a mad mind. No such doubt hangs over *Recital I*. Like the poem, it moves through quotations and macaronic patches, but that path clearly leads into madness, ending in a trembling prayer.

With those final Sanskrit lines, *The Waste Land* merely alludes to a ritual. *Recital I*, on the other hand, enacts one – the concert. That difference adds a layer of pastness to the latter work. The poem, as discussed above, continually looks back to the past, quoting bits of what it finds there. The musical piece not only recalls the past but becomes part of it. Rituals are both a means by which the past is preserved and of the past itself, ceremonies repeated over centuries. In other words, *Recital I*, by presenting itself as a concert, becomes part of a tradition, instead of just referring to one. It is from the past and at the same time a vessel of history, holding treasured songs and arias. No wonder the protagonist feels so trapped. She is stuck in a ceremony as old as the repertory that she has accumulated. "Liberation" from both that vessel and that repertory are what she desperately needs.

Mad Kings and Popes

Bacon's *Study after Velázquez's Portrait of Pope Innocent X* and Maxwell Davies's *Eight Songs for a Mad King* are even more stuck in the past. The two move beyond rituals and step into that period itself. Bacon's painting looks back at and settles into Velázquez's *Pope Innocent X* (1649–50, see Plate 3.1), transforming the stern Pontiff into an embodiment of "the human cry" (see Plate 3.2).[42] Maxwell Davies's composition recreates historical events rather than a specific art work. The piece stages tableaux of eighteenth-century England featuring characters, music, speech, and writings of the period. In contrast to *Erwartung*, *The Waste Land*, and *Recital I*, there are no anonymous characters in the present looking back to the past. These characters have names – they are real-life historical

---

[41] Koestenbaum, *Double Talk*, 137.

[42] For a different approach to madness in Bacon's works, see Donald Kuspit, "Hysterical painting," *Artforum* 24 (January 1986), 55–60.

Plate 3.1 Velázquez, *Innocent X*, Galleria Doria-Pamphili, Rome

figures after all – and they don't recall the past because they have never been able to leave it. They are trapped in time, a fate reinforced by the various cages in which they are placed. Those confines – both temporal and physical – not surprisingly lead to madness.

As an example of one artist's fixation on the work of another, Bacon's Pope paintings are perhaps unprecedented in twentieth-century art. Admittedly obsessed with Velázquez's work, he incorporated it into over forty-five paintings during a sixteen-year period (1949–65). These paintings are often referred to as the "screaming Popes," a phrase that applies to arguably the best-known of the group: *Study after Velázquez's Portrait*

Plate 3.2 Francis Bacon, *Study after Velázquez's Portrait of Pope Innocent X*, Des Moines Arts Center © The estate of Francis Bacon/SODART 2003; used by permission

of Pope Innocent X (1953, see Plate 3.2). What lies behind that scream has fascinated viewers, who have seen the Pontiff responding to such various states as horror, death, pain, and madness. For his part, Bacon refused to limit his paintings to one emotion or condition, aiming instead to capture a "cluster of sensations" that the image produces in him.[43] With the Velázquez works, that cluster is especially dense, as he once commented that the original "opens up all sorts of feelings and areas of imagination, even in me."[44]

Bacon never mentioned if madness was one of the "areas of imagination" explored in the Pope series. He, however, suggested that madness rises to the surface in other paintings. Questions about the agonized male figures in many works prompted him to respond: "I suppose, in attempting to trap this image, that, as this man was very neurotic and almost hysterical, this may possibly have come across in the paintings."[45] Madness comes across in some of the other reworkings of earlier canvases. During the 1950s, simultaneous with the Velázquez studies, Bacon elaborated upon paintings by van Gogh, particularly *The Painter on the Road to Tarascon* (1888), completed during a period of increasing mental instability that led up to the artist's suicide. That instability appears in the Van Gogh figure, whose body and facial features are melting away from the intense colors of the landscape, colors that exceed Van Gogh's in their brightness and contrast.[46] Pope Innocent X may never have gone insane, but in Bacon's hands he is no different from Van Gogh and other anguished male figures, his body contorted and left to scream into nothingness. In that context, madness may be one of the states behind that painful cry. *Erwartung*, *The Waste Land*, and *Recital I* suggest that it is, as, like the characters in those works, the Pope is tormented by the past, a past he cannot leave.

Of those three works, *The Waste Land* offers the most insights into the Pope's madness; however, it is not the protagonist to whom we should turn but the Sibyl of Cumae.[47] Both she and the Pontiff have lived for centuries and will live for centuries more. Velázquez's Pope may never have made a foolish wish to live forever, but he has had that fate thrust upon him. He has become a treasured image that will endure, preserved in the painting itself and the countless reproductions of it. Bacon's painting allows us to imagine a Pope who has not been so well preserved, one that has aged the over three hundred years since the original was completed. That Pope is remarkably similar to the Sibyl. He

---

[43] Quoted in Michel Leiris, *Francis Bacon: Full Face and in Profile*, trans. John Weightman (New York: Rizzoli, 1983), 32.

[44] David Sylvester, *Francis Bacon Interviewed by David Sylvester* (New York: Pantheon, 1975), 24.

[45] Ibid., 48.   [46] See especially *Study for Portrait of Van Gogh III* (1957).

[47] The Eliot analogy is not entirely fanciful. Several of Bacon's paintings refer to works by the poet, including *The Waste Land*. See *A Piece of Waste Land* (1982). John Russell also mentions a possible connection between *Painting 1978* and the poem; Russell, *Francis Bacon* (London: Thames and Hudson, 1993), 180–81.

too has withered. His flesh has thinned to a diaphanous gray. His body no longer dominates the canvas; shrunken, it flickers in the background.

The Sibyl's withered body was placed in a small cage and put on display. The Pope sits helplessly on a throne positioned behind a railing, itself positioned behind a curtain. Bacon added one more enclosure, directing that the canvas, like all of his others, be placed behind a plate of glass. The Pope remains trapped behind that covering, for even if he could crawl from underneath the railing and curtain, he could never get beyond that last layer of his cage, never be able to reach out and harm the museum goers looking at him. The glass not only protects viewers but it also places them in the scene. In museum spaces, the plates often reflect the image of the viewers, letting them see themselves looking at the Pope. Gathered around him, they have become the boys rushing in to see the Sibyl. Instead of ridicule, they may offer looks of shock and disgust for the ravaged figure.

There may also be looks of pity. Just as the Sibyl had been reduced from enigmatic eloquence to death screeches, the Pope has fallen. His emaciated body writhing, he has lost his regal countenance, as well as all signs of Papal authority, namely the ring and Holy Writ in the original. Both the Pope and the Sibyl have been eroded by time. For the two characters, there is no future to look forward to, their future being nothing more than an extension of the past, bringing with it more memories and torture. With her death wish, the Sibyl envisaged one way out of that agony. The Pope's scream is beyond words and could never be reduced to such a stark phrase. Yet in that cry, there is at once a look of madness and a plea for release from it. As with the Sibyl, that desire will go unfulfilled, the Pope facing not death but only continued deterioration.

The Sibyl's body may disintegrate, but it remains her own. The same cannot be said for the Pope. Deathlessness metes out a special punishment for artworks like Velázquez's *Portrait*. Over centuries, those works become part of the pool of images sustained by cultural memory, a reservoir consisting of everything from classic canvases to quotidian sights. In that realm, images can easily become confused. They may even begin to merge, parts of one seeming to fit with another. For treasured images like the Pope, this melding is one more ordeal of excessive age. It amounts to a loss of identity, as the once unique work no longer stands out by itself but instead becomes part of a blur of images. The older the painting, the more susceptible it may be to this agony. The deteriorated figures in those works can do little to fend off the foreign images that they encounter. Indeed, their decaying frames may attract those outsiders, who spot and claim the empty patches, the shrunken limbs, and faded faces.

In Bacon's painting, a variety of foreign images prey upon the Pope's body and pictorial space. They include a still of a screaming nurse from Sergei Eisenstein's 1925 film *Battleship Potemkin*, a shot that for Bacon captured the "human cry" and one which he used in several other works. Centuries removed, created in different media, and seemingly unrelated, the still nonetheless has found its way into Velázquez's painting, or one man's memory of that painting. The once commanding Pontiff offers little resistance to the intruding image, which robs him of his most distinctive feature: his face. On top of the holy vestments and diminished figure now lies the Nurse's head, broken glasses and all. This new visage could not be more different from the Pope's. His grim stare conveys control, of himself and those around him, whereas the Nurse's scream is an effusion of fear and pain, a rush that cannot be controlled.

Innocent X is tormented not only by screaming women but by other Popes as well. Bacon's *Study* draws upon two other images of church officials: Titian's *Portrait of Archbishop Filippo Archinto* (1561–62) and a contemporary photograph of Pope Pius XII blessing a crowd of worshippers while being lifted above them on a *sedia gestatoria*.[48] These images do not alter Innocent X's body but rather disturb his surroundings – insidious redecorating that adds to his agony. He and the throne now sit on the *sedia*, suggested by the raised platform and railing. This new support calls attention to the absence of any worshippers surrounding the decrepit Innocent X, who appears unable to bless anyone even if they were there. The only people he may see are the museum goers, themselves keeping a safe distance behind the glass and railing. The Pope is also separated from them by a curtain, an element borrowed from the Titian painting, which has a transparent drapery covering half of the Archbishop's body. That curtain reminds the viewer that Church officials operate in a removed world, one unknown to the faithful. With Innocent X, the drapery hides nothing. We see the Pope's madness and frail body, sights that formerly would have been hidden behind the Vatican walls. The curtain, though, does not expose everything. It has little to say about the droplets of blood covering it, nor does it make clear on which side those stains originated – his or ours?

In *Eight Songs for a Mad King* (1969), little, if anything, separates us from the insane monarch: no curtain, railing, or glass, instead only that imaginary wall dividing the stage and audience. On that stage, King George III rampages and, as the title promises, sings. The title specifically refers to an organ belonging to the King that played eight tunes. As a note within the instrument explained: "This Organ was George the

---

[48] The image of Pius XII can be found in a photo collage included in Sam Hunter, "Francis Bacon: the anatomy of horror," *Magazine of Art* 45 (January 1952), 12.

third for Birds to sing."[49] Teaching birds to sing was one of George's pursuits during his years of madness. Maxwell Davies reenacts those otiose lessons by placing members of the ensemble (flute, clarinet, violin, and cello) in birdcages and having the male singer interact with them. George, however, is also taught. The percussionist plays the role of the King's "keeper," making sure that he never gets too far out of line.

The "keeper" and ornithological teachings are only two bits of George's madness that the work has drawn from the historical record. The libretto by Randolph Stow presents other incidents and includes lines spoken by the King. The sixth song, ironically titled "The Counterfeit," consists entirely of one of his rants, recorded by Fanny Burney, the Queen's attendant.[50] Even the musical quotations are historically based. George often rasped melodies by Handel, here represented by two recurring phrases from *The Messiah*: the opening line from "Comfort Ye My People" and that for "the kingdom of our Lord" from the "Hallelujah Chorus." Maxwell Davies adds to the period flavor with several bits of "counterfeit" eighteenth-century music, including a suite and a Handelian recitative and aria.

That music is not so much fake as distorted. In the recitative, for instance, the continuo plays cluster chords accompanied by a dijeridu. The *Messiah* quotations are similarly contorted, often sung in a phantom falsetto or once neighed "like a horse."[51] Not only eighteenth-century works are subjected to such distortions. *Eight Songs* borrows the ensemble from *Pierrot lunaire*, adding to it a percussion part and substituting a male singer for the female reciter.[52] These are minor changes compared to the various ways the work exaggerates the sounds and roles of Schoenberg's already mad world. Going beyond the spectral lilt of *Sprechstimme*, the singer screams, jumps into extreme registers, and stretches his voice across chordal sonorities, among other effects.

An eighteenth-century monarch romping through the sound world of a fin-de-siècle clown recalls the chronological mergers in Bacon's paintings. The two works do combine elements from different periods, but they each concentrate on one large block from the past: George III's ravings or Velázquez's painting. In both cases, this extensive borrowing creates the impression of having reentered the past. *Eight Songs* revives the lunacy of the King, whereas Bacon's *Study* returns to and situates itself

---

[49] Peter Maxwell Davies, *Eight Songs for a Mad King* (London: Boosey & Hawkes, 1971), preface.

[50] Much of the historical material was drawn from Christopher Hibbert, *The Court at Windsor: a Domestic History* (New York and Evanston, IL: Harper & Row, 1964), 124–45.

[51] Score direction from the seventh song.

[52] The work was originally performed by the Pierrot players, a group formed by Maxwell Davies and Harrison Birtwistle in 1967. On other works that incorporate the Schoenberg ensemble, see Watkins, *Pyramids at the Louvre*, 307–9.

within the portrait of Innocent X. As is clear in their twentieth-century idioms, the two have never left the present, that is, the present that they share: 1950s–60s England. Both works, though, still look more backward than forward, never being able to turn away from the past. Bacon later mentioned how he was "hypnotized" by Velázquez's painting.[53] For his part, Maxwell Davies was so dependent on the past that, when it came time to depict madness, he drew upon two earlier manifestations of that state: the words of George III and the sounds of *Pierrot lunaire*.[54]

Fixated upon the past, *Eight Songs* and *Study* reveal yet again how much the art of previous periods dominated the twentieth century. The two works, though, do not merely capitulate to that dominance. In both, borrowing from the past provides means of assailing that period, or "inflicting violence" upon it, as Alan E. Williams suggests *Eight Songs* does with its "historical musics."[55] The musical work and painting link the past with figures of power, a King and Pope. Struck insane, they no longer hold sway. The Pope shrinks from his followers and lets out a painful cry. Governed by a "keeper," the King proclaims in a hollow voice: "I shall rule with a rod of iron." By toppling these leaders, the present appears to ascend the chronological throne, wielding the power to alter treasured works and to make gross spectacles of earlier rulers.

The present, though, is only a pretender. Rather than being usurped, the dominance of the past is ultimately reinforced by these works. The madness used to bring down these rulers and the past takes the form of distortion. When used in such excessive ways, that approach comes across as derivative, an action performed on other works. Moreover, in the case of *Study* and *Eight Songs*, it is not a bold artistic choice but one of the few approaches that could be used. With such large blocks of past materials, there is little room to add anything new. About all that can be done is to act upon those materials, and the more one distorts them, the less decisive and original the challenge to the past. Such a realization

---

[53] Quoted in Hugh Davies, *Francis Bacon: the Early and Middle Years, 1928–1958* (New York: Garland, 1978), 99.

[54] Maxwell Davies returned to representations of madness in two later works: *Miss Donnithorne's Maggot* (1974) and the ballet *Caroline Mathilde* (1991). Both are based on historical subjects. The former is a monologue by Eliza Emily Donnithorne, an Australian woman who was the inspiration for Dickens's Miss Havisham. Like *Eight Songs*, this work employs an expanded form of the *Pierrot* ensemble. *Caroline Mathilde* returns to the Court of George III, telling the story of the King's sister who was married to King Christian VII of Denmark, another monarch suffering from insanity. The work also includes parodies of eighteenth-century styles.

[55] Alan E. Williams, "Madness in the music theater works of Peter Maxwell Davies," *Perspectives of New Music* 38 (2000), 85–86.

may have led Bacon to dismiss the Pope paintings as "failures," nothing more than "distorted records" of Velázquez's *Portrait*.[56]

That there is no triumph over the past is made clear by the two works themselves. In both, the authoritative figures may be distorted and pummeled but they never die, and, as long as they live, so does the past. Death, and its promise of release from that period, is evoked but never attained. In the last number of *Eight Songs*, George III announces in a normal speaking voice "the King is dead." By the end of the number, that voice has given way to screaming and the pronouncement overturned by his last words: "the King will die howling." As of 1969, the King was still howling and very much alive, living on in the contemporary fascination with madness and the past.[57] Bacon's Pope makes no such royal decrees. Yet his body – so frail, so in pain – teeters on the edge of death. He too, though, never passes away, still gripping his throne in the 1953 painting.

By denying death, the two works create open endings, it never being clear when and where the Pope and King will die. The three works discussed earlier also feature such conclusions. At the end of *Erwartung*, the Woman greets the dawn with the line "I was looking..." The closing chromatic ascent, trailing off like an ellipsis, suggests that she has not found what she was looking for and that she will continue her desperate search over an endless series of days and nights. The singer of *Recital I* looks for liberation in either applause or death, her abridged Requiem Mass. Neither comes, and we are left with her gasping at the end of prayer, unsure of what will happen to her next. Finally, the protagonist of *The Waste Land* also finishes with a prayer, but his fate is no more certain as we leave him in a cloud of madness.

In works from previous centuries, that madness would have led to death. Insanity was an extreme state, a realm of chaos and darkness from which there was no return. The only escape was to something more extreme: death. From that perspective, death was a form of "divine mercy," a final kindness bestowed upon the hopeless.[58] Many of the characters

---

[56] Quoted in Sylvester, *Francis Bacon*, 37, and Davies, *Francis Bacon*, 99. It should also be noted that Bacon never saw Velázquez's original painting, instead always working from reproductions of it. When having the opportunity to do so during a visit to Rome, he declined, later explaining: "But I think another thing was probably a fear of seeing the reality of the Velasquez after my tampering with it, seeing this marvelous painting and thinking of the stupid things one had done with it." Sylvester, *Francis Bacon*, 38.

[57] In contrast to this view of the King as trapped in time, Ruud Welten argues that the character personifies the postmodern disintegration of the subject, a figure who no longer conveys a unified identity but has been splintered into different identities, as heard in the King slipping into so many different styles. Welten, "'I'm not ill, I'm nervous' – madness in the music of Sir Peter Maxwell Davies," *Tempo* 196 (April 1996), 21–24.

[58] Foucault, *Madness and Civilization*, 31.

discussed earlier received that blessing. As a final punctuation to a murderous run, Hieronymo kills himself on stage. We never see Ophelia or Lucia die, but that is fitting, for both women make musical exits, leaving the stage with mad songs that are eventually silenced. Ophelia's lilting "goodnight ladies" is hushed by a stream, whereas Lucia's coloratura is reduced to the resonance of a lone offstage funeral bell.

The above five works offer their characters no such deliverance, choosing instead to draw out indefinitely the chaos and darkness. That darkness is not just of madness but also of the past. The use of open endings is telling in works that focus on the oppression of the past and memory. Such conclusions provide no future, giving no hints of different directions that impending events will take. They instead create a limitless expanse into which the past can flow, our only possible understanding of the future being as a continuation of what has happened before. With such outcomes, the past has subsumed the present and the future, and time itself has become an embodiment of insanity. In his discussions of earlier conceptions of madness, Foucault described how insanity united opposites – day and night, vision and blindness – to become "ultimately nothing." He called this state "unreason."[59] These five works have created temporal "unreason," spheres in which the lines between the past and the present as well as the past and the future have faded, creating voids of time.

That chronological delirium conveys a larger cultural anxiety over the past. As will be discussed in chapter four, other twentieth-century works drawing upon past materials do not share that fear, viewing instead the blend of past and present as regenerative and enriching. The differences between the two become apparent when contrasting the above five works with the third movement from *Sinfonia*. Like the former, the movement contains a voice suggestive of madness: the constant murmuring of the character from Beckett's *The Unnamable*. Moreover, that literary character also faces an unceasing bleakness, which he pushes his way through with exhortations of "keep going." In his new musical surroundings, however, he finally does reach some sort of conclusion, and perhaps relief from his despair. The movement has a definite ending – not only does the Mahler foundation come to an end, but so does the performance itself. In the final minute, the first tenor, the part that has delivered most of the lines by the Beckett character, formally winds things up by announcing "it's done, it's over," introducing his fellow performers, and, after the last note of the Scherzo, thanking the conductor. Ever so aware of concert protocol, the singer in *Recital I* yearns to take such a final bow, one that would allow her to leave the stage to the sound of applause. The other characters discussed above

[59] Ibid., 107.

desire any type of conclusion, whatever it takes to free them from the past.

In *Sinfonia*, however, the past is not something from which to escape. It is instead one of many elements that the work embraces. The movement initiates a constant process of expansion. From the Mahler base, it pushes outward by linking together scraps from musical pieces, literature, and speech. That expansion creates a musical world that promises inclusion, that everything, even compositions from the past and present, can be united to make something new. The five works discussed here unleash a different type of expansion, one that leads to absence. In those works, the past is a growing void. It slowly encroaches on the ever-new worlds of the present and the future, reclaiming them as realms of crumbling memories and madness.

4

The promise of the past: Rochberg, Berio, and Stockhausen

They showed so much promise, the "class of '45," a group consisting of Boulez, Pousseur, Stockhausen, Henze, Maderna, Nono, and Berio. During the 1950s, this youthful brigade congregated at Darmstadt and developed the plans for integral serialism. Under them, music appeared to have crossed the modernist bridge and attained a style in which "the past had gone for ever."[1] Guided by rigor and logic, this style instead led into a "trap." It had moved too far beyond the past, forgoing even the most basic of "contexts," such as motive and counterpoint. From here, the logical schemes quickly unraveled, and in no time at all new music went from banishing the past to sinking back into it.

It is difficult to avoid a suspicion that the decline of modernism as a certain pathway to the future was indirectly responsible for the onset of a nostalgic form of musical cannibalism – of a tendency to ingest bits of the past (or of the ethno-elsewhere) before regurgitating them as (at worst) an unabsorbed mish-mash of stolen traditions even less honest (because more knowing) than the poverty-stricken recyclings of the pop music industry.[2]

It is with this scene of "cannibalism" that Susan Bradshaw concludes her account of the rise and fall of the "class of '45." That group of young composers took the European musical world by storm in the 1950s with their crusading vitality. By the end of the decade, however, "creative exhaustion" had set in, and the nadir was reached in the 1960s with the "cannibalism" and "regurgitation" of the past. Bradshaw does not cite any particular "cannibalistic" works, but it is not hard to deduce that she is talking about the large number of collage pieces written during that decade, compositions that amass disparate elements, including quotations of earlier pieces, into thick, heterogeneous textures.[3] Many

---

[1] Susan Bradshaw, "The class of '45," *Musical Times* 136 (March 1995), 139.

[2] Ibid., 141.

[3] For a detailed list of compositions in this vein, see Michael Hicks, "The new quotation: its origins and functions" (DMA diss., University of Illinois at Urbana-Champaign, 1984), 16–27.

composers, including members of the "class of '45," turned to this idiom. Indeed, the best-known work in the style, if not the decade, is by a class-mate: Berio's *Sinfonia*.

It is not clear whether Bradshaw would dismiss that celebrated composition as "mish-mash," but it is clear what she thinks of the collage style and the gesture of quotation upon which it is based. Her essay wears down an already worn view of quotation as a symptom of creative desperation. For that opinion, she need look no further than Boulez, the leader of the scattered class, who, writing in 1971, called quotation "a shrunken and accepted form of death."[4] Bradshaw similarly regards the gesture as an emblem of death – in this case, the death of modernism.

How to respond to such a condemnation? One fitting way is with a quotation.

They showed so much promise, the members of the "class of '45" who broke away from the orthodoxies of serialism. From the late 1950s through the following decade, these defectors – Berio, Stockhausen, Henze, Pousseur, Nono, and Maderna – created new styles, ones no longer set on the modernist prize of annulling the past. For them, the tight logical schemes in integral serialism had created a Gordian knot. Realizing the futility of this dense abstraction, they went from banishing the past to building upon it.

It is difficult not to see that for many composers who turned away from serialism the forging of new styles as a certain pathway to the future was through the past. There was an onset of musical quotation – of a tendency to draw upon earlier works and combine them with current styles to produce (at best) vibrant mixtures of old and new that revitalized contemporary music.

Like a musical quotation, this passage does not merely restate Brad-shaw's text but transforms it. The transformation is admittedly not too imaginative – revitalization is merely substituted for decline. However, like a good quotation, this one makes us read Bradshaw in a new way. In particular, the measured prose of the transformation should draw attention to the mass of grisly metaphors and parenthetical asides that support her over-the-top, and itself not too imaginative, response to quo-tation. The transformation is largely intended to make the reader look at the 1960s collage works in a new way, one free from Bradshaw and Boulez's taint of creative sterility. This new perspective can be summed up in the word used to introduce Bradshaw's account and my transfor-mation of it: promise.

Promise, in the sense that quotation had much to offer composers at that time, especially those who had abandoned serialism or, at least, rigid forms of it. Three such composers were Berio and Stockhausen,

---

[4] Pierre Boulez, *Orientations* (Cambridge, MA: Harvard University Press, 1986), 358.

two errant members of the "class of '45," and George Rochberg. In the early 1960s, all three either questioned or rejected outright the premises of serialism and began to search for new idioms that would redress its limitations. Quotation played a key role in that effort. From the way they wrote about quotation and used it in their collage works, it is clear that borrowing was a source of promise, a gesture that opened up new possibilities. These new paths were cut and followed in the works to be discussed in this chapter: Rochberg's *Music for the Magic Theater* and Third Symphony, the third movement from Berio's *Sinfonia*, and Stockhausen's *Hymnen*.

The promise of collage idioms centered around two dynamics: expansion and connection. For these three composers and others, quotation expanded the field of musical resources, opening up worlds of unequaled breadth and richness. Whereas serial composers looked inward, tinkering with ever more intricate operations, composers of collage works looked out at a vast realm beyond the row, one full of, among the infinite array of sounds, the music of Beethoven, the novels of Beckett, and the noises of a Chinese market. Tantalized by that vista, many composers left the confines of the row and ventured into that space. Quotation offered a means of taking the first steps and bringing back the music and sounds heard there into new works. The collage pieces created from these excursions reveal how much quotation had changed the mapping of the compositional world from the 1950s to the 1960s. In the earlier decade, composers charted, as Stockhausen recalled, a musical sphere disconnected from the "known" uses of melody, harmony, and rhythm. By the 1960s, these composers had used quotation to embrace the "known," be it Bach or the sounds of automobiles. Their musical reality was no longer an isolated abstract realm but, as Berio put it, "the totality of the sonic world."[5]

Quotation not only expanded the scope of musical materials but also the scope of what composers could do with those materials. In particular, it allowed them to push further the explorations of simultaneity undertaken in serial works and other complex idioms of the 1950s and early 1960s. In those works, composers experimented with superimposing different musical layers, such as the different tempos in Rochberg's Second String Quartet (1961) and the three orchestras in Stockhausen's *Gruppen* (1955–57). Such experiments did not come to an end with quotation; on the contrary, they were intensified. The gesture allowed composers to bring in a greater variety of materials to use as layers, say Mozart and cluster chords as opposed to two different tempos, and, above all, to create greater contrast and tension between those more easily distinguishable strands. The third movement of *Sinfonia*

---

[5] Michel Philippot, "Entretien: Luciano Berio," *La Revue Musicale*, 235–36 (1969), 90.

offers a particularly rich collage cross-section, one in which the rings of materials – Mahler, Beckett, and other quotations – are stratified.

This expansion of the range and layering of materials brought both challenges and promises. The main challenge, especially for reformed serialists, was to find a means of uniting these elements instead of fortuitously throwing them together as in a "happening" type of performance. According to Stockhausen, how to avoid such random juxtapositions was the most pressing problem facing composers in the 1960s. If solved, that problem could become a source of promise, a means of controlling the limitless sonic terrain that composers had opened up, or at a least a sliver of that terrain. The solution that Stockhausen, Berio, and Rochberg explored was to connect elements, to create links where apparently none had existed before. For these composers, the act of connection was one of the main fascinations of collage works, a fascination that comes through in Berio's talk of "interrelationships," Stockhausen's models of "intermodulation," and Rochberg's accounts of *ars combinatoria*.

One connection that captivated these composers was that between past and present. In its post-war apogee, serialism, along with other avant-garde styles, had stanched the past, attempting to create music that could exist without the blood of tradition. Quotation allowed composers to remove these obstructions and to have the past circulate in the present. Not only could the past flow in the present but the present could also flow into the past. This confluence of different periods was at the heart of an approach to time put forth by Bernd Alois Zimmermann, another serial composer who turned to quotation (although without necessarily giving up serialism). Zimmermann bent conventional linear views of time into what he called the "sphericality of time," a space in which the past, present, and future were all equidistant from the center.[6] As his tributes to St. Augustine, Henri Bergson, and James Joyce reveal, this view of time had circled around for centuries and would continue to do so for centuries to come. Rochberg, Berio, and Stockhausen added to this circle by offering their own variations on Zimmermann's theme. For all three, "radial" time, to use Rochberg's phrase, exposed the delusion behind the modernist renunciation of the past and offered a vision of time in which all three periods were interconnected.

It is an extravagant vision but no more so than some of the other visions created by these composers. So strong was the promise of quotation that almost anything seemed possible. Taken by the gesture and

---

[6] On Zimmermann's use of this concept, see Carl Dahlhaus, " 'Kugelgestalt der Zeit': zu Bernd Alois Zimmermanns Musikphilosophie," *Musik und Bildung* 10 (1978), 633–36; and Lisa Viens, "Stratégies citationelles dans *Die Soldaten* de Bernd Alois Zimmermann," *Canadian University Music Review* 17 (1996), 1–19.

its possibilities, Rochberg and Stockhausen went so far as to pursue idealistic designs. The former proclaimed a "renewal" of music, in which quotation would play a key role. The gesture would allow him and other composers to revitalize new music by synthesizing the rich harmonies and melodies of earlier periods with modern styles. Stockhausen was even more visionary, using quotation as a means of creating utopia. Brimming with quotations of national anthems and other real world noises, *Hymnen* draws a sonic map of the world. For over two hours, it travels between countries before concluding in a new utopian realm, a country that offers a vision of world peace. Berio aspired to no such grand schemes, but *Sinfonia* still offers a striking compositional vision. The third movement begins with a bang, a musical big bang. From that explosion, a new musical universe is born, one that constantly expands by taking in pieces of the past and the present.

Universes, utopia, renewal, and "radial" time are far removed from the chaos and darkness of madness discussed in the last chapter. Those mad scenes offered visions of time in which the past eclipsed both the present and reason. However, bedlam and utopia may not be that far apart, at least they are not in 1960s collage pieces. Individual composers traveled back and forth between the two. Berio turned to the collapsing psychological timbers of *Recital I* only a few years after exploring the promise of collage idioms in *Sinfonia*. In pieces by different composers, the wracked monarchy of *Eight Songs for a Mad King* and the peaceful kingdom of *Hymnen* appeared within two years of each other. These works are typical of the different responses composers had to the past during this time. Having released the past after several years of blocking it, they had to come to terms with the magnitude of that period. Works such as *Recital I* and *Eight Songs* show that some found that magnitude to be overwhelming, whereas *Sinfonia* and *Hymnen* are a sign that other – and sometimes the same – composers viewed it as inspirational, drawing upon its riches to create vast new compositional worlds.

If madness describes the chronological scenes created by the works in the preceding chapter, promise best captures the scenes evoked by *Hymnen*, *Sinfonia*, and Rochberg's compositions. These pieces spring from a fascination with expansion and connection and a hope that past and present can be reconciled. Such optimism in turn inspires the dreams of renewal and utopia. The works abound with promise; however, not all of it is fulfilled. In particular, the dreams of renewal and utopia are not realized. Those failures will hardly come as a surprise. Renewal, on the scale predicted by Rochberg, has not occurred, and utopia is by its nature visionary. These predictable outcomes may tempt us to dismiss renewal and utopia as mere pipe dreams, but that would be a mistake, for, as is so often the case, it is the big dreams and the bigger failures that have much to tell us. So it is with renewal and utopia. The collapse of these dreams points to the looming obstacle that composers of collage pieces confronted: the past. Whereas the past offered composers much in terms of resources, it also offered them many difficulties. In Rochberg and Stockhausen's works, the past proves unwieldy, resisting attempts to control and build upon it. Rochberg's renewal often succumbs to nostalgia, grasping at a past that remains out of reach, whereas Stockhausen's utopia, seeking to move into a perfect future, gets caught in a hollow past and present. Although not pursuing such idealistic designs, the Berio movement still confronts an unpredictable past. In this expanding musical universe, the past comes close to collapsing in on itself, forming a black hole into which the universe, or movement, could sink.

These dangers and thwarted promises remind us once again how tense the relationship between past and present is, even in works that have supposedly achieved a rapprochement between the two periods. The mad characters of the last chapter would only chortle at such crushed dreams, reveling in the dashed hopes of those who thought they could manipulate the past. They, however, should not laugh that long, for these works do live up to some of their promise, including the bridging of past and present. Despite the intractability of the past, these compositions do integrate the two periods to a considerable degree, as heard in the vigorous blends of earlier pieces and new styles. The three composers also realize the promises of expansion and connection by creating works that constantly reach out to the past and intertwine what they find there. With such dynamic expansions, connections, and chronological blends, it is not surprising that composers began to dream of renewal and utopia. These promises, fulfilled and unfulfilled, make it clear that in the wane of serialism, quotation and collage were not part of a decline but rather a new, and much needed, inspiration.

Rochberg

Rochberg took his first steps into collage composition in 1965 with a work entitled *Contra mortem et tempus*. Several years later, he defended his Third String Quartet (1972), a work which in many ways represents the culmination of this new path, by declaring: "Through art we are all Don Quixotes battling Time and Death."[7] Challenging these two foes is an even more visionary pursuit than the renewal of music, or utopia

---

[7] Rochberg, "On the Third String Quartet," in Rochberg, *The Aesthetics of Survival: a Composer's View of Twentieth-Century Music*, ed. William Bolcom (Ann Arbor: University of Michigan Press, 1984), 241.

for that matter. Rochberg apparently realized as much, literally calling the campaign quixotic. Nonetheless, like the Spanish knight, he still charged Death and Time. Death was a pressing foe. *Contra mortem et tempus* arose from the grief over the death of Rochberg's son Paul a year earlier. That loss impelled him to abandon serialism, which he believed lacked the expressive depths to confront his sorrow.[8] He found music that did possess such depths in the past, a discovery that began the trail of quotations extending from *Contra mortem et tempus* through later pieces.

By summoning the past, Rochberg eyed his second foe: time. In many ways, though, time was not an enemy, but rather the foundation of Rochberg's music. Through the quotation of earlier pieces, his works open up vast fields of time. Rochberg explored these fields not only in his music but also in a series of essays dealing with musical renewal from the late 1960s and early 1970s.[9] These articles provided a forum in which to denounce serialism and to hold up collage composition as a way out of that compositional dead end. In making his case, Rochberg returned repeatedly to the topic of time. He dwelled upon the relationship between past and present, reiterating a group of ideas – circular time and *ars combinatoria* – to support his attempts to unite the two. That union was crucial, for it lay at the heart of the grand vision of musical renewal.

True to his claim of being Don Quixote, Rochberg was battling time; however, he was not taking on time, but rather a specific notion of time: history. In his essays, he drew a distinction between the two. History is a linear conception in which time pushes forward from one stage to another. Leaving behind a wake of disappearing pasts, history was the accomplice, if not the leader, of Rochberg's foe Death. Time, on the other hand, remains still and at once encompasses the past, present, and future, an infinite realm in which death is meaningless. Hoping to subdue Death, or at least to flout it, Rochberg embraced this infinite view of time. Other composers developed similar perspectives, though none out of a quixotic attempt to battle Death. Zimmermann saw time as a broad sphere in which all periods were equally within reach. Rochberg depicted time as "radial," a space in which he too was surrounded by

---

[8] Rochberg has mentioned that he considered abandoning serialism as early as 1961, three years before his son's death. In a recent interview, he recalled "I wasn't sure how to work my way out of the cul-de-sac [the rigidities of serialism]. These things take time." Allan Kozinn, "Concert connects new with newer," *New York Times*, 28 April 2000, sect. B, p. 8.

[9] These essays include the articles "No center" (1969), "The avant-garde and the aesthetics of survival" (1969), "Reflections on the renewal of music" (1972), and "On the Third String Quartet" (1974). They have been collected in Rochberg, *The Aesthetics of Survival*.

all periods: "I stand in a circle of time, not on a line. 360 degrees of past, present, and future. All around me."[10]

The music that could capture this panoramic view was part of what Rochberg called *ars combinatoria*. Taking the form of a collage, that art is based upon, as Dahlhaus said of Zimmermann's sphere, the "simultaneity of the unsimultaneous."[11] Or as Rochberg rhapsodized: "simultaneous streams of events, gestures, perceptions...of sounding bodies. A vibrating galaxy of suns, moon, and planets. Each different. Each unique. Coming together, colliding, penetrating, attracting, and repelling."[12] Rochberg's "galaxy" is notably far removed from the ordered space of serialism. As if wanting to get as far away as possible from that precision, the composer leapt into a chaotic realm wracked by apparently random collisions. Whereas the "external logic and methodology" of serialism have been abrogated in that realm, other laws, albeit much more general ones, hold sway there.[13] *Ars combinatoria* is governed by the two underlying forces of expansion and connection, the same two forces that shape much collage composition at this time. Such art arises from, as Rochberg put it, the pressing "need to expand our sources" beyond the narrow stylistic dictates of the present.[14] Drawn from the wealth of the past, these new sources are not to be merely thrown together but rather combined, or connected. In his practicing of *ars combinatoria*, Rochberg created those connections by drawing intervallic links between quotations of past works and passages in modern styles, a motivic cord stringing together, for instance, Beethoven, Mahler, and an atonal outburst.

Those ties, however, are already there, made before Rochberg even conceives of a piece. Elaborating upon an essay by Borges, Rochberg describes what he calls the "universal mind," an infinite field of consciousness in which all ideas and feelings – those of past, present, and future – are enfolded.[15] Given that all musical works and ideas exist in a state of interconnectedness, Rochberg's motivic links admittedly prove redundant. Nevertheless, these connections are still vital, as they broaden the play of expansion in *ars combinatoria*. Each link takes us one step further into the "universal mind," serving as a means for us to hop from one musical idea to another. These connections also expand the consciousness of listeners, making them sense the expanse of the "universal mind" and glimpse the "patterns" underlying that realm.

---

[10] Rochberg, "No center," 158.   [11] Dahlhaus, "'Kugelgestalt der Zeit,'" 636.

[12] Rochberg, "No center," 159.   [13] Ibid., 160.

[14] Rochberg, "On the Third Quartet," 241.

[15] Rochberg, "Reflections on the renewal of music," 232; Jorge Luis Borges, "Pascal's sphere," in *Selected Non-Fictions*, ed. Eliot Weinberger, trans. Esther Allen, Suzanne Jill Levine, and Eliot Weinberger (New York: Vintage, 1999), 351–53.

As depicted by Rochberg, *ars combinatoria* is a chain reaction of expansions and connections. All that is necessary to set off that reaction is a single quotation, and, once initiated, it could go on forever until all possible combinations of past and present had been made. This idea of a single act or idea opening up to infinity runs through Borges's writings. In his story, "A survey of the works of Herbert Quain," each of the chapters of a novel by Quain leads independently to new chapters that explain events and characters mentioned in the original chapter, a "ramification" that results in an unending succession of new novels.[16] Rochberg imagined the expansions and connections of *ars combinatoria* similarly pointing toward infinity, stretching out over the limitless "universal mind": "the use of every device and every technique appropriate to its specific gestural repertory in combination with every other device and technique, until theoretically all that we are and all that we know is bodied forth in the richest, most diverse music ever known to man: *ars combinatoria.*"[17]

This grandiose vision is how Rochberg concluded a 1972 essay entitled "Reflections on the renewal of music." The crowd of superlatives provides a fitting end to his equally grandiose conception of renewal. Rochberg proclaimed a renewal of vast dimensions, one that would sweep over new music in general, raising it from the "cultural exhaustion" into which it had fallen.[18] He first perceived the need for renewal as far back as "the early sixties," the period during which he grew disillusioned with serialism, a disenchantment that hardened into antipathy with his son's death.[19] As Rochberg repeatedly asserted in his essays on renewal, new styles, including serialism, had atrophied, becoming lifeless to listeners. In attacking those styles, he focused on the act of listening, an act ignored by most serial composers writing on music. From the position of the listener, the shortcomings of this music were all too clear. It had no expressive range, what little it could express being limited to "overintense" extremes.[20] For Rochberg, expression was a key concern. It was in many ways the driving force behind renewal, a quality that was desperately needed in contemporary styles. This interest was not shared by Berio, Stockhausen, and other serialists turned collage composers, who, keeping up their modernist detachment, viewed quotations of past works more as materials to manipulate than as distant voices of sorrow and love. Rochberg also held that new idioms failed in

---

[16] Borges, *Collected Fictions* (New York: Penguin, 1998), 106–11.

[17] Rochberg, "Reflections on the renewal of music," 238.

[18] Rochberg, "No center," 158.

[19] Rochberg, liner notes, Third String Quartet, Nonesuch Records H-71283 (1973). Rpr. in Joy DeVee Dixon, *George Rochberg: a Bio-Bibliographic Guide to his Life and Works* (Stuyvesant, NY: Pendragon, 1992), 140.

[20] Rochberg, "On the Third Quartet," 239.

the equally fundamental role of music to create a corporeal connection with listeners. Modern works, he argued, could never stir a listener to sing or dance. As with emotional expression, that quality needed to be reclaimed: "The renewal of music lies in the direction of reasserting both [singing and dancing], simply and directly."[21]

The way to revive this moribund art was to connect it with the past. Such connections, as Rochberg mentions, had occurred frequently in music history, be it the Florentine Camerata's recreation of Greek drama, Brahms's use of the passacaglia, or Stravinsky's refashioning of eighteenth-century idioms.[22] Never before, though, had new music been in such a perilous state and never before had it been so isolated from the past. This renewal would need to be on a much larger scale, nay on a visionary scale. Rochberg was calling for composers to initiate that infinitely expanding *ars combinatoria*, a wave that would go beyond borrowing a specific style or form and encompass all of the past and all of the present. In his more practical moments, he encouraged composers to draw from the past resources that he found lacking in the present, including melodic lyricism, harmonic richness, resolution, formal grandeur, and incisive rhythms.

Rochberg never intended for composers to reject present styles outright and to return to older idioms – the present had too much to offer to be discarded, and it did, for better or worse, capture a contemporary spirit. Nor did he call for them to synthesize the past through the present as done in neoclassicism – the past was too rich and distinct to lose its identity. Renewal should instead take the form of *ars combinatoria*, in which unaltered pieces of past and present butt up against each other. These encounters, Rochberg believed, would renew both periods.[23] Enriched with the melodic lilts of Mozart and the rhythmic swerves of Beethoven, the present would take on whole new musical dimensions and regain the power to connect with listeners, perhaps even inspiring them to sing and dance. Conversely, proximity with the present would give the past new stylistic dimensions and increase listeners' appreciation of earlier works by pushing those works out of the familiar and into new contexts.

Renewal, *ars combinatoria*, and "radial" time are all means by which Rochberg approached the relationship between past and present. There is another way, though, that is not mentioned in the essays on renewal. That way is nostalgia. Rochberg elaborates upon that sensation in a 1973 article on Schoenberg. The inventor of the twelve-tone system was, for Rochberg, a tragic figure, a man "unable to relate any longer to those traditions from which he came, compelled to leave behind

---

[21] Rochberg, "Reflections on the renewal of music," 238.
[22] Ibid., 233.   [23] Ibid.

whatever security those traditions offered – yet always longing for them."[24] Having set the stage for the nostalgic Schoenberg, Rochberg immediately distances himself from any such "longing." He assures us that his many glances back to the past arise from wholly compositional interests:

I used to think that it was pure nostalgia, a longing for a past Golden Age which always brought me back to the supremely wrought clarities and identities of old music. Now I realize that it was not nostalgia at all but a deep, abiding personal need for clear ideas, for vitality and power expressed without impediments, for grace and beauty of line, for convincing harmonic motion, for transcendent feeling – all qualities which have no specific historical location or inherent stylistic limitations but which supersede theory and aesthetics or the parochialisms of cultish attitudes ("music of the future," avant-gardisms, etc.).[25]

How curious then to read about "nostalgic beauty" in the composer's notes to *Music for the Magic Theater* and "metaphysical nostalgia" in those for the Third Symphony.[26] These brief phrases tap into the rich veins of nostalgia running through these works.[27] The conception of nostalgia used here is similar to the one elaborated upon in the chapter on Ives (just how similar will be pointed out). As Rochberg describes it, nostalgia is a "longing." Nostalgic longing, as we have seen, emerges from a loss. Ives's nostalgia stems from the loss of childhood, whereas Rochberg's comes from that of a distant, yet just as pressing, past: the common practice era. Nostalgia attempts to fill that loss by animating the past, making it appear, as with Ives's re-awakened childhood campgrounds, that it has returned and that one can re-experience it. Rochberg's works give the impression that the music of the common practice era has been restored and that its emotional expressivity and rhythmic dynamism can be used to enrich the present. In nostalgic evocations, the past ultimately recedes and falls apart, leaving the reminiscing figure disconsolate in the present. Some, but not all, of Rochberg's collage compositions make this attempt to grasp the past only to have it disintegrate.[28] That futile effort is enacted in an elaborate scene: the past is evoked through quotations; it is given a vitality suggesting that one can build upon it and use it for

---

[24] Rochberg, "Reflections on Schoenberg," 47.

[25] Ibid., 49–50.   [26] Dixon, *George Rochberg*, 94 and 160.

[27] In his study of quotation, Michael Hicks divides composers into three groups: evolutionists, eternalists, and nostalgists. Rochberg is listed among the eternalists, composers who write a music free of time in which all styles and periods can exist. Hicks, however, calls Rochberg a "sometimes nostalgist"; Hicks, "The new quotation," 38–39.

[28] Such scenes do not appear in other of his contemporary quotation works, notably *Nach Bach* (1966), *Carnival Music* (1971), and *Caprice Variations* (1970), in which Rochberg viewed the past from other perspectives in these works, such as the "commentary" angle taken in *Nach Bach*.

renewal; it becomes part of a mounting chaos spurred on by the attempt to remember more and to hold on to the increasingly fading memories; and, finally, it is shattered into fragments by that chaos, remaining forever out of reach.

If nostalgia appears so vividly in these compositions, then why does Rochberg disavow it? One obvious reason is to avoid the taint of sentimentality and conservatism attached to that term. Perhaps there was no greater opprobrium in the innovation-obsessed 1960s than to be called nostalgic, especially for a recovering serialist like Rochberg. He most likely wanted to free not only himself from that taint but also his designs for renewal. If that word were dropped even once into his essays, it could threaten to permeate his vision. Who could take seriously plans for revitalizing the present from a composer enthralled by "nostalgic beauty?"

That question suggests that renewal and nostalgia are antithetical. In many ways they are. The two pull in opposite directions. Renewal expands and connects, whereas nostalgia shrinks and separates. Nostalgia undoes Rochberg's slogans of renewal. It creates broken, not "radial," time, and it is an art of division rather than of combination. In Rochberg's works, there is a give and take between these two forces. More specifically, renewal gives, and nostalgia takes away. The former gives new idioms fresh energy by importing elements from the past that are needed in the present. Nostalgia, on the other hand, takes away some of these elements and hides them in an inaccessible past, leaving the present desolate and in even more need of the past. This tension plays itself out differently in the two works discussed below. Each creates a unique mold of renewal by drawing upon different elements from the past, thus showing us two pieces arising from Rochberg's infinite *ars combinatoria*. In these works, nostalgia also assumes unique forms, but, no matter what the guise, it obstructs renewal.

This impediment speaks of the difficulties that composers of collage works faced in dealing with time. They sought to manipulate the fraught relationship between past and present; Rochberg going so far as to bend the two into a circle and combine every minuscule fragment in those endless realms. Time resisted such efforts. It did more than resist. For the visionary composers like Rochberg, it set up traps, each tailor-made for the individual. Rochberg's trap was nostalgia: the belief that he could capture and shape the past, only to have it fall apart in his hands. With these works, Rochberg became not a Don Quixote battling Time but an unwitting and tortured Penelope. He could weave together strands from the past and present but during the course of the work that tapestry would unravel – although never all the way. For, as we shall see, Rochberg did build from the past, often creating vital works, though that vitality is sapped by a fading past.

The play being put on in *Music for the Magic Theater* (1965) stars a fading past.[29] As the accompanying program for the work tells us, that drama focuses on the relationship between the past and the present.

Act I: in which the present and the past are all mixed up... and it is difficult to decide or to know where reality is.

Act II: in which the past haunts us with nostalgic beauty... and calls to us from the depths of inner spaces of heart and mind... but the past is all shadow and dream-insubstantial...and we can't hold on to it because the present is too pressing...

Act III: in which we realize that only the present is really real... because it is all we have... but in the end it too is shadow and dream...and disappears...into what?[30]

Rochberg stages his three-act drama in a theater that Hermann Hesse built for his novel *Steppenwolf* (1927). The Magic Theater is a psychological space entered by the protagonist Harry Haller, who finds there a realm free of time and full of infinite possibilities. In other words, it is a theater of *ars combinatoria*, in which the "hundred thousand pieces" of Haller's life are continually combined in new ways.[31] He, for instance, meets Mozart, who, far from enchanting him with beautiful music, chills him with icy laughter and mocks the emptiness of his life work. Other encounters prove no less surprising and troubling, as Haller finds himself rushing through an emotional corridor, experiencing such states as love, fear, murder, and savagery. Having survived the show in the Magic Theater, he realizes that he must accept all these "pieces" of his life, no matter how painful, and take it upon himself to keep combining them in different ways. This self awareness leads to personal renewal or, as Hesse put it, "healing."[32]

Music for the Magic Theater similarly combines numerous pieces – the quotations and passages in modern styles – and searches for renewal in those pieces. Like other Rochberg works, it rummages through the past, looking for one particular element to add to the bereft present. That one element is harmonic resolution. In his article on Schoenberg, Rochberg described "the cadential problem" facing the composer – that is, the difficulty of achieving closure in the absence of tonal direction and momentum.[33] Some fifteen years after Schoenberg's death, the modern passages in *Music for the Magic Theater* have not solved this problem. Far from it, they can only calibrate degrees of dissonance and cannot offer release and repose. Neither can the tonal quotations. They have the means but are prevented from doing so. Rochberg cuts off

---

[29] Appendix 2 lists the quotations in the work.   [30] Dixon, *George Rochberg*, 94.
[31] Hermann Hesse, *Steppenwolf*, trans. Bais Creighton (New York: Henry Hold, 1990), 217.
[32] Ibid., vi.   [33] Rochberg, "Reflections on Schoenberg," 50.

these borrowings before they reach a concluding cadence. Be it an eight-measure phrase or an entire movement, they are all left incomplete.

On these torn pages of the past is written the tension between renewal and nostalgia that runs through the work. Possessing the treasured means of resolution, the quotations point to renewal. That means, however, is never gained, as the borrowings are abruptly shorn before reaching a close. As incomplete sheets of the past, the quotations no longer point to renewal but instead to things lost. Strewn throughout the composition, the tattered tonal borrowings as a group arouse a feeling of nostalgia. They reinforce the perception that the past is fragmentary and cannot live fully in the present. Just when it seems that we can clutch that time, it always falls apart and leaves us stranded in the restless dissonances of today. Each fractured quotation heightens the question: will the past recede completely and keep its needed means of closure or will it offer that prize and allow the present to be renewed?

Before looking at how *Music for the Magic Theater* responds to that question, a few general remarks about endings are in order. In the works discussed in this chapter, endings, particularly those of movements and of the work itself, loom as significant events. They mark a crucial border between past and present. When evoking both periods – especially when laying out such extensive stretches of earlier works as Rochberg and Berio do – a concern arises over which period the piece will conclude in. Will it come to a close in the pastness of the quotation or in the present? The works by Rochberg, Berio, and Stockhausen negotiate that border in contrasting ways, reaching endings in the past (Berio), the present (Rochberg), and the present/future (Stockhausen). In each case, that border is tense, and the tensions that say much about how these composers have approached the relationship between past and present.

In *Music for the Magic Theater*, the most important ending is that of the second movement. That movement is a "transcription" of the Adagio from Mozart's Divertimento No. 15 (K. 287), a new version that involves Rochberg's rescoring of almost the entire movement.[34] It is this music, as the program states, that lures us back into the past with its "nostalgic beauty." The "beauty" is largely Mozart's – his cantabile violin melody is preserved, as well as the cushioning accompaniment. The "nostalgia" is all Rochberg's. His rescoring gives the Adagio a faded hue. The violin line, shared mostly by solo violin and piano, is performed very softly and an octave higher in an ethereal register, made all the more so as

---

[34] For a discussion of this movement that draws upon Jameson's views on postmodernism, see Robert Fink, "Going flat: post-hierarchical music theory and the musical surface," in Nicholas Cook and Mark Everist, eds., *Rethinking Music* (Oxford: Oxford University Press, 1999), 128–32.

the violin plays "sempre quasi flautando." Rochberg similarly veils the string accompaniment by having it play "sempre quasi sul tasto." With such touches, the Adagio sounds as distant as two centuries. It is also distant from the stylistic storms of the outer movements, in which harsh modern idioms batter fragmentary quotations of older works. As an eye within the storm, the central movement offers a nostalgic respite in which we can lose ourselves. This vision of Mozart comes close to the one that transported Harry Haller away from his own personal storms. Prior to his venturing into the Magic Theater, Haller sits in a restaurant and hears in his head "Mozart's *Cassations*" (the genre title used by Leopold Mozart in describing K. 287), a music in which "there was a feeling of time frozen into space, and above it a never-ending and superhuman serenity."[35]

Haller's fantasy serenade is interrupted by his lover sneaking up on him; Rochberg's is broken off by calamity. The recomposed Adagio follows the pen of Mozart up to the cadenza, and, at the brink of that fermata void, it cuts off right before the I_4^6 chord, unable to venture beyond the original. As the program describes, the present rushes into that empty space. The first sounds we hear are of 1965, a trumpet with Harmon mute that calls to mind Miles Davis, a possible allusion to Pedro, Hesse's jazz trumpeter and owner of the Magic Theater.[36] With jazz following Mozart, the stylistic flux thickens. Pouncing on the trumpet solo are quotations of Webern and Stockhausen (serial patriarch and scion), joined from below by Mahler fragments heard in the first movement. The Adagio seems left behind, especially as the orchestra starts looking forward to what's next. At fig. 57, the winds play shrieking chords that foreshadow the opening sonorities of the third movement, whereas the strings state a phrase from the sixth and final movement of the Divertimento. We do return to the Adagio, but just briefly. Underneath these premonitions of subsequent movements, the brass and double bass sustain the delayed I_4^6 chord, which fades away into silence.

Followed by no solo violin and left unresolved, that flickering chord is the most prominent example of a blocked ending in the work. As heard in the Adagio, those endings play two roles. On one hand, they execute the moment of nostalgic interruption, the moment captured in the final scene of Rochberg's Act II: "we can't hold on to [the past] because the present is too pressing." On the other hand, they call attention to the need for resolution. That need is at the heart of a tension between the outer

[35] Hesse, *Steppenwolf*, 155.

[36] Rochberg directs that the solo is "to be played like Miles Davis – intense, felt, singing." It has also been suggested that the solo is a quotation of a Davis performance of "Stella by Starlight." The solo, however, bears little resemblance to any recording by Davis of that tune, and it also does not fit well the harmonic progression of the song, even by Davis's ingeniously expanded standards. Dixon, *George Rochberg*, 190.

movements. The two follow the same general design. Both open with loud, dissonant passages, move to episodes featuring sustained pitches that lead to tonal quotations, reach a climax at roughly the same spot, and conclude with a scattering of Mahler fragments. The beginnings and endings may be similar, but what happens at the high points – the sections where resolution is demanded – is quite different. One climax points to obsolescence, the other to renewal.

The first movement drops us into a realm where, as the program says, "the present and the past are all mixed up." In other words, we have entered the chaotic "galaxy" of *ars combinatoria*. The opening of the movement offers one of Rochberg's most dynamic realizations of that art.[37] It indeed appears to be "mixed up"; however, it too follows the general laws of *ars combinatoria*. The musical sphere expands quickly, starting off with a dissonant fanfare that announces the present and then shoots out into quotations of Mahler's Ninth Symphony and Varèse's *Déserts*. It soon becomes clear that we have not been blown hither and thither between these sections but rather we have been led by a trail of connections. Running through all three passages is a brief descending motive (E–E♭–D), a thin thread in the deep, intricate cross-stitching of the "universal mind."

This motivic connection soon breaks off, and past and present go their own ways. Opening movements are supposed to be in sonata form, or so argues the past by asserting themes from the introductory Allegro from the Mozart Divertimento. Here is a form, the past seems to be saying, that provides balance, resolution, and conclusive endings. The present remains scornful. Dissonant chords heckle a quotation of the B♭ major first theme of the Mozart and cut it off before it can reach a cadence. The modern idioms continue with a "turbulent" flurry of pitches, out of which emerges a series of sustained Fs in the brass. The links of *ars combinatoria* appear again as these Fs anticipate the following quotation of the F major second theme of the Mozart Allegro. Just as it appears we might be able to piggyback that sonata form and have it lead us out of this stylistic turmoil and to an ending, the theme breaks apart and the Mozart movement is never heard from again.

Traces of another sonata form, though, appear and offer us a new path. Starting at fig. 23, individual lines from a section before the coda of the first movement of Mahler's Ninth are extensively quoted; however, these lines also never reach their destination. A "fast as possible" succession of pitches in the winds rips us away from this sonata form and hurls us into the climax of the movement: a quarter-tone cluster chord played

[37] A discussion of the first movement of the work, one that focuses on the use of Mahler references, can be found in Lisa Robinson, "Mahler and postmodern intertextuality" (Ph.D. diss, Yale University, 1994), 91–131.

ffff (RH 29). This is a climax by virtue of weight and force. Unlike the arrival of a recapitulation or coda, no harmonic logic has prepared this chord and none will lead us out of it. The cluster cannot resolve, but only dissipate, which it does do for twenty-five to thirty seconds until it reaches *pppp*. It is an extreme gesture, one that calls to mind the close of a Rochberg piece bearing an extreme title – *Apocalyptica* (1964)[38] – in which there is only silence after the final cluster chord. In contrast, *Music for the Magic Theater* provides music to follow the apocalypse. The closing section consists of motives from the Mahler symphony. They are only fragments, and some not even in the original key, leaving us in a bleak and ambiguous terrain, after which the dulcet Mozart Adagio is a relief.

The serenity of the Mozart is destroyed by both the uproarious cadenza and the opening of the third movement. With that disruption, the present has returned. As the third movement makes clear, it is a period of extremes, reinforcing Rochberg's view of serialism and other modern idioms as confined to the edges of emotional expression. This movement takes us to the edge of "noise – chaotic without shape or form." Within that fracas are buried phrases from Rochberg's Second String Quartet.[39] It is hard not to hear this quotation as a self-reproach. So disenchanted was the composer with serialism that he was willing to damn one of his own twelve-tone works to this chaos. The once striking features of the piece – the incisive melodic lines, the quicksilver imitation – are lost, now only brief tremors in an unstable sound world.

This instability abruptly gives way to another extreme gesture, sustained sonorities played very slowly and softly (fig. 71). Within this stasis, the pitch E♭, the key of the Mozart Adagio, stands out. Just as the Fs in the first movement pointed to the Mozart Allegro second theme, this pitch also finds a tonal release, not in Mozart but in Beethoven – a phrase from the String Quartet no. 13 (fig. 79). This quotation marks the first appearance of the tonal past in the movement, and, as made clear in Beethoven's intact score direction *beklemmt* (oppressed), it struggles to break through the tyranny of the present. Having emerged, the past, led by E♭, quickly assumes prominence. That pitch plays a key role in the next episode, which is not a quotation but a passage in the style of a tonal cello concerto (fig. 81). Tonal, that is, to everyone but the cellist. As the orchestra winds its way through a circle-of-fifths sequence beginning on E♭, the cellist plays two twelve-tone collections. The atonal–tonal

---

[38] The chord could also be heard as a critique of the dense clusters used in the contemporary works of Ligeti and Penderecki.

[39] Dixon states that there are also references to Rochberg's Sonata-Fantasia for Piano Solo. I have not been able to identify any quotations or references; however, it is possible that the extended piano solos in the last movement could draw upon the earlier work. Dixon, *George Rochberg*, 202.

muddle clears up as the cellist joins the orchestra in heading toward a cadence. But even with the soloist on board that resolution also is thwarted.

The obstruction this time comes from a startling reprise of the opening of the first movement, which, along with the piano solo that follows, appears as a desperate attempt to steer the piece away from tonality and back into the present. The effort fails. The jagged piano solo smooths down to a cadential trill, which, unlike the tonal passages, reaches its goal, a resolution in E♭. At that moment, the final measures of the Mozart Adagio appear, those measures that would have followed the soloist's concluding trill in the cadenza (fig. 89). The Mozart fragment is still played in that ghostly high register, but, even at a whisper, it marks the climax of both the movement and the piece – the one cadence in a work that constantly subverts resolution. Unlike the massive cluster chord in the first movement, this is a climax achieved and resolved by harmonic means. But, although a cadence has been realized, uncertainty lingers. As in the opening movement, the closing section is filled with Mahler fragments (stated in the original D and Mozartian E♭) as well as B♭, the final pitch from the Mozart cadence, which together create a mysterious realm suggesting Rochberg's question "into what?"

The answer is renewal. The Adagio cadence offers a glimpse of what is needed in the present. Resolution can provide composers a resource with which to enrich modern idioms and temper the extremes of those idioms. However, as is so often the case with Rochberg's objects of renewal, more is lost than is gained. The Mozart cadence is heard but not grasped. It remains out of reach in a faded past, far from the shrill present. Time is still divided, not "radial." Moreover, little is learned from the Adagio cadence. After the final chord, we do not hear another cadence, only unresolved fragments of the past. We find ourselves in the same ambiguous terrain which was earlier cleared by the "apocalypse" chord. The only difference is that this time we have the promise of resolution.

The Third Symphony (1969) promises grandeur. According to Rochberg, the work was "the most ambitious project" in the series of quotation pieces beginning with *Contra mortem et tempus*.[40] The Symphony is ambitious in both size and subject.[41] Rochberg marshals an impressive body of performance forces, including a large orchestra, organ, double chorus, chamber choir, and four soloists. The imposing ensemble matches the solemnity of the subject. Rochberg thought

---

[40] Ibid., 75.

[41] The Symphony has yet to be commercially published or recorded. I would like to thank Theodore Presser for allowing me to examine a score and recording of the work.

of the composition as part of a *Passion [According to the Twentieth Century]*.[42]

For a composition "according to the twentieth century," the Symphony draws amply from the past. That large debt does not come as much of a surprise, given Rochberg's views on the expressive constriction of modern idioms. Such abstruse styles could never bear the grandeur and spiritual profundity called upon by a Passion. For those qualities, it was necessary to return to past works that possessed greater depths. The group of compositions that Rochberg brought back in the Symphony include Schütz (*Saul, was verfolgst du mich*), Bach (Chorale Prelude on *Durch Adams Fall*, BWV 637), Beethoven (*Missa Solemnis* and Symphonies nos. 3, 5, and 9), Mahler (fanfares from Symphonies nos. 1 and 2), and Ives (*The Unanswered Question*). With quotations of large sections from these works, Rochberg reached for more than a cadence, seeking now to renew music with the grandeur of the past.

The work is one continuous movement and lasts around forty minutes. It is built around three extended borrowings, here called blocks: a complete statement of Schütz's Grand Concerto, the fugato from the "Eroica" Funeral March, and an extended passage from the coda of the first movement of Beethoven's Ninth Symphony. To create grandeur, Rochberg not only states these imposing passages but also builds them up by adding new lines and formal sections. The Beethoven fugato undergoes the most extensive construction. Rochberg latches his own fugue on to Beethoven's, creating that contrapuntal skyscraper, the double fugue. Not only does he add new parts but also two different texts, creating not so much a skyscraper as a behemoth: a double choral, polytextual double fugue. All of that in the space where once stood an orchestral fugato.

In all three blocks, the gradual enlargement of the past throws more and more weight on the borrowings, causing them to collapse. Each follows a similar path: the borrowings begin relatively pristine, more and more layers are added (some not even integrated into the originals), and the escalation of these new parts leads to an inevitable crash that scatters pieces of both the borrowings and the layers. At the end of the Schütz quotation, for instance, the rapidly multiplying calls of "Saul" are banged out in a "rock rhythm," a rush of contemporary rhythmic energy that pushes the quotation to a breaking point, at which burst out of the orchestra Mahler's fanfares and the last wind figure from Ives's *The Unanswered Question* – Rochberg's not so subtle response to the plea made by the Schütz work. The Beethoven Ninth borrowing, the final section of the Symphony, suffers the most dramatic cave-in. Its chromatic windings are burdened with cries of "Saul," a percussive

---

[42] Dixon, *George Rochberg*, 159.

recitation, Mahler fanfares, and this time the trumpet figure from *The Unanswered Question*. All of this occurs along with an increase in tempo. The building chaos overwhelms the quotation, which breaks apart and is left incomplete. With no original as a foundation, the chaos, and the Symphony with it, rapidly disintegrates into nothingness.

The Ives quotations not only add a philosophical twist to the Symphony; they also shed light on the nostalgia running through the work. These dashed blocks call to mind the nostalgic scenes in Ives's works, a close resemblance to which *The Unanswered Question* quotations hint at. The "memory pictures" in such works as *The Fourth of July* follow a basic pattern: a slow introduction filled with fragmentary quotations, the materialization of a borrowed tune from these fragments, an escalating chaos of additional layers and quotations, and a quick collapse. This pattern conveys the gradual recollection of past events, the immersion in reminiscence creating the illusion that one has returned to the past, and the inevitable crash as it becomes impossible to sustain that illusion. Rochberg's Symphony closely adheres to this scheme, except for the initial probing of fragments. Rather than gathering up mere pieces, the Symphony disinters intact slabs of the past and builds them up. That enlargement creates the impression that the past can be reclaimed, that it can live again in new styles. As in Ives's works, chaos escalates, resulting from the attempt to grab more of the past and to fend off the encroaching present. That chaos crushes the past, and the present gradually reemerges in its rubble. For Rochberg, Ives was the "first and foremost" practitioner of *ars combinatoria*.[43] The collapsing scenes in the Symphony suggest that Rochberg also recognized him as the leading practitioner of the art of nostalgia.

In Ives's compositions, there is only ever one chaotic climax, whereas Rochberg's Symphony has three. One is all that is necessary to capture the flow of expectation and disillusionment in nostalgia. Three is too much and speaks of exaggeration. Exaggeration gets at the heart of the way the work approaches the past. Aspiring to reclaim a lost grandeur, the Symphony only apes such splendor by adding new parts to the borrowed passages, making them sound not grand but hyperbolic and ultimately hollow. Rochberg's contrapuntal scaffolding, for instance, obscures the pathos of the Beethoven fugato, encasing it in an outer shell of an overblown and stolid double fugue. Nostalgia also suffers from exaggeration. Rochberg overwrites Ives's script. The present is not so much melancholic about recovering the past but is instead desperate to do so. It repeatedly goes back to the past, even after there is apparently nothing left. In addition, the means of reminiscence have grown contrived. Memory is not realized just through

[43] Rochberg, "No center," 156.

quotations but has become a quotation itself, taking the form of Ives's method.

Where could renewal go after the Third Symphony? With that work, it had reached an impasse. On one side lay nostalgia, on the other, hyperbole – or the even more dangerous pitfall, hyperbolic nostalgia. Renewal, though, did not crumble with the Symphony. Several works of the 1970s, notably the String Quartets nos. 3–6, continue to propel the infinitely expanding *ars combinatoria*. Nostalgic spells momentarily appear in these works, notably the tranquil slow movement of the Third Quartet, but that sentiment does not dominate as in earlier pieces. The dream of renewal similarly began to fade. After the flurry of essays written to defend the controversial Third String Quartet, Rochberg never again addressed renewal in such an elaborate manner. The polemical moment had come and gone, and his views changed. Gone, or very much downplayed, are the visions of *ars combinatoria* and "radial" time. In lieu of such fantastic ideas, Rochberg blankly referred to his use of past materials and styles as leading to a reconnection with tonality.[44] The concept of renewal, though, never completely disappeared. As long as Rochberg has continued to rail against serialism and modernist extremes, it still appears in the background of his attacks. In a 1998 interview, he encouraged young musicians to forsake grasping for the new and to "regain contact with the tradition and means of the past."[45]

Berio

In a 1968 newspaper article written three months before the premiere of *Sinfonia*, Berio warned American audiences about an enemy gathering outside the gates of the concert hall.[46] That enemy was the twelve-tone system. As he described it, serialism was a Trojan horse, a compositional approach that seduced with talk of rigor and historical inevitability but that inevitably led to the rigor mortis of abstraction. In alerting the citizens of Troy to this danger, he was joined on the city ramparts by Rochberg. Some citizens may have easily confused the two sentries, for there are some general similarities between them. The two, for instance, had once composed serial works and thus knew the enemy well.

---

[44] This idea of a reconnection with tonality first appears in the essays on the Third String Quartet. It becomes the main focus in such later articles as "Can the arts survive modernism? (A discussion of the characteristics, history, and legacy of modernism)," *Critical Inquiry* 11 (1984), 317–40, and "Guston and me: digression and return," *Contemporary Music Review* 6 (1992), 5–8.

[45] Paul J. Horsley, "For an early post-modernist, a day of overdue vindication," *New York Times*, 12 July 1998, sect. 2, 35.

[46] Luciano Berio, "Meditation on a twelve-tone horse," *Christian Science Monitor*, 15 July 1968. Rpr. in *Composers on Modern Musical Cultures*, ed. Bryan Simms (New York: Schirmer, 1999), 182–87.

Berio's use of serialism, however, was relatively short-lived and highly individualistic.[47] Berio and Rochberg also repudiated that enemy in like terms. For the former, serialism had developed into a "formalist" and "escapist" pursuit, divorced from the sonic vitality and "poetics" of music.[48]

The two composers diverted citizens away from the deceptive horse by offering them similar visions of a new type of music. Rochberg conjured the magic of *ars combinatoria*, whereas Berio dazzled with a music of "interrelationships," which, like Rochberg's art, reached out to and connected a diverse collection of seemingly unrelated elements.[49] The third movement of *Sinfonia* overlays Mahler, Beckett, and a host of smaller musical and textual quotations. Perhaps the most far-reaching of these works is the anti-opera *Opera*, which simultaneously levitates three different musical/dramatic layers: excerpts from Striggio's libretto to Monteverdi's *Orfeo*, the sinking of the Titanic, and a contemporary experimental play called *Terminal*.

Berio also sought to bring together different layers of time. Peering into that realm, he searched for the ultimate connection: the bond between "the present and the past and a maybe Utopian future." His works would not be creating this "continuity" as much as following one that already existed. As he claimed, artistic works embodied all of time. Adding his own view of blended time to those of Rochberg and Zimmermann, he commented: "Every experience carries with itself traces of past experiences and the seed of future ones to be discovered. Every form has a memory and is a premonition. Historical time is a quality, not a quantity."[50]

That "quality," as we know, posed difficulties for collage composers, and Berio was no exception. At times, it appears that the *Sinfonia* movement might suffer a fate similar to the crumbling behemoths of Rochberg's Third Symphony. Like Rochberg's bloated fugato, it lays down a foundation from the past – the Scherzo from Mahler's Second Symphony – and piles on top of it new layers through expansions and connections, which, as Berio remarked, are constantly "proliferating."[51]

---

[47] On Berio's use of the twelve-tone system, see David Osmond-Smith, *Berio* (Oxford and New York: Oxford University Press, 1991), 5–8, 16–19.

[48] Berio, "Meditation on a twelve-tone horse." It should be noted that Berio did not think that the twelve-tone system by itself produced sterile music. On the contrary, he claimed that composers such as Schoenberg used it in a "responsible" and creative way. Berio objected to overly theoretical approaches to the system and to "the composer who loudly declares his disregard for the audience's reaction," an arrow most likely intended for the camp of Babbitt and other isolationists.

[49] Ibid.

[50] Simon Emmerson, "Luciano Berio talks with Simon Emmerson," *Music and Musicians* 24 (February 1976), 26.

[51] Philippot, "Entretien: Luciano Berio," 88.

The incessant combining of past and present, though, often appears as if it has spun out of control, the "proliferating" connections taking on a life of their own. This frantic process poses two dangers. On one hand, the Mahler foundation, similar to Rochberg's blocks, could be crushed by the weight of the new materials, a possibility raised by the frequent eclipse of the Scherzo. On the other, the quotations could sweep us far away from the Mahler and into new, and seemingly unconnected, musical realms. Both threats jeopardize the "creative continuity" between past and present that Berio has tried to achieve. Will that continuity hold? As so often is the case with quotation pieces, it all comes down to the ending.

Before turning to the end of the movement, some introductory remarks are in order. The third movement, like the others in the five-movement piece, is scored for large orchestra and eight amplified vocalists, who both sing and speak. It rests upon a statement of the Mahler Scherzo. Another foundation supports the movement: Beckett's novel *The Unnamable* (1952). The relationship between these two works – not to mention that between both of them and Berio's music – has fascinated writers on the movement, each arriving at his or her own interpretation of that bond. These views differ in regard to whether one of the two pieces serves as a focal point, and, if so, which one. Michael Hicks contends that "the movement is best viewed as a setting and interpretation of [the Beckett] text. It is a book turned into music."[52] As such, Berio's and Mahler's music cooperate to illustrate Beckett's themes, including alienation and monotony.

David Osmond-Smith, on the other hand, places the Mahler at the center of his analysis, viewing the novel, Berio's music, and the quotations as all commenting on the Scherzo.[53] As he has described elsewhere, Berio has engaged in the approach of "commentary" throughout his career. This technique involves infusing pre-existent works, his own and those by other composers, with new materials that elaborate upon the original.[54] His *Chemins*, for instance, orchestrally expand solo instrumental *Sequenza* works, whereas the *Sinfonia* movement "explores [the Scherzo] from the inside."[55] According to Osmond-Smith, that internal exploration focuses on the form of the Mahler, especially how it can be taken apart. "Commenting" on this commentary is the chattering

---

[52] Michael Hicks, "Text, music, and meaning in the third movement of Luciano Berio's *Sinfonia*," *Perspectives of New Music* 20 (1981–82), 207.

[53] David Osmond-Smith, *Playing on Words: a Guide to Luciano Berio's 'Sinfonia'* (London: Royal Musical Association, 1985), 39–71.

[54] David Osmond-Smith, "Berio and the art of commentary," *Musical Times* 116 (1975), 871–72, and *Berio*, 42–55.

[55] Luciano Berio, *Two Interviews*, trans. David Osmond-Smith (New York and London: Marion Boyars, 1985), 107.

Table 4.1 *Formal outline of Scherzo from Mahler's Symphony no. 2*

mm. 1–103	Scherzo (C minor)
mm. 104–149	Trio I (F major)
mm. 149–189	Scherzo (C minor)
mm. 190–347	Trio II (C major; D major; E major; C major)
mm. 348–406	Scherzo (C minor)
mm. 407–544	Trio I and Trio II (F major and C major)
mm. 545–581	Scherzo (C minor)

voice from *The Unnamable*, which Osmond-Smith claims opines on both "processes at work within the movement" and "the situation within the concert hall itself."[56]

This study sees the Mahler and Beckett as two equals that run side by side in their new musical environment. They comment on each other, the Beckett calling attention to a feature in the Scherzo, and the latter building upon a mood or idea in the novel. That conversation is hectic but friendly, for, although they may never have encountered each other before being brought together by Berio, they prove a complementary pair, having some basic things in common. That bond can be better appreciated by discussing each of the two elements individually.

What the Mahler is doing in *Sinfonia* is a question perhaps second only to what to make of the Scherzo itself. Mahler frequently addressed that question, leaving behind various programmatic interpretations of the movement. These glosses differ in tone and imagery, but they all bewail an unending monotony, called at different times the "ceaseless flow of life" and the "deafening traffic of mundane affairs."[57] The most vivid of the programs depicts a forlorn character spying on a dance from the darkness outside a ballroom.[58] Unable to hear the music, he sees the dancers as silent automatons endlessly "turning and twisting," a distorted vision that incites a scream of despair. The music to which Mahler sets this silent dance is appropriately in triple meter and has an unrelenting flow of sixteenth notes. It is a *perpetuum mobile*, a music that pushes unabated through the various formal sections of a scherzo with double trio, emerges from the tumultuous cry, and finally comes to a halt (see Table 4.1 for a formal diagram of the movement).

In Beckett's novel, another anonymous character observes life from afar. What he sees and where he sees it from, not to mention who he

---

[56] Osmond-Smith, *Playing on Words*, 55.
[57] Quoted in Hicks, "Text, music, and meaning," 210.
[58] Two different versions of this scenario can be found in Hicks, "Text, music, and meaning," 210, and Osmond-Smith, *Playing with Words*, 54.

is, is never made clear. All that we can gather is that he exists in limbo, surrounded by a mysterious "they." He may be alone in that state, but he is not alone in Beckett's oeuvre. The Unnamable is one of the author's numerous characters who are condemned to speak forever, powerless to stop. Speech is at once his damnation and salvation. Salvation in that it allows him to fill up the void that surrounds him. In one particularly hopeful moment, the character even suggests that there are a series of magic words that when spoken could end his nattering and perhaps his life. "Keep going," he exhorts himself to push through this Sisyphean monologue. Beckett offers another type of *perpetuum mobile*, though one in which the "ceaseless flow" of words goes nowhere. There is no climactic cry of despair and no conclusion. The novel does end, but the final words – "I can't go on, I'll go on" – only acknowledge the inevitable.

Having the *perpetuum mobiles* of Beckett and Mahler chug alongside each other creates one of the numerous interrelationships in the movement. Around both works swarm a flock of musical and textual quotations, which create even more links. The quoted composers include, among others, Bach, Beethoven, Berlioz, Strauss, Debussy, Schoenberg, Stockhausen, Hindemith, and Boulez. Berio adds to these fragments of past and present his own modern passages, notably heavy cluster chords. The spoken quotations draw upon a poem by Paul Valéry, opera librettos, an article by Berio, student protests, and variety of other sources. With these two large blocks and several smaller musical and textual quotations, Berio has several pieces to connect and comes up with many different ways to do so.[59] As the following examples illustrate, he draws upon both direct and general links. The Mahler and many of the quotations share specific intervals and motives, such as the prominent use of a fourth in the melodic lines of the Scherzo and the violin solo of Hindemith's *Kammermusik no. 4*, which, similarly moving in steady thirty-second notes, is a little *perpetuum mobile* itself.[60] Elsewhere, the quotations elaborate upon various associations of the Scherzo. The Berlioz, Strauss, and Ravel waltzes give us an idea of some of the other music heard in Mahler's ballroom of the damned. Text and music also intertwine. The opening notes of the Hindemith borrowing prompt the second tenor to muse "nothing more restful than chamber music," an alteration of the Beckett line "nothing more restful than arithmetic." In other cases, the music follows the lead of the text.

---

[59] For detailed discussions of the intricate interrelationships in the work, see Osmond-Smith, *Playing with Words*, 39–71; Hicks, "Text, music, and meaning," 199–224; and Peter Altmann, *Sinfonia von Luciano Berio: eine analytische Studie* (Vienna: Universal Edition, 1977).

[60] On such connections see Robinson, "Mahler and postmodern intertextuality," 138–52; and Osmond-Smith, *Playing with Words*, 47–51.

"I have a present for you" announces the first tenor. The orchestra provides the gift with a borrowing from Boulez's "Don" – the French word for "present."

Such bilingual puns are a means not only of making connections but also of expansion. Each one of these individual links forms an offshoot from the Mahler and Beckett trunks, creating the impression of a work that is constantly branching out. Expansion – both outward and forward – is central to Berio's views of the movement. He has compared the Mahler to a "container" that is filled up with "a large number of references," a pile that grows larger and larger until it is on the brink of spilling over.[61] He has also likened the Mahler to a "river," a "voyage," and a "process."[62] All three imply direction, each moving forward and heading either toward some location or to completion. But what is the destination? Berio does mention a "voyage to Cythera"; however, that mythical island of pleasure seems well beyond the horizon. The more pressing question is not so much where are we headed as will we ever get there.

That question arises from the treatment of the Mahler. As mentioned earlier, the Scherzo disintegrates during the course of the movement. According to Osmond-Smith, the overall "shape" of the movement is created by a process of "incremental obliteration."[63] In a way, the whole movement is put together by taking apart the Scherzo. As Osmond-Smith also points out, this disintegration ties in with *The Unnamable*, which forms the third part of a trilogy that "accomplishes a gradual dissolution of traditional narration and character."[64] The fractured, scattered thoughts of Beckett's character lost in some sort of after-life limbo mingle with the broken, isolated phrases of the Scherzo lost in some sort of after-life fracas.

Osmond-Smith's claims of "obliteration" may seem overblown, that is until one surveys the damage. A remarkable view of that destruction can be found in Karl Aage Rasmussen's *Berio-Mask* (1977). Turning the tables on Berio, that piece quotes the entire *Sinfonia* movement and then erases all the borrowings and Berio additions until there is left only the traces of the Mahler as they appear in *Sinfonia*, now overlaid with some of Rasmussen's own music. What remains is a fragmentary, disjointed Scherzo, one that grows more so as it progresses. Rasmussen's removal of Berio's layers reveals how much weight has been placed on the Mahler

---

[61] Berio, liner notes, *Sinfonia*, Columbia MS 7268.

[62] Berio, liner notes; and "Luciano Berio on new music: an interview with David Roth," *Musical Opinion* 99 (September 1976), 549–51.

[63] Osmond-Smith, *Playing with Words*, 39. For detailed accounts of the disintegration of the Scherzo, see 44–53, and Robinson, "Mahler and postmodern intertextuality," 166–74.

[64] Osmond-Smith, *Playing with Words*, 55.

and how much it has crumbled underneath that load.[65] That weight does not fall just anywhere: it presses down at key formal moments in the Scherzo, particularly the junctures between the major divisions. For instance, the return of Scherzo 2 (fig. S) is submerged under a quotation from the drowning scene in *Wozzeck*.[66] The two central modulations in Trio 2 (figs. K and M) are similarly squelched by Berio's cluster chords. With its beams and hinges shattered, the Scherzo falls apart, becoming a broken and sputtering *perpetuum mobile*.

That oxymoron captures a tension underlying the movement. On one hand, the movement constantly expands; on the other hand, the Mahler foundation falters. These two tendencies are not opposites but rather are interconnected. The expansion causes the faltering by encumbering the Scherzo, yet at the same time it is dependent on the Mahler, which is the base from which the outward links are made. That dependency raises the concern, mentioned above, of whether or not the Mahler will break apart before it reaches its proper ending. In other words, will the "process" be forever incomplete, the "river" blocked, or the "voyage" unfinished? If so, the prospects are bleak. We could be left without an ending, worse yet we could be stranded in one of the quotations – say a patch of Brahms or Webern – forever removed from the music to which we have been clutching. No wonder the voices repeatedly urge "keep going." They are trying to push the Mahler along and to avoid the fate of Rochberg's Symphony.

Such a peril appears near the end of the *Sinfonia* movement, at which point the Mahler is on the verge of completely disappearing. As if that disintegration were not worrisome enough, a new threat arises. In the final moments, the Mahler confronts several musical and textual quotations of beginning and ending passages. These borrowings threaten to serve as new openings or peremptory conclusions. In other words, such passages could supplant the Scherzo by having us begin again with a new foundation or finish with the ending of an undamaged work. Either way, the multiplying connections could rip us away from the Mahler and place us in a new musical work, leaving us desperate to get back to the foundation of the past on which we began.

The first of these traps appears at fig. AA, which features not a quotation per se but a reprise of the opening measures of the movement

---

[65] Berio commented that "Mahler's music seems to bear the weight of the entire history of music." In the *Sinfonia* movement, it appears that he is forcing that weight down upon the Scherzo. Berio, liner notes.

[66] This quotation is one of many examples of double-quotations: borrowings of passages in works that are borrowings themselves. For instance, the chromatic ascent in Berg's opera draws upon the ascent used to close Schoenberg's *Erwartung*. These double borrowings further suggest the interconnectedness of musical works. For a discussion of possible borrowings in the Scherzo, see Osmond-Smith, *Playing with Words*, 41–43.

(which, though, are full of quotations). Before discussing the reprise, it is necessary to say a few words about the initial appearance of that passage. The movement begins with a bang, a massive orchestral cluster, out of which springs in the brass a quotation of the fourth of Schoenberg's Five Pieces for Orchestra op. 16. The quotation springs out even further as the vocalists announce the title of that movement: *Peripeteia*, the Greek word for an unexpected reversal. The word "unexpected," in both Greek and English, reappears throughout the movement, pointing to the unending surprises of hearing well-known compositions in new contexts. Such startling transformations of the familiar, according to Berio, were one of the main areas of fascination for contemporary composers, an interest fueling the burst of collage composition at the time.[67] For listeners, the ricochet of quotations of Schoenberg, Debussy, and Mahler's Fourth Symphony in the cramped space of the opening six measures is surely unexpected – as is the emergence of the Scherzo, which, once the creaky gears get going, is put into motion and sets us on our way.

When the opening bang returns at fig. AA, it is a true *peripeteia*. So unexpected is the reprise that it leaves the first tenor pondering "when they ask, why all this, it is not easy to find an answer." It isn't. Nothing in the Mahler foundation suggests such a recapitulation. We are in the middle of the second Trio, nowhere near the return of the Scherzo. As the second soprano suggests in her quotation of Valéry, one answer is that the work is trying to *"recommencer,"* perhaps this time without the Mahler. At this moment it seems that the Mahler may not emerge. Leveled by the previous cluster chords, it has disappeared for the longest stretch of time in the piece so far. A new foundation could arise, one that is desperately needed, since the Scherzo has deteriorated so much.

A similar gesture occurred in the final movement of *Music for the Magic Theater*, where the initial measures of the first movement reappeared as a last-ditch effort to divert the work away from tonality and the past. It didn't work there and it doesn't work here. The Mahler foundation does surface, although it takes longer than it did in the opening, and it returns with a vengeance. The Scherzo resumes at the climax, the cry of despair (fig. BB). That climax marks an imposing assertion of the Mahler – a passage just as forceful as any of the preceding clusters and, taking a cue from those clusters, strong enough to push aside other music, particularly quotations, from disturbing its ferocity. The Scherzo defiantly holds its ground.

The raging climax, though, does not intimidate the vocalists or keep them from speaking, or shouting as they now have to do. Mahler's wordless cry is given words. The first tenor elaborates upon lines from Berio's recent newspaper article: "it can't stop the wars, can't make

---

[67] Philippot, "Entretien: Luciano Berio," 88–89.

the old younger, or lower the price of bread . . ."[68] Where Mahler's hero screams at the unending tedium of life, Berio's tenor cries out against the social irrelevancy of new music brought about by serialism and other abstract styles. That plight preoccupied the composer at the time and it is worth taking a moment to see how he saw works like *Sinfonia* as remedying that situation. As Berio admits, music, new or old, cannot do the things that the tenor screams about; nonetheless, we, as the tenor later says, "must believe that it is true," in other words, believe that new works are what Berio calls a "social act."[69] That act is to invigorate listeners and rescue them from the passivity forced upon them by society. Typical of the promise placed in them, collage idioms had much to offer in this effort. First, the "unexpected" twists on the familiar would encourage listeners to experience things around them in constantly new ways.[70] Moreover, the interrelationships created in such pieces could "educate people to find, even to invent relations among things," an effort that Berio considered "maybe the most important role of music in our society."[71]

No sooner has Berio made his cry against the social decline of new music, than it, along with the Mahler climax bolstering it, gradually dwindles into traces. If that fortified passage cannot endure, then what can? A conclusion of the Mahler seems even more in doubt, prompting the first tenor to repeat the Beckett conundrum: "it [I] can't go on." The Scherzo doesn't go on. It disappears as we find ourselves walking down a corridor of doors, a group of quotations opening up to possible new endings or beginnings. The first door that opens before us is a conclusion, an excerpt from the final scene of *Der Rosenkavalier* (fig. DD). This borrowing offers us a late Romantic ending with which to replace the now silent Mahler. The Strauss, though, turns out to be a nostalgic deception. No sooner have we relaxed in its harmonic luxury, than it vanishes, cut off by a loud chord that returns us to the present. "Present" in terms of both period and gift. "I have a present for you" the first tenor states, an offering that, as mentioned earlier, takes the form of a quotation from Boulez's "Don" (1962), the first movement of *Pli selon pli* (fig. EE).

With the Boulez, we have gone from the endings of the past to the beginnings of the present. The Boulez composition is all about beginnings. "Don" deals with the creation of the artwork, symbolized by the birth

---

[68] The original reads "We all know that music can't lower the cost of bread, is incapable of stopping (or starting, for that matter) wars, cannot eradicate slums or injustice." Berio, "Meditation on a twelve-tone horse."

[69] Ibid.   [70] Philippot, "Entretien: Luciano Berio," 88–89.

[71] Quoted in Jack Bornoff, "Music, musicians, and communication," *World of Music*, 16/2 (1974), 40.

of a child. From that piece, Berio quotes the opening crashing chord and the following sustained string harmonics. We, though, never hear that work nor do we hear the child grow up, as a different quotation settles down upon the string sonorities. That borrowing is of another beginning, the first measures of the fifth movement from Webern's second Cantata (op. 31). The Webern lasts longer than the Boulez, leading us again into a new work and farther away from the Mahler, which has not been heard since the Strauss quotation. However, Cantata too is cut off, or, should we say, extended. The violin solo from the Webern work flows into a violin solo from Stockhausen's *Gruppen* (1958). With this passing of the torch, Berio, like Rochberg in holding up the Webern–Stockhausen pair in *Music for the Magic Theater*, has evoked the "Darmstadt trinity," the serial father and two of his sons.[72]

This serial block completely obscures the final return of the Scherzo, the only formal juncture in the movement in which we hear neither the music before nor after the change in section.[73] This eclipse adds to the anxiety that the Mahler will not finish, as the formal event that sets up the conclusion has failed to occur. In lieu of that reprise, the serial quotations assume the role of a new section. They assume more than that, positioning themselves as a new beginning, not only for the movement but for the present as well. With avant-garde arrogance, the Darmstadt School saw itself playing such a historical role. *Sinfonia* argues otherwise. Written six years after the Boulez work, it offers a musical vision strikingly different from Darmstadt serialism, one that is indebted to the multi-layered design of serial works like *Gruppen* but at the same time has realized the necessity of reaching out beyond the row and into the surrounding musical universe. This is the music to follow serialism, a music that nothing else was supposed to follow. In addition to this historical riposte, the movement conveys how abstruse these quoted compositions can be, especially when compared to the Mahler and the surrounding web of "unexpected" connections. The serial block is a lifeless space, the one section in the movement in which there is almost no motion – an affront to a *perpetuum mobile*. To the first tenor, this music is akin to a dead, or dying, body. Delivering a post-mortem, he observes: "he is barely moving now, almost still."

However one perceives this section, it is not a welcoming space, making us even more anxious to return to the Mahler. That desire is keyed up by other means. With the Boulez and Webern quotations as well as the earlier reprise of the opening passage, we experience the frustration over

---

[72] Osmond-Smith, *Playing on Words*, 48.

[73] This section of the Scherzo has disappeared to such an extent that, in *Berio-Mask*, it is represented by three successive G.P. markings.

"suspended beginnings" felt by the protagonist in Italo Calvino's novel *If on a winter's night a traveler* (1979).[74] In that work, the lead character continually comes across the opening chapters of different novels, all of which are left uncontinued. Like him, we feel ourselves being drawn into new pieces, a strong pull given the collapsing Scherzo. However, as in the novel, these incomplete beginnings do not so much make us want to jump into the new works and abandon the old ones as build up our desire for conclusion in general, a desire that can only be met with the ending of the work we originally began. For Calvino's readers, that conclusion comes with the marriage of the two characters who have pursued all of these interrupted novels over the course of the book, whereas, for us, it will come with the closing bars of the Mahler.

We too must deal with our own "suspended beginning" of a novel. During all of these serial quotations, the first tenor has resumed reading from the Beckett, now focusing on lines drawn from the first page.[75] As with the earlier reprise of the initial measures of the movement, it appears that the Beckett is trying to begin again. But it would be hard for it to do so, considering that the novel never really began in the first place. Beckett's work is a *perpetuum mobile*, one not only without a definitive ending but also without a clear beginning. As the protagonist tells us, he is not sure when he started speaking and less sure of when he will stop. In this light, the novel comes across as a transcript of a brief segment from a timeless monologue. Also timeless is the "show" that the Unnamable describes, a speech which Berio extensively quotes (figs. L–R). This show never begins, and the "show" becomes the endless waiting for a beginning that will never happen and for an even more improbable ending. The quotations of both the opening lines and the show episode add to the numerous portents that the Mahler may not reach a conclusion. It could either be sucked into the beginning or ending of another work, or it could become, like the novel, lost in a constant babble.

The Mahler is spared such a fate. After the Stockhausen quotation, the Scherzo resumes. The last measures are thinned out and fragmentary, but they do reach a conclusion. Moreover, the musical quotations have come to an end. The rest of the movement is all Mahler up to the final low C. All Mahler, that is, except for the spoken lines of the first tenor.

---

[74] Calvino was a friend of Berio's and contributed texts for many of his works, including *Allez Hop* and *La vera storia*. Calvino, *If on a winter's night a traveler*, trans. William Weaver (Toronto: Lester, Orpens, and Dennys, 1981).

[75] The final block of text is provided here with the lines from the first page underlined:

There must be something else. Otherwise it would be quite hopeless. But it is quite hopeless. Unquestioning. But it can't go on. I say it, not knowing what. It's getting late. Where now? When now? [I have a present for you.] Keep going, page after page. Keep going, going on, call that going, call that on.

Having broken off from the Beckett, he confirms that we have arrived at an ending: "But now it's done, it's over." The singer makes it official by engaging in such concert formalities as introducing his fellow vocalists and thanking the conductor. These are conventions that the audience gathered for Beckett's show so want to hear, for with them the show will conclude, along with their perpetual waiting. With the last "thank you," we have been delivered from limbo and have at last found an ending. The final cadence provides a conclusion in more than one way. The close of the Scherzo also resolves the tension between obliteration and expansion. The Mahler continues to be buffeted until the end, but it should not be overlooked that the Scherzo does close, even if in pieces. All the metaphors of expansion have been realized: the "container" has been filled, the "process" has been completed, the "river" has run its course, and the "voyage" is finished.

Berio called the third movement of *Sinfonia* "perhaps the most 'experimental' music I have ever written."[76] He never identified a specific experiment undertaken in the movement, but one could easily see it as study of time, specifically how to connect pieces of past and present. It is an experiment, though, that almost gets beyond his control. The connections multiply so quickly that they come close to overwhelming the Scherzo and also to whisking us into musical realms far away from the Mahler. Near the end of the movement, we find ourselves thrown into such a realm, the serial works of the present. The Scherzo, however, returns and, with it, the last connection has been made and the conclusion we have been seeking has been attained. In other words, the experiment has succeeded. Berio's experiment with time shows how difficult it is to control that force. Time never topples his work as it does Rochberg's renewal and Stockhausen's utopia, but we are given the impression that it could. Above all, *Sinfonia* shows us that time acts in so many "unexpected" ways.

Stockhausen

Now on to the composer who has stood for the present in both *Sinfonia* and *Music for the Magic Theater*: Stockhausen. On the basis of *Hymnen*, the designation fits.[77] An electronic work of unprecedented scope and technological intricacy, it not only speaks of the present but also proclaims the future. Berio and Rochberg, though, do not quote from this work or any of the ones immediately preceding it. They instead find the present in compositions from the late 1950s: *Gruppen* (1955–57) and

---

[76] Berio, liner notes.
[77] This study only discusses the electronic version of *Hymnen*. Stockhausen later composed versions of the work for soloists and tape as well as orchestra and tape.

Zeitmasse (1955–56), respectively. However, from the vantage point of *Hymnen* (1967), those pieces were not the present, but very much the past.

Between *Hymnen* and those earlier works, Stockhausen's music had shifted course.[78] During the 1950s, his compositions scrutinized the new formal possibilities opened up by integral serialism. *Gruppen* and *Zeitmasse*, for instance, plotted some of the myriad relationships that could be drawn between pitch and time. Stockhausen's preoccupation with that relationship extended into such early electronic pieces as *Studie I* (1953) and *Studie II* (1954), in which he could use the new medium to realize his schemes with unequaled precision. These works also attained an unequaled abstraction, as Stockhausen recalled in a radio interview conducted after the premiere of *Hymnen*.

For many years in music – in my music at least – a certain expungement of all musical "objects" has been noticed. Since 1951, I had attempted to compose neither known rhythms nor melodies nor harmonic combinations nor figures: in other words, to avoid everything which is familiar, generally known or reminiscent of music already composed. I wanted to quasi create a music ex nihilo: a completely non-figurative, extra-objective music which existed outside of the world of objects.[79]

Like many serial and electronic composers, Stockhausen found that he could not abandon "the world of objects." To do so was to walk further and further into a desert of abstraction. He eventually changed course and headed back to that world. In other words, Stockhausen, like Rochberg and Berio, expanded his musical realm by drawing upon the recognizable. For him, the recognizable was not quotations of past concert works but – befitting the electronic medium on which he focused – familiar sounds. One of the first works in this direction, *Gesang der Jünglinge* (1955–56), introduces into a structured sphere of sine and impulse tones a boy singing the *Benedicite*, a voice many of the original audience members could have heard any Sunday at church. Grabbing their hands, the child guides listeners through the foreign electronic

---

[78] For discussions of *Hymnen* and its role in the composer's oeuvre, see Johannes Fritsch, "Hauptwerk *Hymnen*," *Schweizerische Musikzeitung* 116 (1976), 262–65; Jonathan Harvey, *The Music of Stockhausen* (London: Faber & Faber, 1975), 102–9; Nicholas F. Hopkins, *Hymnen: Tractatus Musica Unita*, Feedback Papers 37 (Cologne: Feedback Studio Verlag, 1991); Robin Maconie, *The Works of Karlheinz Stockhausen* (London: Oxford University Press, 1976), 216–26; Maconie, "Stockhausen at 70: through the looking glass," *Musical Times* 139 (Summer 1998), 4–11.

[79] Karlheinz Stockhausen, "Hymnen – Nationalhymnen (zur elektronischen Musik 1967)" in Rudolf Frisius, ed., *Karlheinz Stockhausen* (Mainz: Schott Musik, 1996), 275. An English translation of this essay is included in the liner notes to the CD recording of *Hymnen* produced by Stockhausen Verlag (CD 10, p. 130). All subsequent references to this essay will be from that translation.

landscape, a known sound among so many strange ones. *Hymnen*, as the sparse title states, finds the familiar in national anthems. According to Stockhausen, "national anthems are the most familiar music imaginable."[80] In other words, any listener could spot these songs, along with such other recognizable sounds as folk music, cheers from state ceremonies, and the noises of a Chinese market. Listeners will need to hold on to such sounds, as the work surrounds them with electronic materials that "make a completely abstract impression and are not reminiscent of anything."[81]

Having expanded his musical realm to include everything from the "completely abstract" to the "most familiar," Stockhausen faced the challenge of connecting such varied materials. These connections were crucial for they would distinguish his works from a mere collage. If Stockhausen was adamant about one point it was that "the composition *Hymnen* is *not* a collage" (original emphasis).[82] As used by him, collage was an approach in which elements were superficially and/or randomly juxtaposed, without being integrated into a larger structure. Such loose mixtures were a pitfall for composers seeking to work with diverse elements. The problem confronting him and other such composers was to find a means of unifying those materials. It was a pressing problem. Indeed, Stockhausen viewed it as "the problem since 1960, not only in the field of music."[83]

Stockhausen's solution was "intermodulation." This technique was born out of new electronic technologies. It allowed the composer to connect two sounds by blending them into one.[84] Two examples given by Stockhausen include the coalescing of Japanese and African idioms and the synthesis of the rhythm of one fragment with the harmony of another and the "dynamic envelope" of a third.[85] In both cases, he argued, the originality of the individual components would be heightened and a new element would emerge. Comprising all those components, that unique element would provide a deep level of unity. The preoccupation with unity of different parameters harks back to Stockhausen's explorations of integral serialism. Indeed, as he pointed out, that exploration was not over, it had just shifted course. "General serial form" and "musical through-organization" were still concepts that shaped his music, the two now being broadened by the technique of intermodulation.[86] Stockhausen held that the fundamental ideals of serialism were still

---

[80] Stockhausen, Introduction, *Hymnen* (Vienna: Universal Edition, 1968), ix.

[81] Stockhausen, liner notes, 136.

[82] Stockhausen, Introduction, ix.   [83] Stockhausen, liner notes, 138.

[84] On this technique, see David Ernst, *The Evolution of Electronic Music* (New York: Schirmer Books, 1977), 61–66.

[85] Stockhausen, liner notes, 138, and Introduction, ix.

[86] Stockhausen, liner notes, 138.

valid.[87] More than valid, they were crucial in connecting the different materials with which he worked. "Serialism," he emphasized, "tries to go beyond collage, beyond the incoherent multiplicity of things."[88]

Stockhausen also sought to unify the larger sonic categories of the "abstract" (the pure electronic sounds) and "concrete" (the anthems and other bits of the familiar). Recent music, with its unprecedented sonic variety, demanded a new understanding of the relationship between these two areas, one that no longer split them into a "dualism." That split, Stockhausen argued, could be sealed by having the two "simultaneously in play."[89] He similarly aimed at erasing the division of past, present, and future that orders our notion of time. Like Rochberg, Berio, and many other contemporary artists, Stockhausen was entranced by interconnected time. Indeed, the "whole compositional project" of *Hymnen* is to merge past, present, and future, to have them exist "simultaneously."[90] Anthems were the perfect material for this endeavor, as they had already achieved a certain synchronicity by being, in Stockhausen's words, "charged with time, with history – past, present, and future."[91]

---

[87] Berio made a similar claim, stating that *Sinfonia* "would not have been possible without the experience of serialism" (Philippot, "Entretien: Luciano Berio," 88). As could be argued elsewhere, collage offered composers a way of extending the life of serialism, which, by itself, especially in the extreme forms of the 1950s, had become untenable. Composers used collage in several different ways to give serialism new life. In Zimmermann's works, quotation acts as a new dimension – a pocket of the familiar and tonal – in the larger serial whole. It breaks up the stylistic uniformity and adds expressive and symbolic elements to the music. Rochberg goes further in this direction, creating a musical space in which dissonant atonality and earlier tonal styles coexist, with the latter taking a new role as a stylistic foil. Finally, Stockhausen and Berio hold on to ideals of serialism, even when it means stretching those ideals and placing them in much different sound worlds.

[88] Peter Heyworth, "Spiritual dimensions," *Music and Musicians* 19 (May 1971), 34.

[89] Stockhausen, liner notes, 137.

[90] Stockhausen made this comment while discussing a passage from *Hymnen* that consists of studio chatter between him and his assistant David Johnson (Region II). They are discussing Stockhausen's decision to mix together the current West German anthem with the *Horst Wessel Lied*, a song adopted by the Nazis. As he was told, the inclusion of the latter may arouse "ill feeling"; however, Stockhausen brushed aside such concerns saying that he was using the song only as "a memory." During the studio conversation, the verb *sagen* is conjugated in the present, past, and pluperfect tenses, giving different layers of past and present. According to Stockhausen, in that discussion the "present, the past, and pluperfect become simultaneous." The future can also be seen as part of this scheme, as we hear a studio discussion (an event of the present) about the Lied (a song of the past) and possible "ill feelings" (a possible future) ensuing from the inclusion of that song. Stockhausen's visionary interpretation of mundane studio talk offers him another way to avoid confronting the troubling impact of his quotation. Stockhausen, Introduction, viii.

[91] Stockhausen, Introduction, ix.

But, contrary to that claim, *Hymnen* sequesters its anthems in the past. Throughout the work, they come across as relics of both past events and, even more remote historically, the days of acoustic instruments and tonality. The anthems have no awareness of the electronic sound world, which, in contrast, is not only aware of those antique sounds but can grab and manipulate them. That world, full of new sonorities and unlimited possibilities, stretches out from the present into the future. It is between these two periods that Stockhausen stakes his claim. The past was a realm to which he had no desire to return. By itself, he argued, the past is "useless." Only when experienced within the context of the present – say, as part of an electronic work – could it have any relevance. Turning the tables on Rochberg, Stockhausen upheld that the past could be "renewed" – given a new life and purpose – by the present.[92]

Hymnen reaches out not only to all of time but also to all the world. The work has global dimensions, in terms of both its unprecedented length and its structure. By incorporating anthems, *Hymnen* draws a map of the world. With that map unfolded, we can see that the work divides into four large sections, called regions. Each of these regions has several "centers," anthems around which others with melodic or historical affinities circulate. The first region, for instance, establishes the *Internationale* as a center and then later the *Marseillaise*. The second and third regions share the Soviet anthem as a center. The former ends with that piece surrounded by a flock of African anthems, whereas the latter opens with the Soviet anthem by itself. The fourth region has two centers. It begins in Switzerland and then steps into an unknown land: "Hymnunion in Harmondy under Pluramon." What at first sounds like the foreign language spoken in that mysterious country is actually Stockhausen's intermodulation of familiar words. Here is a realm where "hymns" (anthems) are in "union"; where *harmonia mundi* reigns; and finally where pluralism and monism intermingle, a dualism which, like the abstract/concrete opposition, has been sealed. It is, as Stockhausen states, a "utopian" realm, one in which the musical unity forged through intermodulation offers a vision of "the unity of peoples and nations in a harmonious human family."[93]

---

[92] Stockhausen, liner notes, 138–39.

[93] Ibid., 124. This idea of global unity was part of a larger move toward a *"Weltmusik,"* an idea that Stockhausen pursued in *Telemusik* and *Hymnen*. Luigi Nono criticized Stockhausen's conception of *Weltmusik*, claiming that the composer blindly tossed together musics of different cultures and political regimes without being sensitive to the historical and political connections between them. He also believed that Stockhausen's handling of the music of non-Western countries had imperialistic bearings. Nono, *Texte: Studien zu seiner Musik*, ed. Jürg Stenzl (Zurich: Atlantis, 1975), 205–06, 249. For a discussion of the development of Stockhausen's idea of *Weltmusik*, see Gernot Gruber,

This vision of unity is far removed from the sonic welter heard earlier in the work. *Hymnen* opens at the desk of a shortwave radio operator, whose constant turning of the dial churns a mix of shortwave noises, anthems, Morse code patterns, and voices.[94] These chaotic initial minutes capture *Hymnen* at its best. In these days of microsampling and editing, they still captivate. It is not only the sonic volatility that thrills, but the sense of expansion as well. Through the conceit of the radio, Stockhausen takes us across the world. He also takes us into the world of electronic sound, which can be heard in the bracing electronic dissonances and the swoosh of sonic glissandos.

This expansion is driven by what Stockhausen calls "searching," specifically the search for unity.[95] That search will be repeated throughout the work and take different forms. In the opening passage, our radio operator restlessly turns the dial in an attempt to hold on to a signal. Finally, after six minutes, that signal is found. Fragments of the *Internationale* gradually emerge and take shape, an electronic version of Ives's cumulative form. A call to workers to band together, the *Internationale* offers one vision of unity. But it is a political and musical vision that falls short. Interrupted and gradually distorted, the anthem never takes full form. A swooshing electronic sound disperses it, and the searching resumes.

One other anthem appears prominently in this opening radio scramble: that of the USSR. Even the most attentive listener, however, would not recognize the song, as it has been transformed into a series of dissonant electronic chords. Stockhausen distinguishes the Soviet anthem as the only one to be presented with purely electronic sounds. He also subjects the song to a new "harmonic process," which proceeds from "diatonic tonality via modal Hungarian minor to whole tone and finally ending in chromatic-dissonant atonality."[96] In this new guise, the anthem is splintered into 112 individual chords, which often appear separately or in small groups. At once sonically tied to the electronic medium and melodically and harmonically connected to the original, it occupies a liminal position within the abstract/concrete scheme of the work, making it the centerpiece of the ongoing tension between the two areas. In the opening passage, though, the anthem comes across as abstract, for, without a full context, it emerges as a series of bracing electronic dissonances that disrupt the surrounding anthems.

"Stockhausens Konzeption der 'Weltmusik' und die Zitathaftigkeit seiner Musik," in *Internationales Stockhausen-Symposium 1998*, ed. Imke Misch and Christoph von Blumröder (Saarbrücken: Pfau, 1999), 103–10.

[94] A discussion of this opening section with references to relevant pages from Stockhausen's notebooks can be found in Richard Toop, "Stockhausen's electronic works: sketches and work-sheets from 1952–67," *Interface* 10 (1981), 191–95.

[95] Stockhausen, liner notes, 135.   [96] Ibid., 151.

A full context does emerge midway through *Hymnen* in an extended passage that features a nearly complete statement of the USSR anthem.[97] From the last center of Region II to the first of Region III, the anthem crawls from one sustained sonority to another, taking around ten minutes to reach the final chord. Along the way, it also reaches for abstraction. At the end of Region II, the electronic anthem already stands apart from the acoustic and tonal African melodies surrounding it. However, the opening chords of the anthem, despite Stockhausen's timbral transformations, still adhere to the melody and diatonicism of the original, a tether that keeps it connected to the familiar. By the opening of Region III, the anthem, following Stockhausen's "harmonic process," has cut that bond and moved further into abstraction. In addition, the backdrop of the familiar, the African anthems, has vanished. The Soviet anthem has entered a realm of pure electronics, where it becomes sound treated as sound. The electronic sonorities of the anthem are subjected to timbral distortions, each a sonic event in itself.[98] The distortions gradually increase, reaching a climax with the 112th chord, which no longer comes across as a chord, dissonant or consonant, but as a sonic mass on the verge of breaking apart.

Or, from a different perspective, that mass is trying to break free – that is, attempting to move beyond the anthem and to cross over into the realm of abstraction. It cannot, however, because when the anthem ends, it does, too. There is no life beyond the 112th chord. The sonic abstractions will always remain tied to the anthem. Unable to venture beyond that point, the last chord slowly dwindles. In its dying trail, the sounds of the familiar return. First, Morse code patterns produced by sine tones pulsate, blips that resume the searching executed by the shortwave radio in the opening scene. As in that episode, the searching attempts to push through the unrelenting pops of anthem fragments. After about one hour, we find ourselves back where we began, lost in sonic chaos and once again searching.

The final utopia appears even more out of reach. Within that initial hour, though, we have already experienced several different visions of utopia. *Hymnen* rests upon various utopian premises and references besides the dream of the final episode. The work adheres to two fundamental aesthetic outlooks – collage heterogeneity and sonic purity – which are utopian in that they strive to achieve the perfection of a certain compositional ideal. The former can be heard in the tumble of anthems throughout the opening section. It is a state that harbors diverse materials while finding unity amid that diversity. Creating that state is

---

[97] All the chords but the twenty-second are stated.

[98] For a detailed discussion of the electronic manipulation of the anthem, see Stockhausen, liner notes, 151–61.

the drive of expansion and connection, the reaching out to and creating links between the seemingly disparate. This ideal of multiplicity inhering in oneness was explicitly viewed as utopian by some of Stockhausen's Darmstadt alumni, a point to be explored below. That concept overlaps with another utopian scheme: blended time. Like Berio and Rochberg, Stockhausen believed that past, present, and future could be simultaneously experienced. Time too could be conceived of as multiplicity existing within unity. Not surprisingly, Stockhausen claimed, as we have seen, that the "whole compositional project" of the work was to realize the unified spectrum of time.

The other central aesthetic premise – that of sonic purity – dominates the section featuring the anthem of the Soviet Union, itself a reference to an envisaged utopian society. The plodding march of the anthem takes us to the brink of that ideal, a realm of sound as sound.[99] Much art of the twentieth century staked out such domains of perfection, spaces in which an art form concentrates on the essence of its medium. Within the realm of sonic purity, the extraneous and the heterogeneous, the stuff of collage, will have been shredded. Unity is not to be achieved by connecting this to that, but rather by narrowing in on a singular state. This absolute state has also been achieved through the use of electronic technologies.[100] With the advent of studio resources in the early 1950s, many composers prized that technology as utopian, especially in the ways in which it would allow them to work with sound. Stockhausen, for instance, claimed that as long as he wrote for the "classical orchestra" the idea of having different timbres "germinate" from a single source and form part of a continuum would always remain a "Utopian concept."[101] In the studio, however, that vision of sonic unity could be attained, as the composer already sought to do in his earliest electronic works.

A discussion of the different utopian streams – collage heterogeneity, blended time, sonic purity, and electronic technology – running through *Hymnen* helps us to interpret the closing vision of utopia, that of the far-away land of "Hymnunion in Harmondy under Pluramon." Here is a realm of ideal unity, where pluralism and monism merge into a larger whole. That belief leads us to expect that the aesthetic outlooks of collage heterogeneity and sonic purity, manifestations of those two categories, will coalesce. Rather than synthesizing the two, "Hymnunion" sets them against each other. It creates a clash of utopias. At the center of that conflict stands the past, which captures the differences between

---

[99] The inability of that chord to cross over that brink may be a comment on how cruelly short the USSR had fallen in reaching its political ideals. It could also be viewed as Stockhausen's rebuke of that country for banning his music.

[100] For a discussion of Stockhausen's interest in the purity of the sine tone, see Richard Toop, "Stockhausen and the sine-wave," *Musical Quarterly* 65 (1979), 379–91.

[101] Stockhausen, "Two lectures," *Die Reihe* 5 (Bryn Mawr: Theodore Presser, 1961), 61.

the two ideals. It seeds the heterogeneity of the work with anthems, crowd noises, and voices. At the same time, those elements spoil the sonic purity striven for by *Hymnen*. As we enter "Hymnunion," the question becomes whether this utopia has a past, and, if not, what kind of utopia it is.

"Hymnunion" initially sounds very peaceful. We make our way into that land through Switzerland. The first half of the fourth region concentrates on the Swiss national anthem, a choral chord of which is transformed (or intermodulated) into a resounding bass sonority that supports the initial section of "Hymnunion." The sonic turmoil of the opening radio scene does not rattle this realm. It is a tranquil sound world, consisting of the lulling bass chord and a few other sonic layers. That chord once again metamorphoses, becoming now the sound of Stockhausen breathing. Over this new foundation occur a series of "reminiscences" of anthems heard earlier in the work. The closing sound is not an anthem but Stockhausen's breathing, which stands for "the breathing of all mankind."[102]

The tension between the two utopian aesthetic premises of the work occurs during the "reminiscences," which are also called "insertions" since they are "inserted" into the continuous stream of Stockhausen's breathing. The former is the more fitting term, as the first four of these passages recall materials – the *Internationale* and Ghanaian, British, and Soviet anthems – that have been previously stated. The fifth and sixth insertions, in contrast, present new materials – the Indian anthem and noises from a Chinese market – but they may as well be reminiscences, since they are just as much part of the world that we have left behind upon entering "Hymnunion." What we have not heard before and what there is little to prepare us for earlier in the work is what happens to these memories. They are "framed," that is, enclosed by thick electronic sounds on all sides. The first reminiscence is undisturbed, but the second one is hammered by a "left frame," a jarring sonority that precedes the anthem statement. With the following four passages top, bottom, and right frames are added – sounds above, below, and at the end of the reminiscences. The anthems and folk sounds are gradually confined. They cannot break out of these containers. The upper and lower frames are in such extreme ranges that there is no crawling above or beneath them. Even if that were possible, the anthems would crash into the closing right frame.

The anthems have not only been contained, they have also been effaced. Beginning with the third reminiscence, Stockhausen smothers them with the dissonant electronic chords of the Soviet anthem. By the time of the sixth passage, the Chinese market noises can barely rise above

---

[102] Stockhausen, liner notes, 170.

the din of the Soviet chords, bottom and top frames, and the final thud of the right frame. In six brief steps, the anthems have been methodically erased. The seventh frame finishes the job. It is an "empty frame," just the four containing sonorities with nothing inside, not even the Soviet anthem. All we hear is the frame itself, which amounts to a mass of pure electronic sounds. Coming after the erasure of the reminiscences, it is a menacing sound, one that will not let us go, as Stockhausen sustains it for seventy-seven seconds. The only way to top this imposing gesture was with the seventy-nine seconds of his breathing that immediately follows and closes the work.

Utopia has been achieved – the utopia of sonic purity. The final frame erects a monument to that ideal. It is not a monument of unity.[103] Before the last frame, Stockhausen says the word "pluramon," an incantation that supposedly enacts the blending of opposites. But the empty frame mocks that spell. It is all monism, pure electronic sound. Rather than attempting to merge the two utopian streams, the series of frames expunges the ideal of collage heterogeneity. What is especially surprising is how that depletion is accomplished through such an unsparing, systematic process. The conclusion even flaunts the ascendancy of sonic purity by placing the Soviet anthem in the frames. That anthem had earlier attempted to cross over from the concrete to the realm of abstract sound. Now it has been placed in the frames with the other anthems, humiliatingly reduced to their level, and suffering the same fate.

The triumph of sonic purity may not be much of a triumph at all. It could be viewed as a concession to the inherent difficulties of representing utopia. As historian Laurent Gervereau has described, utopia "is, on the face of it, resistant to iconographic (and *a fortiori* material) fixity in all its forms."[104] To represent that realm necessitates the

---

[103] Hopkins strongly disagrees. He views the last Region as attaining a deep level of unity, one based on the synthesis of the "two major tendencies" of the work, specifically "plurality and monism." His discussion of how that synthesis is achieved and what form it takes is vague, at times relying on Stockhausen's claim of such unity. Hopkins, though, does draw attention to many intricate formal relationships in the work that provide a more conventional type of structural unity. In particular, he reveals the importance of the number seven on both the local and large-scale formal dimensions. He also points to formal parallels between the opening and closing Regions. His account, however, never scrutinizes Stockhausen's claims of utopia, nor does it probe the treatment of the past. Hopkins, *Hymnen: Tractatus Musica Unita*, 31–44. In another discussion of unity in the work, Michael Rigoni argues that the dimensions of the First Region are based on the Fibonacci series. Rigoni, *Karlheinz Stockhausen* (2nd edn, Paris: Millénaire III Editions, 1998), 231–32.

[104] Laurent Gervereau, "Symbolic collapse: utopia challenged by its representations," in *Utopia: the Search for the Ideal Society in the Western World*, ed. Roland Schaer, Gregory Claeys, and Lyman Tower Sargent (New York and Oxford: New York Public Library and Oxford University Press, 2000), 357.

depiction of details, exact conditions, places, laws, etc. Such attempts to solidify the imaginary will ultimately lead to its "dissolution," as utopia succumbs to our own embittered experiences of those specifics.[105] Not surprisingly, artists have often evaded such details and emphasized instead more abstract conceptions. Many depictions of utopia, for instance, are built on the shapes of circles, squares, and rectangles. These figures of geometric purity bestow upon those representations a sense of perfection. In his account of utopian imagery, Gervereau focuses on the circle, "utopia's first figure." The shape not only possesses an ageless purity but it also conveys enclosure, an inside space separated from the outside by the border of that classic and impenetrable form. Of note is the round island settled by many utopian representations, a "closed" land "doubly hemmed in by water and walls."[106] That realm reinforces the purity claimed and sought as utopia, since it excludes the extraneous and defiled – in other words, the materials of our world.

In depicting his utopia, Stockhausen also avails himself of perfect shapes. During a discussion of the piece, he attempted to clarify the series of frames by means of an illustration, which shows a blob figure, the anthems, gradually enclosed by heavy lines, the frames.[107] The concluding "empty frame" takes the form of a rectangle, four stark lines with nothing inside them. Turning to Gervereau, we can see how that shape places "Hymnunion" in a larger tradition of utopian representations. First, it has us hear the "empty frame" for the abstract sound that it is, just as abstract as an isolated rectangle.[108] The purity of both the shape and the sound belie the compulsive talk about the synthesis of disparate materials. Like the round island, the rectangle excludes, but with a telling difference. Whereas the island uses its border to keep out the foreign, the "empty frame" eradicates such material from within its confines. "Hymnunion" is a utopia based upon a grand purge, not upon isolation.

One element that is purged is the past. More than any other moment in the work, the final section compels us to hear the anthems as from that time. They are, as Stockhausen calls them, "reminiscences," recollections of the world that we have left behind in crossing over the border to "Hymnunion." Those reminiscences are erased and as they disappear so does the past that they preserve. By the time of the seventh frame,

---

[105] Ibid., 357.   [106] Ibid., 357.

[107] Jonathan Cott, *Stockhausen: Conversations with the Composer* (New York: Simon and Schuster, 1973), 146. Another version of the diagrams can be found in liner notes, 172–73.

[108] The sound may not be completely abstract, as Stockhausen says it calls to mind a "lion roaring." Cott, *Stockhausen: Conversations with the Composer*, 147.

there are no traces of memory and thus no traces of the past.[109] *Hymnen* instead locks us into an electronic sound that has no past, in the sense that it has not been heard earlier in the work. Moreover, it seems almost interminable, as if it stretched well beyond seventy-seven seconds. In other words, *Hymnen* has locked us into a static present.

Stockhausen's perpetual present accords with other conventions in the representation of utopia. Contrary to the ideal of blended time upheld by collage heterogeneity, such realms disconnect themselves from both the past and the future, settling into an amorphous present. Regarding the future, utopias are by nature anti-evolutionary, there being no higher state toward which the already perfect society can develop.[110] As Matei Calinescu puts it in his commentary on utopia, "the future – the begetter of change and *difference* – is suppressed in the very attainment of perfection, which by definition cannot but repeat itself *ad infinitum*."[111] In such a scheme of time, the future exists only as a continuation of the present, thereby endlessly elongating it. Besides neutralizing the future, utopias sever ties with the past.[112] These realms can exist only free of the failures and burdens accumulated during that period. To that end, some utopian groups have sought such isolated spaces as islands or rural areas to begin anew, to create their own Gardens of Eden. On a grander and more desperate scale, many political regimes, like the USSR, have sought to cleanse their lands of emblems of the past, eradicating them through revolution, upheaval, and murder.

Such movements make clear the mass of violence and destruction that must be marshaled in the attempt to raze the past. *Hymnen* makes a similar point. The end of the work is striking for its sonic brutality. Even such a devout admirer of the piece as Nicholas Hopkins has commented on the "violence" and "aggressiveness" unleashed in the series of frames. He, though, never questions the reasons for that fury or how it fits into the deep levels of unity that he sees the work attaining in the final scene. Other scholars, however, have pointed to the ferocity in the work and viewed it as marring, if not outright quashing, Stockhausen's claims of unity and utopia. Luigi Pestalozza and Brunhilde Sonntag have described scenes of "catastrophic destruction" and "death" at the

[109] As Stockhausen has commented: "In this last loud section, you can't think of anything any more – figures, melodies, anthems – it's all gone." He refers to this process as "washing out," which to him is meant in the "general sense: brain washing, cleansing out of the brain." Such an interpretation contrasts with an earlier statement in the interview. Describing the vision of utopia in the last section, he says: "It's kind of a utopia, a union of all the anthems, but they're still all together, they're not washed out – a union of the hymns." Cott, *Stockhausen: Conversations with the Composer*, 144, 147.

[110] Gervereau, "Symbolic collapse," 360.

[111] Matei Calinescu, *Five Faces of Modernity: Modernism, Avant-Garde, Decadence, Kitsch, Postmodernism* (Durham, NC: Duke University, 1987), 66.

[112] Gervereau, "Symbolic collapse," 363.

end of the work.[113] According to Pestalozza, Stockhausen's utopia is nothing more than a realm into which he can withdraw and hide from the violence rampaging throughout *Hymnen*.[114]

Ironically, Stockhausen went the furthest in associating *Hymnen* with violence. Placing the work in an apocalyptic scenario, he prophesied that *Hymnen* would be one of his pieces that would stir utopian inspirations for the reconstruction of society after an impending cataclysm.[115]

This is an age of purification, and after it will come rebirth. But rebirth can only happen when there is death. A lot of death. Things cannot go on the way they are. So they must die out – and they will... What I'm trying to do, as far as I'm aware of it, is to produce models that herald the stage after destruction. I'm trying to go beyond collage, heterogeneity, and pluralism, and to find unity; to produce music that brings us to the essential ONE. And that is going to be badly needed during the time of shocks and disasters that is going to come. Models of coming together, of mutual love, of love as a cohesive force. I'm sure that if I'm in my best state, my music will have a unifying effect.[116]

Stockhausen's doomsaying captures the utopian fantasies built around apocalypse. That event amounts to the ultimate form of erasing the past. Not surprisingly, it plays a prominent role in utopian representations, for only total destruction can lead to the total rebirth necessary to create the perfect society. The anxieties over nuclear catastrophe that haunted the Cold War era roused many such visions of the future, as seen in such an unlikely pairing as Stockhausen's utopian predictions and *Star Trek*. In the latter, the ravages of nuclear war led survivors to band together and build the peaceful Earth featured in the television series, a society that has attained "the essential ONE." Placing *Hymnen* in the context of such utopian representations raises more questions about the work's evocation of that realm. Stockhausen's comments reveal that a brutal erasure of the past forms an integral part of his conception of

---

[113] Luigi Pestalozza, "Stockhausen und der musikalische Autoritarismus," *Schweizerische Musikzeitung* 116 (1976), 270; and Brunhilde Sonntag, *Untersuchungen zur Collagetechnik in der Musik des 20. Jahrhunderts* (Regensburg: Bosse, 1977), 164.

[114] Pestalozza, "Stockhausen und der musikalische Autoritarismus," 270.

[115] This chapter was written before Stockhausen made his controversial comments regarding the terrorist attacks of 11 September 2001. The following discussion of apocalypse will not deal with those remarks. It, though, does provide a context for the comments, showing to what extent Stockhausen had already been fascinated by scenes of grandiose violence.

[116] Heyworth, "Spiritual dimensions," 38. In his interviews with Cott, Stockhausen directly mentioned *Hymnen* as part of a similar apocalyptic vision. See Cott, *Stockhausen: Conversations with the Composer*, 23–24. A poetic gloss on the apocalyptic resonance of the work can be found in Jean-Noel Der Weid, "L'apocalypse de Stockhausen," *Silences* 1 (1985), 170–71.

utopia. If that is the case, then what can we make of the final framing episode? Is it the model of utopia that Stockhausen holds it up to be? Or, with its upheaval of the past and its sonic detonations, is it a representation of apocalypse?

There is another way of approaching the ambiguity of that scene: does "Hymnunion" synthesize the past or does it erase it? It was suggested above that that imaginary land dreams of the former but comes closer to achieving the latter. This tension marks the culmination of an ambivalence toward the past which runs throughout the entire work, an ambivalence shaped by the two competing aesthetic outlooks. On one hand, *Hymnen* builds around the past an ideal of diverse yet integrated time, part of its vision of collage heterogeneity. On the other hand, the work appears ill at ease with the past, viewing the acoustic and tonal anthems stemming from that period as materials that need to be purified. In a telling moment, the act of memory, the means by which the past takes life, is extirpated. Only after the past has been blotted out can pure sound finally, after nearly two hours, be achieved.

What is left at the end of *Hymnen* is a monumental emptiness, that empty frame. What is left at the end of the climaxes in Rochberg's Third Symphony is rubble, and in the final measures of the third movement of Berio's *Sinfonia*, mere threads. All three works conclude with depleted, if not erased, forms of the past. Like Berio's and Rochberg's works, *Hymnen* succumbs to difficulties in handling the past. However, whereas the former two composers attempt to build upon the past, Stockhausen approaches it in a conflicted way, at times trying to synthesize it into a greater whole and at other times seeking to purify it into nothingness. The past is not so easily molded. The conclusion of *Hymnen* attests most strikingly to that intractability. Stockhausen cannot transcend the past, either through unity or through purity. The violence resulting from that effort mars his utopia, turning it into a realm of static vacuity. At the moment when the promise of collage composition is to reach apotheosis, it is dashed by vain attempts to coerce the past.

There is one other empty sound in this final passage that needs to be discussed: Stockhausen's breathing.[117] Although that sound is supposed to represent the respiration of humankind, it comes across only as the breathing of one man, the man who created or breathed life into this utopia. With his world coming down around him, Stockhausen struggles to shore it up with symbols of unity – the breathing and the magic word "pluramon." Moreover, through his respiratory grandeur,

---

[117] The breathing could be interpreted as an assertion of the concrete. The sound, however, comes across as existing outside of the abstract/concrete relationship. Breathing is a familiar sound, but, as used in *Hymnen*, it is removed from the other concrete noises, especially the anthems and voices enclosed by the frames.

he asserts his presence, telling us that he is in control and urging us to believe his vision.[118] We are to breathe and dream in lockstep with him.[119] Many of the same scholars who have been shocked by the swath of destruction in *Hymnen* have also recoiled at such scenes of megalomania, viewing the two as interrelated. Pestalozza sees authoritarian and destructive impulses running throughout the work and culminating in the final vision of utopia, which amounts to nothing but a mystification.[120] Sonntag similarly detects an authoritarian fantasy being played out in the land of "Hymnunion," the utopian creed of which she dismisses as mere dogma.[121] To both authors, that land is ruled by a demagogue.

Demagoguery, violence, the purging of the past, and the push for purity are more the foundations of a dystopia than a utopia. In many ways, "Hymnunion" could be viewed as such. The darker side of the realm especially emerges when comparing the end of *Hymnen* to Jean-Luc Godard's contemporary film *Alphaville* (1965). The film engages many of the same issues raised by *Hymnen*, particularly the role of the past, but places those issues in a dystopian scenario. *Hymnen* and *Alphaville* can be seen as participating in a contemporary debate over those issues, a debate that in the 1960s was often pitched in the extreme terms of utopia and dystopia.[122]

Alphaville is a city ruled by a computer, Alpha 60, which controls not only the daily running of the city but also the thoughts and feelings of its citizens. One thought that has been expunged is that of the past. To prevent citizens from recalling the emotions and ideas that filled their lives before its inception, Alpha 60 programs them to think of time as an infinite present, a period existing in and by itself. The citizens of "Hymnunion" have similarly had their minds erased of anthems and noises of the past, existing in a static empty frame. Both peoples find themselves in technocracies, one run by a computer, the other by electronic studio equipment. Each of these machines attempts to create worlds in its own image, be it a realm of machine-like efficiency or a world of pure electronic sound. Moreover, in an eerie parallel, the citizens of both worlds cannot escape the sound of breathing, that of the

---

[118] It should also be noted that Stockhausen uses studio technology to enhance his breathing to take it beyond the patterns and lengths of normal human breathing. For instance, there are moments of successive inhales and the inhale-exhale pattern occurs at a very slow pace. With these alterations, Stockhausen has taken himself beyond the merely human and into the realm of technology.

[119] The technological enhancement of the breathing makes it difficult to join him, a fact that works against the ideal of a collective breath.

[120] Pestalozza, "Stockhausen und der musikalische Autoritarismus," 268–72.

[121] Sonntag, *Untersuchungen zur Collagetechnik*, 165.

[122] The polar positions in that debate are summed up in the title of a book by R. Buckminster Fuller dealing with the potential of new technologies: Fuller, *Utopia or Oblivion: the Prospects For Humanity* (New York: Overlook Press, 1969).

halting respiration made by Alpha 60 and the steady flow of the other technological overlord, Stockhausen.[123]

With *Alphaville*, Godard strongly warned against the equation of technology with utopia made by Stockhausen and other contemporary figures.[124] That link, as he shows, leads to dehumanization and a benighted view that the past is irrelevant, that it can be forgotten or even erased. Fittingly it is the past that brings down Alpha 60, just as the ineradicable memories of that period reduce "Hymnunion" to a void. In the film, the defender of the past is a figure of that time, a cliché figure we have seen so often as to have it embedded in our cultural memories. Lemmy Caution is a trenchcoat detective who walks straight out of early film noir and into the futuristic society of Alphaville.[125] His mission is to stop both the scientist who built Alpha 60 and his creation.[126]

Stopping the scientist is easy. Like any gumshoe, Caution just shoots him. Gumshoes, though, don't usually have to deal with computers. Caution rises to the challenge. He sabotages Alpha 60 by asking it a riddle about time. Having solved the riddle, the computer is forced to acknowledge the full range of time and destroys itself. With its city collapsing around it, Alpha 60 delivers a final soliloquy about how it is inescapably enmeshed in time:

Time is the material of which I am made... Time is a stream which carries me along... but I am Time... it is a tiger which tears me apart... yet I, too, am the tiger. For our misfortune, the world is a reality... and I... for my misfortune... I am myself – Alpha 60[127]

These lines are actually a quotation from Borges's essay "A new refutation of time," which portrays time as a "stream" of past, present, and future, not the isolated present upheld by some philosophers as well as

---

[123] The voice of Alpha 60 is not electronically produced, but is instead that of a man who lost his vocal chords and learned to speak from his diaphragm. Godard wanted a voice that, like the people of Alphaville, was "killed," or had become almost inhuman. This idea of having technology deplete the human contrasts with Stockhausen's using technology to enhance his breathing into some sort of superhuman respiration. Richard Roud, Introduction, *Alphaville: a Film by Jean-Luc Godard*, trans. Peter Whitehead (London: Lorrmier, 1966), 16.

[124] For a discussion of such views, see Huyssen, *After the Great Divide*, 193.

[125] The actor Eddie Constantine played the character Lemmy Caution in a series of French films from the 1950s and 1960s.

[126] Like *Hymnen*, Alphaville deals with the banal, or very familiar, which includes not only detective movies, but also Esther Williams films and low-budget science-fiction fare – all of which, like the anthems, are mixed together. By doing so, Godard upholds an aesthetic outlook of collage heterogeneity, setting that perspective against the uniform, narrow world created by Alpha 60. Moreover, the film does not hold these materials in contempt but instead values them and the cultural memory in which they belong.

[127] Translations of the screenplay have been drawn from *Alphaville: a Film by Jean-Luc Godard*, 78.

by Alpha 60.[128] The final shot of the film floats up and down that stream, presenting an experience of blended time. As Caution and his girlfriend, the scientist's daughter, drive away from the burning city, they are at once driving into a future free of Alphaville and into the formulaic film noir endings of the past.

Promise

Stockhausen was not the only composer to associate collage composition with utopia. He was, however, the only one to go so far as to name a utopia and to depict its birth (or dissolution). Henri Pousseur, another "class of '45" member who found his way out of serialism and into collage idioms, connected the two in ways resembling Stockhausen's conception. For Pousseur, utopia similarly arose from a deep level of unity. To be specific, it achieved a state of "supra-unity," in which, as "Hymnunion" aspired to, fundamental dualisms, including that between unity and contradiction, are synthesized. Like Stockhausen, Pousseur believed that the "supra-unified" musical realm could offer models of social organization that would lead to utopia; however, unlike Stockhausen's vision, Pousseur's utopian schemes would not have to wait for an apocalypse to inspire humankind.[129]

Pousseur's linking of utopia and collage begs us to reconsider that connection and not to dismiss it as a Stockhausen fantasy. Indeed, the concept of utopia does offer insights into the cultural and compositional idealism of the new idiom. Utopia, however, is a problematic topic to introduce into discussions of 1960s arts, specifically those, like collage works, that have been viewed as postmodern. As Jameson has described, postmodernism has been seen as antithetical to utopia, particularly the two main veins of it that run through the first half of the century: leftist political ideologies, notably Marxism and its offshoots, and the pure aesthetic realms of modernism. The battering that these two ideals took in the decades after World War II, though, did not mean

---

[128] Borges, *Selected Non-Fictions*, 332. An earlier lecture given by Alpha 60 draws upon lines from Schopenhauer's *The Will and Representation*, which are excerpted in the Borges essay. Compare *Alphaville: a Film by Jean-Luc Godard*, 43, and Borges, *Selected Non-Fictions*, 331. These lines uphold the view of an infinite present, a view that both Borges and Godard refute. It is difficult to know what to make of these quotations. Are they Godard throwing in poetic bits of Borges (and Borges's quotations of Schopenhauer)? Or are they Alpha 60 recalling works by Borges and Schopenhauer that have been processed in its memory banks?

[129] Pousseur, "Composition and utopia," *Interface* 12 (1983), 75–83. Pousseur may not have perceived a utopia in *Hymnen*. In his discussion of the final passage of the work, he does not mention that term or any related concept. Pousseur, *Fragments théoriques I sur la musique expérimentale* (Brussels: Institut de Sociologie, Université Libre de Bruxelles, 1970), 184–85.

an end to utopian thought, or to those two views for that matter. Quite the contrary, the 1960s, as Jameson argues, witnessed "a whole explosive renewal of Utopian thinking and imagination." On the political and social fronts, "utopian impulses" fueled such movements as hippie culture and student riots, both of which were inspired by dreams of a more peaceful and egalitarian future.[130]

These "impulses" also ran through collage works. Pousseur, for instance, has mentioned how his utopian musical ideals were shaped by the May 1968 riots, which, along with changes in "artistic practice," were part of "an important revolution that, if it was not going to take us to the pure realization of Utopia, would at least take us to something very close to it."[131] Stray pieces of student protests and talk – "we need to do something. Something is going to happen" – ring out in the text of the *Sinfonia* movement. Stockhausen compared his vision of a peaceful "one family" in works like *Hymnen* to those held by "the movement of young people – the hippies."[132] Rochberg too evoked the hippies, viewing them, black militants, LSD, and his own works, among other things, as part of the vibrant *ars combinatoria* of American society.[133]

Besides drawing upon new social energies, collage idioms responded to a second vein of early twentieth-century utopian imagination: the self-contained aesthetic realm focused on the essence of its medium, such as the compositional worlds created by integral serialism and the pure sound realms sought by *Hymnen* and other electronic works. As has frequently been mentioned, postmodern styles wreaked havoc with those realms by sullying them with the familiar and flouting their systematic precision with seemingly random juxtapositions. What has not often been discussed is how many of these postmodern idioms, including collage works, created their own utopian worlds. Whereas composers may have rejected a "twelve-tone utopia" (to quote Berio), they did not necessarily give up on the concept of an ideal musical space.[134] That enduring vision may come as a surprise, given the commonly held perception of postmodernism as being so steeped in irony and skepticism as to be dismissive of any idealism. Moreover, if such works do create aesthetic realms, they are usually depicted not as utopian but as voids – spaces with no borders (open to anything), no depth, and full of empty play.[135]

---

[130] Jameson, *Postmodernism*, 159–60.   [131] Pousseur, "Composition and utopia," 75.

[132] Heyworth, "Spiritual dimensions," 38. The sixth frame is also supposed to include the sounds of a student protest amid those of the Chinese market.

[133] Rochberg, "No center," 155–60.   [134] Berio, "Meditations on a twelve-tone horse."

[135] The lack of depth refers to Jameson's formulation of "depthlessness." Jameson, *Postmodernism*, 9. The phrase "empty play" refers to Keith Hartwell's description of a "play of empty signs" in postmodern music. Hartwell, "Postmodernism and art

Collage works, contrary to such theoretical models, opened up vital musical worlds full of dynamic play. In addition, composers often viewed and realized these worlds in utopian ways. The ideal was a constantly expanding realm that embraces all of time and connects all the materials, no matter how diverse, that come within its reach. Rochberg perhaps best conveyed this idealism with his dream of an infinite *ars combinatoria* that would yield "the richest, most diverse music known to man."[136] Pousseur described a "plural space" in equally utopian, if less poetic, terms: "a space of coexistence of all sorts of possibilities, a much vaster space than the one explored up to that date and in which different structural possibilities can be dialectically confronted according to an 'equipotential' principle."[137] In his music, Stockhausen aimed to reach a fundamental unity by connecting different elements, a unity that would go – musically and spiritually – beyond that plumbed by integral serialism.

These aesthetic and social "utopian impulses" bring us back to a point raised in the opening of this chapter: the promise of collage composition. Such idealism bears witness to how much promise composers saw in that idiom. For many of them, it would have come as a surprise to read Michael Hicks's 1983 pronouncement that "in one decade" composers had "exhausted what seemed to be a technique of promise."[138] Surprising, but true. Having pounced on it as a new "technique," one desperately needed after the demise of the serial master plan, they intensively pursued collage composition and eventually, as Hicks claims, depleted it. By the mid 1970s, Rochberg, Berio, and Stockhausen and many others – Maxwell Davies, Crumb, and Henze to name a few – had for the most part walked away from the idiom. Of course, collage works continue to be written, but the heyday of the style has long passed.

There are several possible reasons for this exhaustion. One is that collage idioms offered composers little surface variety. Just as integral serialism produced atomized textures in which the gestures only ever seemed to get more minuscule, collage works created chaotic surfaces that could only become more chaotic. Along these lines, the surprising

music," in *The Last Post: Music after Modernism*, ed. Simon Miller (Manchester and New York: Manchester University Press, 1993), 45.

[136] Rochberg, "Reflections on the renewal of music," 238.

[137] Pousseur continues to state that Webern gave "the most reduced model but also the purest one" of "plural space," a comment that shows how for some composers these two notions of utopia were related. Pousseur, "Composition and utopia," 80. For a discussion of Pousseur's concept of utopia, see Pascal Decroupet, "Henri Pousseur: composition, perception, and utopia," in Mark Delaere, Helga de la Motte, and Herman Sabbe, eds., *New Music, Aesthetics and Ideology* (Wilhelmshaven: Florian Noetzel, 1995), 182–92.

[138] Hicks, "The new quotation," 126.

juxtapositions soon made the "unexpected" rather expected. With all sorts of combinations being made, it became harder to keep up the thrill of having Schütz wander into Mahler (to give an example from Rochberg). What at first appeared to offer so much soon became limited, at times even hackneyed.

Viewed from a different angle, collage idioms may have been too demanding. Such works present tremendous difficulties in handling the past. In reading composers' commentaries on their pieces, it is surprising how much confidence they show in approaching that period. Stockhausen boasted about making the past "useful," whereas Rochberg sought to redirect its flow into the present. Such confidence is perhaps exceeded only by the audacity of the integral serialists in trying to annul the past. Many of those same composers, of course, later turned to collage composition, and their chronological arrogance once again led them into a trap. If integral serialism traveled too far away from the past, collage idioms got too close to it. Such works wind around large, bald pieces of the past, actual blocks of Mahler or Beethoven, not mere fragments or allusions. Those blocks cast a strong presence with which composers must contend. The works discussed above show different responses to that presence. In his compositions, Rochberg is pulled in by the past and succumbs to nostalgic scenes of collapse. Caught in the excitement of connection and expansion, Berio, in contrast, propels his movement further and further away from the Mahler foundation, a wild ride that threatens to get out of control and to crash both the movement and the foundation. Stockhausen does try to crash the past – that is, to erase it in an effort to reach utopia. He, though, comes close only to erasing his own work.

These struggles with time may have dimmed the promise of collage for some composers. Such difficulties, though, should be seen as part of the promise that was collage. Promise is never pure. Some of it is fulfilled, but much of it gives way to impasses and failures. The promise placed in collage works proves no different. The pieces did achieve much. Above all, they turned many composers away from the narrow focus on the present that was dictated by serialism and made them behold the richness of the past. Drawing upon both past and present, these artists created vibrant mixtures of time, which, as in the *Sinfonia* movement, still startle us with the "unexpected" some thirty years later. As described above, though, the challenges of handling the past press down upon those mixtures, creating shards of past and present.

The two sides of that promise create two different chronological scenes. On one hand, these pieces reveal dynamic spaces shaped by the forces of constant expansion and connection, realms that reach out into endless horizons of time and hope. On the other hand, those spaces ultimately collapse in on themselves, creating scenes of emptiness and rubble. Such contrasting visions are yet another way in which these works are unique, for rarely do compositions offer more than one chronological scene, especially such dissimilar ones. That contrast speaks to how much those compositions had opened themselves up to the realm of time, experiencing both the bounty and the dangers of that realm. What is most striking about those explorations of time is the idealism that inspired them, as these three composers ventured into that territory with dreams of renewal, new experiments, and even utopia.

5

Sampling and thievery

It is a question that has been asked before, but for pop-music critic Neil Strauss it bore repeating after the summer of 1997: "Sampling is (a) creative or (b) theft?" During that summer, Puff Daddy, the "king of sampled hits," reigned, flanked by the princes Wyclef Jean and Will Smith. All three were guilty of "riding stolen songs," pieces that sampled extensively from earlier records. Puff Daddy's "I'll Be Missing You" digitally resuscitated guitar and bass lines from The Police's "Every Breath You Take," whereas Wyclef Jean's "We Just Be Trying to Stay Alive" resurrected the chorus and bass line from the Bee Gees' "Staying Alive." For Strauss, little if anything new was added to the originals, except for a few banal melodies and lines of rap. Even with such cliché trappings, or perhaps because of them, these old hits once again climbed the Top 40. Shaking his head, Strauss could only conclude: "Nostalgia, not creativity, made the song[s] a success."[1]

That swipe clearly rules out (a) as the correct response. Many musicians and listeners would respond similarly to Strauss's question. Sampling has often been dismissed as unoriginal, a mere assembling of other musicians' sounds and melodies. Despite the either/or phrasing of his question, Strauss backs off from such a broad condemnation, pointing out that there are musicians who use samples imaginatively, which makes the hijacking of old hits by Puff Daddy and others all the more inexcusable. He praises Public Enemy and the Chemical Brothers for taking earlier songs and "making [them] in their own image." Even during that dark summer of 1997, there appeared a popular single that reminded listeners what sampling could offer. Strauss holds up Janet Jackson's "Got 'til it's Gone," which engagingly mixes together bits from Joni Mitchell's "Big Yellow Taxi" with a vocal melody by Jackson and rap by Q-Tip.

As far as Puff Daddy and the others are concerned, though, the answer to Strauss's question is (b). "Theft" is a word that has often circulated around sampling, meaning different things to different people.

---

[1] Neil Strauss, "Sampling is (a) creative or (b) theft?" *New York Times*, 14 September 1997, sect. 2, p. 28.

For Strauss, it is the opposite of creativity, the act of uninspired musicians who lift hit tunes and try to cash in on their past success. As Tom Rowlands of the Chemical Brothers puts it: "There is that hangup of people who think that sampling is just stealing something and not doing anything with it."[2] There are also sampling musicians who think that sampling is stealing, at least that is how they refer to their digital borrowings. Rappers, for instance, often boast about "stealing" beats and other bits from older recordings.[3] They direct these taunts at major labels, which have often claimed that their borrowings are just that – stealing. From its initial commercial appearances, sampling has given rise to accusations of theft – that is, performers violating copyright by using samples without permission. Rappers and non-rappers, from De La Soul to Michael Jackson, have faced such charges, with many having to pay up in one way or another to compensate for their thefts.[4] Having cleared all their samples, Puff Daddy, Wyclef Jean, and Will Smith are guilty only of unoriginal quotation, the ultimate theft for Strauss.

Theft, though, does not necessarily have to be unoriginal. To Strauss's two stark choices, a third should be added: (c) creative theft. What is an oxymoron for Strauss is an inspiring fusion for many artists. That exact phrase has been used by members of the San Francisco group Negativland to describe their use of sampling.[5] The group does "steal," meaning that it samples recordings without permission and openly acknowledges the violation of copyright. Negativland justifies this practice by pointing out how creatively it uses the stolen goods, an originality that keeps it artistically, if not ethically, above Strauss's band of crooks. There are more thieves in the electronic woods than just Negativland. Other musicians – John Oswald, the Tape-beatles, and Scanner – have performed similar versions of "creative theft."[6] Not just musicians have been in on the act. Artists from various disciplines have congregated

---

[2] Quoted in Ken Micallef, "The Chemical Brothers: samplers, stomp boxes, and other sonic secrets," *Musician* 224, July 1997, 80.

[3] The charge of "stealing beats" is bandied about in the song "Caught, Can We Get a Witness" from the Public Enemy CD *It Takes a Nation of Millions to Hold Us Back* (Def Jam Records, 1988). See also William Maxwell, "Sampling authenticity: rap music, postmodernism, and the ideology of black crime," *Studies in Popular Culture* 14 (1991), 6–7; and Thomas G. Schumacher, "'This is a sampling sport': digital sampling, rap, and the law of cultural production," *Media, Culture, and Society* 17 (1995), 264–66.

[4] De La Soul faced charges in regard to the samples for their 1984 CD *3 Feet High and Rising*. In 1992, the Cleveland Orchestra sued Jackson for allegedly taking sixty-seven seconds from a 1961 recording of Beethoven's Ninth and using them in the opening section of the song "Will You Be There" from the *Dangerous* CD (1991).

[5] "Negativland bio (August 1998)," http://www.negativland.com/riaa/negbio_1998.html (30 July 1999).

[6] This article will concentrate on Negativland, the Tape-beatles, Oswald, and Scanner. These musicians are among the best-known artists in this vein and all but Scanner have been on the front lines in the battle against copyright. There are obviously more

worldwide in Festivals of Plagiarism, where they celebrate "thievery" and assail the confining institution of copyright.[7]

It is not surprising that Strauss does not mention Negativland and these other musicians. He and most critics focus on sampling in popular styles. Lurking in what one critic has called "the cut-and-paste 'no copyright' underground scene," these theft musicians are anything but popular.[8] The focus on popular music, though, is understandable, given how extensively sampling is used in Top 40 hits and in such styles as hip-hop and electronica. Coming from the pop music scene, it is not clear what Strauss would make of these "underground" artists. Their works certainly do not resemble the formulaic products of Puff Daddy's nostalgia hit factory. Looking for original uses of sampling, he and other critics could benefit from traveling into the peripheral world of sonic thievery. The pieces found there could offer them new insights into pop music, as many of these works comment on pop hits and the mass media environment in which those hits thrive. Negativland, for instance, sampled bits from U2 to satirize its song "I Still Haven't Found What I'm Looking For" and the radio play that made the tune a success – a satire that led to legal action by U2's label Island Records. In a strange twist, many mainstream groups, including some represented by Island, have sampled without permission works by these theft artists. In other words, they have stolen from the thieves.[9]

Getting past that hypocrisy, the question arises: why would such popular groups turn to these fringe artists? One answer is that they have found rich bits in the imaginative transformations and dense collages of these musicians, so rich that they cannot help but steal them. Students of quotation should also find these bits intriguing, hearing how Negativland and other thieves have taken the gesture to extremes. In their works, quotation – in terms of both the choice of borrowed sources and the uses made of those sources – has reached new limits, points

---

musicians working with stolen materials, including Emergency Broadcast Network, Tom Zé, Otomo Yoshihide, Thievery Corporation, Kopyright Liberation Front, and musicians involved in the CD *Deconstructing Beck* (1998 and released by Illegal Art), which, as the title suggests, takes apart songs by Beck. It should also be noted that these peripheral musicians are not the only ones who "steal." Given how popular sampling is, everyone does so; the technique is so common and pervasive that there is no way all samples can be cleared. Mainstream pop acts have had little problem using materials without permission. Thievery artists, though, stand apart because they make a point of stealing and build their cultural commentary around that act.

[7] See the program published for the 1988 Festival in London. Stewart Home, *The Festival of Plagiarism* (London: Sabotage Editions, 1989).

[8] Vittore Baironi quoted in Todd Kimm, "Meet the Tape-beatles," *Icon*, 6 January 2000, http://www.iconquest.com/backs/%212000/01-06-00/cover.htm (9 January 2000).

[9] Such cases include The Orb's sampling of the Tape-beatles' track "Beautiful State" in the song "Plateau" from their *Live 93* CD.

at which we hear the gesture in new ways. Theft musicians have also taken quotation into new cultural realms. They have enlisted quotation in a battle raging around us. Some listeners may not be aware of the battle, but we are all familiar with the battlefield. These musicians have joined a larger fight against the mass media, a force that various artistic and political groups have seen as over-running modern life. In that fight, quotation, or creative theft, has proven to be a valuable weapon.

These cultural assaults and sonic extremes can be better understood by first discussing sampling in general and its role in the tradition of quotation. Sampling is a means of recording, storing, and manipulating sounds.[10] That basic definition applies to a variety of other technologies, including the tape recorders used by Stockhausen and *musique concrète* composers. The term sampling, though, has been most closely associated with digital technologies that became commercially available in the mid 1980s. That technology allows a sound to be converted to digital data and stored within a computer memory, which preserves it with the fidelity of a compact disc. These sounds can be accessed either at a computer or, as is common in performance situations, through an intermediary keyboard. In either case, musicians often transform the sounds by altering their digital signatures, a reconfiguration that can give the sounds whole new identities.

In pop music, sampling has been used in two general ways. First, many musicians have isolated individual performance sounds, say a bass line, cymbal crash, or vocal cry. Edited and combined together, these parts can create a whole that is more impressive than the sum of its parts. For instance, five or six drum sounds – say classic hi-hats and bass drums – can be put together on one track to "get stuff that a real drummer just can't play."[11] Such amalgams of sampled parts are prevalent in techno styles, in which two stationary guys at a console can produce a body-shaking groove. Sampling musicians have also sought larger prey, working with longer and more involved sounds, such as the Joni Mitchell vocal line used by Janet Jackson. These fragments are not anonymous building blocks, like an isolated rim shot, that disappear into the groove. They are instead interlopers that stand out in the mix, creating a constant give-and-take between the associations of the original source and those of the new surroundings. In other words, these extended samples are quotations.

That designation is pretty apparent. What is not so clear is how sampling fits into the tradition of borrowing. Quotation – recalling – is a

---

[10] For a historical account of sampling and its relationship to earlier electronic idioms, see Hugh Davies, "A history of sampling," *Organized Sound* 1 (1996), 3–11.

[11] Tom Rowlands quoted in Micallef, "The Chemical Brothers," 80.

two-sided gesture: the original and the transformation. With sampling, both sides are expanded: material can be quoted from more sources, and more can be done with it.[12] A computer can hold an unprecedented array of sounds. Sound is the key word. For with sampling, musicians can borrow sound, not just melodies, rhythms, or harmonies. Why use just the melody of "Big Yellow Taxi," when you can have Joni Mitchell singing that melody? The ability to draw upon specific sounds, be it those of a certain performer or those of everyday life, adds new dimensions to quotation. Sampling has also brought new dimensions of transformation. Not only can any sound be borrowed, but also, with the capabilities of computer editing, almost anything can be done to that sound. Mitchell's voice, not to belabor a point, could just as easily be turned into a shrieking bird. Jackson's producers, though, avoid such radical transformations, which would only defeat the purpose of borrowing such a recognizable sound. They lightly shade Mitchell's voice, so that it comes across as a distant, worn old record. In the new digital world of 1997, "Big Yellow Taxi" is an old record as well as a distant memory of a more simple acoustic folk style. The effect of the quotation – nostalgia – is a traditional one, but the focus – sound borrowed and sound transformed – captures the new possibilities offered by sampling.[13]

That new focus has brought new critical attention to quotation. Sampling has frequently been viewed in the light of theories of postmodernism. Indeed, few discussions of the technique do not wander into that theoretical territory.[14] These critical excursions often prove insightful, but they just as often prove shortsighted.[15] In the vast space that they see opened up by digital technologies, many theorists have lost

---

[12] Earlier analog technologies of course can also hold an array of sound and be used to transform them in a multitude of ways. Stockhausen's 1960s works make that point clear enough. Indeed, much of what the theft artists have done can be accomplished with analog equipment. In fact, the Tape-beatles' works prior to 1997 are almost all analog. With digital sampling, though, these capabilities have been expanded. Most importantly, digital technology is more readily available and more practical to use. Musicians from different backgrounds – classical, techno, and rap – can draw upon sampling technologies, a development that has made electronic quotation prevalent and also varied in its different forms.

[13] So quick to accuse Puff Daddy of nostalgia, Strauss fails to recognize how the treatment of the Mitchell sample creates that sensation. Strauss, "Sampling is (a) creative or (b) theft?," 28.

[14] See in particular Peter Wollen, "Ways of thinking about music video (and postmodernism)," *Critical Quarterly* 28 (1986), 167–70; and Paul Théberge, "Random access: music, technology, postmodernism," in *The Last Post: Music After Modernism*, 150–82.

[15] For a critique of many assumptions underlying postmodern accounts of sampling, see Andrew Goodwin, "Sample and hold: pop music in the digital age of reproduction," *Critical Quarterly* 30 (1988), 34–49.

sight of quotation.[16] That space, as described by them, is limitless and made of a single concentrated material. New reproduction technologies, especially computer-based ones like samplers, offer "massive capacity for information storage," a memory bank that can contain an almost immeasurable field of sounds.[17] Sound, particularly recorded sound, is the matter that forms this space, as parts of a recording of one song sit within the recording of another. Here is a realm of pure recordings, the ultimate state of simulacra. In that realm, the line between the original and the reproduction, so long eroded by previous reproduction devices, has now been erased. Recordings of recordings, the nexus of sampling, do away with the idea of an original altogether. For some critics, they may also do away with the act of quotation. Regarding sampling, Peter Wollen states: "Reproduction, pastiche, and quotation, instead of being forms of textual parasitism, become constitutive of textuality."[18] In other words, the act of drawing upon an outside source, which is so crucial to quotation (a parasitic gesture), has been supplanted by a realm of recorded intertextuality, in which different recordings overlap and merge.[19] Quotation is no longer a specific gesture performed by one musician to the work of another but rather it is a ubiquitous act enacted between an unending web of works.[20] So prevalent is quotation that it is everywhere and nowhere at once. In such a state, it has been taken to the points of redundancy and irrelevancy.

In this infinite space of recordings, no one can hear you quote. Or maybe not. The lawyers can hear you. Their accusations of theft announce that a sound has been taken from one recording and placed in another one. That sound has crossed a border, the legal lines of ownership and copyright. Boundaries, the division between the work and the

---

[16] For a study that views sampling as a quotation practice, see Kevin Holm-Hudson, "Quotation and context: sampling and John Oswald's plunderphonics," *Leonardo Music Journal* 7 (1997), 17–25.

[17] Wollen, "Ways of thinking about music video," 169.   [18] Ibid.

[19] Wollen's views accord with the notions of intertextuality developed by Barthes. The latter approaches a text as "a tissue of quotation drawn from the innumerable centers of culture." In that view, there is no clear distinction drawn between the quoting work and the original upon which it draws. Such ideas of source and influence are irrelevant in a space where everything is already connected to dense cultural codes. Barthes, *Image – Music – Text*, trans. Stephen Heath (New York: Hill and Wang, 1977), 146.

[20] This discussion of the relationship between the practice of quotation and theories of intertextuality could be developed elsewhere. The main point to be emphasized here is that such theories often downplay or dismiss clear cases of quotation (x drawing upon y) and instead focus on more open relationships, texts that lie behind or around the corner from each other. One critic who has focused on the act of quotation is Gérard Genette. He sees the practice (along with plagiarism and allusion) as examples of "intertextuality," which for him is one of five subtypes of "transtextuality." Genette, *Palimpsests*, trans. Channa Newman and Claude Doubinsky (Lincoln: University of Nebraska Press, 1997), 1–7.

world surrounding it, are often overlooked in theories of intertextuality, which, instead of discussing the crossing of those lines, focus on the incessant blending of works.[21] By patrolling that line, the lawyers have witnessed only half of the act of quotation: drawing upon a pre-existent piece. They, however, have ignored the transformation and recontextualization of the borrowing that completes a quotation, and creates a new work. Many postmodernist theorists have not perceived even that much. They have not only obfuscated the first half of the gesture with the talk of open recorded space but have neglected the second half as well. Their accounts of sampling pay little, if any, attention either to how the borrowed sounds are altered or to the play of cultural associations between the original and the new work.[22] To do so would involve returning to a mode of "textual parasitism," in which one work isolates, draws upon, and manipulates another one.

Musicians, however, have been more than aware of these aspects of sampling. Rap artists, for instance, have drawn upon samples of such past political figures as Malcolm X to comment on contemporary events and to make young African-American listeners aware of their own past. With samples of James Brown and 1970s funk bands, they have offered similar music history lessons as well. The theft artists discussed in this chapter have perceived sampling as a form of quotation. Negativland refer to their recordings as a "folk art."[23] Folk in the sense that the group sees itself as extending a tradition of taking found items that were used originally for a specific purpose and transforming them into something new with a different purpose (they give as a parallel the example of Caribbean musicians turning old barrels into steel drums). Other musicians have placed themselves directly in the tradition of quotation by evoking the names of Ives and Stravinsky. In either case, Negativland and the others remind us that sampling embraces both old and new. On one hand, it carries on the basic dynamics of quotation, whereas, on the other hand, it brings the gesture into new technological and cultural realms.

One of these new realms is theft. With that topic, Negativland and the previously mentioned theft musicians take center stage in this discussion. Given how unknown these musicians are, some introductions are in order. "An experimental music and art collective," Negativland was formed by four San Francisco musicians in 1979.[24] In their recordings, the group fishes the sonic streams of the mass media, pulling in such

---

[21] As Barthes remarks, the text is "is a multi-dimensional space in which a variety of writings, none of them original, blend and clash." Barthes, *Image – Music – Text*, 146.

[22] This neglect is evident in Wollen, "Ways of thinking about music video"; and Théberge, "Random access."

[23] Quoted in Craig Baldwin, dir., *Sonic Outlaws*, Other Cinema, 1995.

[24] "Negativland bio."

different sounds as popular hits, talk radio programs, commercials, and political speeches – all of which are taken without permission. As the theft half of "creative theft," these materials are rendered "creative" by transforming them and mixing them together in collages. Negativland has turned their satirical collages on targets ranging from the emptiness of classic hits nostalgia radio programming to the psychological manipulation of advertising.

The targets, though, have sometimes turned their attention – legal, not satiric – back on Negativland. In 1991, the group released a single that drew upon the hit song "I Still Haven't Found What I'm Looking For" by U2. Repackaged by Negativland, the rock anthem becomes, among other things, a rock farce, as Bono's swagger is replaced by the whiny speaking voice of one of the band members. The original packager of the tune – Island Records – did not appreciate this new take on their property.[25] They objected not only to the use of samples but also to the actual packaging of the single: a cover prominently featuring the letter "U" and the number "2" bestriding a picture of a U2 spy plane with "Negativland" written below in smaller, but still clearly noticeable, letters. The cover, according to Island, threatened to mislead listeners into thinking that they were buying a U2 recording. Lacking the resources to respond to Island's legal assaults, Negativland gave in to the company's demands. The band was forced to destroy all existing copies, sign copyright over to Island, and pay $25,000.[26] As usual, such corporate bullying ultimately backfired. Negativland became martyrs in the fight for artistic freedom, and its U2 single continues to fly, being available in various locations, most notably on the Internet.

Other artists trawl the media airwaves, although few have faced such high-profile legal actions. The Tape-beatles, a "collaboration" begun in 1987 in Iowa, has similarly built collage works from media fragments and old recordings, which again are sampled without clearance.[27] They subject these materials to "Plagiarism®," the group's trademark technique of creating works from "previously 'finished' works."[28] This brand of plagiarism does not merely copy bits from the media but rewrites them, offering new versions that critique the original media scripts. For instance, the CD *Good Times* (1999) draws upon found

---

[25] Details about and materials relating to the case can be found in Negativland, *Fair Use: the Story of the Letter U and the Numeral 2* (Concord, CA: Seeland, 1995).

[26] In 1992, the group was sued again for its magazine and CD set entitled *The Letter U and the Numeral 2*.

[27] In 1996 The Tape-beatles changed its name to Public Works and released the CD *Matter*. The group returned to its original name in 1998. The Tape-beatles not only produce CDs but also work in video.

[28] "The Tape-beatles: frequently asked questions," http://solo.inav.net/~psrf/faq.html (9 March 1998).

167

sound – Aaron Copland's *Appalachian Spring* and *Fanfare for the Common Man*, a speech by Andrew Carnegie, a trailer for a TV horror film, a Coca-Cola commercial, interviews with food service workers, and Oliver North's testimony before the US Congress – to question the prosperity that the 1990s economic boom had supposedly brought to all segments of American society.

Not only the media airwaves are being scavenged for materials; so are the private airwaves, particularly the ether streams of cell-phone conversations. Scanner, the stage name of the British artist Robin Rimbaud, has used his namesake device to pick up such conversations. Catching voices out of the air is, as Scanner acknowledges, illegal, but if that is the case, he asks, then why make these machines commercially available?[29] They were most likely not made available for the musical purposes for which Scanner has used them. In his recordings and live performances, stolen conversations float in and out of layers of static ambient music. No sooner has one conversation grabbed your attention, than it disappears. These works play off one of the unstated reasons these devices were made available: voyeurism. The musical accompaniment does little to disguise the fact that we are listening to private conversations, hearing the sorrows and anxieties of strangers.[30]

The Canadian composer John Oswald has focused on the more traditional sampling prey of popular recordings. Sampling is just one of Oswald's many musical activities. He also composes acoustic works for orchestra and chamber ensembles as well as performing as an improviser on alto sax. The sampling works, though, have attracted the most attention, both from listeners and, unfortunately, from lawyers. The best known of Oswald's recordings is the 1989 CD *Plunderphonic*, his neologism to describe the practice of selecting and transforming pre-existent recordings. The CD features reworkings of songs by Michael Jackson, Dolly Parton, Bix Beiderbecke, and the Beatles, among others. "DAB," as the title attests, takes apart and puts back together Jackson's song "Bad," and not necessarily in the same order. With this "revised performance," Oswald undoes the precise studio mix, robbing it of the illusion of a live performance and instead revealing it to be, like "DAB" itself, an arrangement of different parts.[31]

Such a critique was lost on Jackson's label, CBS Records, and the Canadian Recording Industry Association (CRIA), which together accused him of violating copyright. Oswald, for his part, had attempted to avoid

---

[29] "Scanner: scanning for realism, and those real juicy bits!" http://geekgirl.com.au/geekgirl/008fruit/scanner.html (22 July 1999).

[30] Scanner does edit out personal references in his recordings.

[31] John Oswald, "Bad relations: plunderography, pop, and weird in DAB," *Musicworks* 47 (1990), 9.

such charges by distributing the CD without charge to libraries and interested individuals and by citing all of his sampled sources. Those precautions made no impression on CBS and the CRIA. The legal skirmish that ensued would serve as a prelude to the Negativland/Island affair. The Oswald case even features an offending album cover, which offered a visual "plunderphone" of Jackson's face grafted on to the naked body of a white woman. As with the Negativland cover, this one was not going to mislead even the most dimwitted of Jackson fans. It only served to nettle CBS. Both the label and the CRIA acted quickly and forcefully. Unable to engage the attack, Oswald settled to their terms, which included destroying the master recordings and all available copies. Such measures again proved shortsighted. The CD is still available, floating around in cyberspace, and Oswald, another martyr to creative freedom, is still plundering recordings.[32]

While working in different idioms, these musicians, particularly Negativland, the Tape-beatles, and Oswald, are united by a rhetoric of theft and an opposition to copyright. "Creative theft," "plagiarism," and "plunderphonics" are just that – rhetoric. These musicians emphasize that they are not really stealing, meaning that, contrary to the accusations of CBS and Island Records, they are not attempting to pass off their works as those of other musicians so as to cut into their earnings.[33] The bandying of theft turns the tables on such accusations. What kind of plagiarism announces up front that it consists of other people's works and then proceeds to transform those sources into something new? This

---

[32] For Oswald's account of the case, see Norman Igma, "Taking sampling 50 times beyond the expected," *Musicworks* 48 (1991), 16–21. A discussion of the CD and of Oswald's sampling practices in general can be found in Chris Cutler, "Plunderphonia," *Musicworks* 60 (1994), 6–19.

[33] This point and the ones discussed in the paragraph below can be found in the following sources: John Oswald, "Plunderphonics or, Audio piracy as a compositional prerogative," *Musicworks* 34 (1986), 5–8, and "Neither a borrower nor a sampler prosecute," *Keyboard* 14 (March 1988), 12–13; the Tape-beatles, "Plagiarism®," http://soli.inav.net/~psrf/Tb/tapebeatles.html (9 March 1998), and "Plagiarism®: an interview with the Tape-beatles," in *Sounding Off! Music as Subversion/Resistance/Revolution*, ed. Ron Sakolsky and Fred Wei-han Ho (Brooklyn: Autonomedia, 1995), 217–24 (this interview is also available at http://soli.inav.net/~psrf/Tb/interview2.html (9 March 1998)); "Negativland bio," "Changing copyright" (http://www.negativland.com/changing_copyright.html (30 July 1999)), and "Fair Use," in *Sounding Off!*, 91–94 (this essay is also available at http://www.negativland.com/fairuse.html (30 July 1999)). For an essay dealing with these arguments, see Brian Duguid, "The unacceptable face of plagiarism," *EST Magazine*, http://taz.hyperreal.org./intersection/zines/est/articles/plagiari.html (6 March 1998).

For a discussion of the ethical and legal issues raised by sampling, see Thomas Porcello, "The ethics of digital audio-sampling: engineers' discourse," *Popular Music* 10 (1991), 69–84; Simon Frith, ed., *Music and Copyright* (Edinburgh: Edinburgh University Press, 1993); and Schumacher, " 'This is a sampling sport'," 266–69.

irony, as the "quotation" of the ® symbol by the Tape-beatles makes clear, targets copyright. That body of law has been used to brand these musicians as thieves. By assuming that title, they brand the law as narrow and muddled. As one member of the Tape-beatles has explained: "We say we're thieves, but we mean that, under the current topsy-turvy ethics of cultural property, we are thieves."[34]

In opposing copyright, the Tape-beatles and the others have armed themselves with more than thin irony. Each of these musicians has developed acute and convincing arguments. Taking these arguments as a whole, several common planks emerge. First, copyright can and does serve a purpose. The law, for instance, is necessary to stop the bald thievery mentioned above. However, as used now, there is no distinction between pirates copying recordings and artists quoting from those recordings. When applied so blindly, copyright becomes an obstacle to creative expression. As Oswald has quipped: "If creativity is a field, copyright is the fence."[35] That fence is in danger of falling down. Copyright rests upon a distinction between copying and creation. Sampling collapses that distinction. The sampler is at once a copying instrument – a recording device – and a creative instrument – a machine used for transformations.[36] Such a technological undermining demands a rethinking of the law. However, even if these issues are not considered, the present law could accommodate sampling "thievery." These musicians contend that their works fall under the Fair Use provisions of copyright, measures allowing for uses of pre-existing materials ranging from academic citation to artistic parody and critique. Deflating a rock super group, exposing the growing gap between rich and poor, and taking apart the studio perfection of a best-selling pop star are all, these artists would argue, creative expressions that fit within the latter category.

These arguments unfortunately have yet to receive any legal clarification. Given that Oswald and Negativland could not afford to respond to the accusations made against them, their views were never heard in court, a forum that might have been more beneficial to them than to the record companies.[37] But, even though the two cases may not have found their way into the court record, they have made it into the history

---

[34] Quoted in Mark Athitakis, "God and country, remixed: the Christal Methodists and Ralph Johnson turn the rhetoric of politics and religious radio against itself," *sfweekly.com* (14–20 April 1999), http://www.sfweekly.com/1999/041499/music1.html (28 July 1999).

[35] Oswald, "Neither a borrower nor a sampler prosecute," 12.

[36] Oswald, "Plunderphonics," 5.

[37] In a 1990 case, the rap group 2 Live Crew successfully used the Fair Use clause to protect its borrowing of Roy Orbison's "Pretty Woman." The group had the financial resources to pursue the case, which went all the way to the US Supreme Court.

of quotation, where they have much to say about the state of the practice in the late twentieth century. They reinforce the point made earlier that sampling has extended the range of quotation to unprecedented degrees. The talk of theft on both sides testifies to that expansion. Theft denotes transgression, suggesting that quotation has reached into new areas, ones that are considered off limits. Indeed, many of these musicians have taken the mass media as their creative field. With that focus, quotation has reached out beyond the realm of musical works and into the vast sonic world surrounding us. In other words, it has claimed the world in which we live.

Sampling musicians have also broadened the range of quotation by pushing the act of transformation. Oswald and others have altered sampled materials in extravagant ways. Theft, it should be emphasized, is not crucial to achieving such results. Similar alterations, of course, can be done with sanctioned materials.[38] Still, it is noteworthy that theft artists have been among those searching the outer reaches of quotation. They have already raised the stakes by turning it into an act of theft. Not stopping there, these artists push quotation from within, driving it to the point at which it can apparently go no further.

Oswald has explored the limits of density. His *Plexure* CD (1993) packs samples from "several thousand different songs" into a little less than twenty minutes.[39] Lasting a second or less, the samples come across merely as sonic sparks rather than as memories of pop hits. Such distortion is what Oswald was after, as he wanted to take those hits to the "threshold of recognizability."[40] *Plexure* brings us to that point, where the Top 40 resembles a sonic debris field. Oswald was not the first to arrive there. That point looms large not just in digital sampling works but in much electronic music, in which composers have been tantalized by the possibilities of pure abstraction. Stockhausen, for instance, took the USSR anthem to that "threshold" in *Hymnen*. Indeed, in the final utopian section, he tried to take the whole work across that line, only to fail.

In the music of Stockhausen, Oswald, and other samplers, that "threshold" has significant implications for the act of quotation. To cross that line would be to annul quotation. In other words, if the borrowed material is transformed beyond recognition, especially if the original

---

[38] As Oswald demonstrates in his "plunder" recordings that use sanctioned materials, such as *Rubaiyat* (1991), in which Elektra allowed him to ransack its catalog, and *Gray Folded* (1994), in which Oswald was invited by the Grateful Dead to sample and transform their works.

[39] For a discussion of *Plexure*, see Holm-Hudson, "Quotation and context," 23–24.

[40] "Interview with John Oswald," conducted by Brian Duguid in September 1994 for *EST Magazine*. Available at http://taz.hyperreal.org./intersection/zines/est/intervs/oswald.html (22 July 1999).

has never been stated, then there is no evidence of a borrowing. Once altered so severely, the dynamics between original and transformation that define quotation disappear, as all that is left is a strange new sound rather than a transformed old sound. Oswald and the other musicians discussed here have come up with a way of countering that risk: theft. If quotation is in danger of crossing Oswald's threshold, theft is a way of yanking it back from the brink. It reminds us that there is an original, the sound that has been stolen. Refocused on the original, we can appreciate more the ways in which it has been altered, changed not just by sonic operations but by the act of stealing itself. Theft gives a sound new associations. It is a fetishistic act that surrounds a sound with an aura of illegality. Even the banal becomes interesting when stolen, as interesting and daring as intercepted cell-phone conversations. Both take on new lives as contraband.

But they do not always take on new sounds. Many theft musicians leave their materials relatively untouched. This downplaying of transformation reveals the degree to which theft has switched the emphasis to the original. Alterations would only obscure the original and thereby cover up the crime used to take it. Without any traces of a crime, the aura of illegality would disappear. To prevent that loss, many musicians carefully display their booty. Far from transforming the voices, Scanner tries to get the cell phone signals as clear as possible so that the audience can eavesdrop. The musical accompaniment, a series of repeated hollow sounds with an unobtrusive beat, does not get in the way of this guilty pleasure, leaving us to enjoy the thrill of stolen voices.

This flow of blank sounds and distant voices is not thrilling to every listener, especially Stockhausen. Yes, the grand man of electronic music and the 1990s electronica *Wunderkinder* have come face to face, or recording to recording. For a 1995 interview, *The Wire* sent Stockhausen recordings by a group of "technocrats," including Scanner. In his response, he comments on the musicians' works and recommends a piece of his own for each of them to listen to and learn from. At the end of the interview, the young techno wizards are given the opportunity to respond to the doyen's counsel.[41] With Scanner, Stockhausen wastes no time in getting to his main critique: "I think he should transform more what he finds. He leaves it too much in a raw state." His advice to Scanner is to listen to *Hymnen*, a work that also pulls down sounds from the airwaves. From the play of anthems and short-wave noises, Stockhausen believes that Scanner could learn "the art of transformation."

---

[41] The comments below from both Stockhausen and Scanner come from this interview; "Advice to clever children," *The Wire*, November 1995. I consulted an on-line posting of the article at the address http://www.isa.dknet.dk/~stigbn/stockau.html (22 July 1999).

Respecting his electronic elders, Scanner claims to take some of Stockhausen's remarks "to heart." He objects, though, to the comments about transformation, contending that he does alter materials. The blips and screeches produced by the scanner, he points out, are frequently turned into bass sounds. The human voices, the objects of thievery, are not mentioned. For Scanner, there has to be a recognizable, and apparently controversial, focal point in the electronic mix. Without one, the music could be, as he claims *Hymnen* is, "too abstract," a "barrage of sound against sound."[42]

This generational quarrel centers around a question that is just as pressing now as it was in the 1960s: if real-world sounds are to be incorporated into electronic music, to what degree should they be transformed? The works of Stockhausen and Scanner answer that question with extremes. Stockhausen goes so far as to take us to the moon. In *The Wire* interview, he describes how "the art of transformation" could render sounds "completely new," just "like an apple on the moon." Scanner keeps us on the earth and presents an apple as an apple. It is this lack of transformation, though, that makes his works just as extreme. If Stockhausen and Oswald have charted the "threshold of recognizability," Scanner and other musicians have turned in the opposite direction and reached the threshold of sameness, exploring how close they can get to an original without stating it exactly. Exactness is not what they are after. The placing of the quotations in new sonic environments makes that point clear enough. Theft also precludes exactness; it serves not only as a means of quotation but also as a means of transformation, giving the borrowings new associations. In other words, a plain apple becomes a stolen apple, a much more interesting and tempting fruit.

At these extremes, quotation can collapse. Either the excessive transformations wipe out any trace of the original, or the close fidelity gives no impression of creative alteration, leaving behind what appears to be merely a recording. Not surprisingly, few theft artists have been willing to take these final steps. To do so, they could lose their grip on quotation and, without a firm grip, they would lose their ability to make any sort of cultural commentary. Artists across the century have drawn upon the play between old and new that is produced by borrowings to comment on different cultural areas, including childhood/adulthood and black/white. Theft musicians are no different. Although theft alone makes a huge statement, these musicians are interested in more than just issues of copyright. They have brought quotation into the

---

[42] Scanner does score a few points against Stockhausen: "I wonder about him putting himself into the recording; is it a vanity thing, or part of the process?... At the end there's a recording of him breathing. It's quite uncomfortable – like being inside his head."

fray of a present-day cultural battle, a conflict raging over the mass media.

The sampler is the perfect weapon for this battle. It allows musicians to infiltrate the sonic world of the media and to raid its major centers, including radio and television. Their loot consists largely of voices, all sorts of different voices. Some come from commercials, some from pop songs, and some from cell-phone conversations. These voices say many different things, but, as used by theft artists, they ask one question: how are we, as individuals, doing in this media environment – have our lives been enhanced or have they been effaced?

Before addressing that question, a related but more basic one needs to be raised: why are voices so prominently featured in these works? The answer has much to do with the electronic sound world of recording. Since the early days of electronic music, composers have confronted the abstract, apparently inhuman, quality of the medium. One way to mollify that abstractness has been to humanize it, to add human voices and sounds. With his *Gesang der Jünglinge* (1955–56), Stockhausen rejected the serial lattices constructed from pure electronic sounds in his *Studien I* and *II* (1953 and 1954) and created a more open sonic terrain around which wandered the voice of a boy. This need to humanize electronic styles still presses upon musicians. The voices lifted by theft artists, for instance, not only offer fodder for cultural critique but also serve, like Stockhausen's *Jüngling*, as familiar faces in the foreign digital spaces. Many popular musicians have felt similar pressures.[43] In his 1999 CD *Play*, the techno star Moby mixed dance beats with samples from field recordings of southern African-American musicians done by Alan Lomax.[44] Like Stockhausen, Moby has been looking for some human element to counter the studio precision of the CD, and what could be more "human," or less techno, than the blues and sacred music of forgotten back-roads black musicians?

Sidestepping the loaded cultural assumptions underlying his sampling, Moby's CD ironically suggests how less human these most human sounds have been rendered in their new surroundings. Sampled in a dance track, these voices have been taken from their original "fields," spliced into small licks, and locked in static loops. They have become, in other words, just another repeating sound in the mix.[45] This digital

---

[43] For a cry against the deadening mechanistic quality of techno styles, see Michiko Kakutani, "Escape artists," *New York Times*, 6 July 1997, magazine section, p. 14.

[44] Moby samples tracks from Lomax's 1961 collection *Sounds of the South*.

[45] Repetition is the key word. Moby's tracks bring together two idioms built upon repetition, but which approach repetition in very different ways. Techno dance music repeats four- and eight-measure units and creates variety by layering additional melodic and/or rhythmic lines with each repetition. Blues styles repeat individual phrases (like those of the A sections in the AAB twelve-bar chorus) and achieve variety through

standardization reinforces a point made by *Gesang* and other early electronic pieces: human elements may soften electronic idioms but only at the expense of their human qualities. Far from being only the unavoidable and unacknowledged outcome that it is in Moby's recordings, this dehumanization is a starting point for theft musicians. To the question posed above about the media and the individual, these musicians assert that the media have a dehumanizing effect. They convey that message through various means. First, voices are stolen (or quoted) and purposely hollowed out in the recorded space, made to sound isolated and fragmented. Second, the voices are placed in media and technological scenarios, which further deplete them. Ranging from cell-phone conversations to infomercials, these scenarios portray sonic worlds in which the voices and thoughts of individuals are slowly being eroded.

In the works of Scanner, one simple piece of technology is all that is needed to wear down those voices and thoughts. A track from the recording of a live 1995 London performance gives us a good idea of how his musical setting of stolen conversations works.[46] Scanner's live performances revolve around the tuning in of clear calls. When such a prize is claimed, a new musical section usually begins. The "umirvelt" track starts with a discussion between two women that dabbles in the quotidian, focusing on the crying of a baby. The accompaniment is both sparse, so as not to overwhelm the voices, and evocative, perhaps to offset the commonplaces. Scanner's background works within the conventions of ambient music, an idiom that features long sustained electronic sonorities that pass through and over each other, short repeating melodies, exotic sounds, and spoken voice samples (not necessarily stolen voices). In "umirvelt," he presents a four-note melody around which dive sonic glissandos, one of which sounds like a woman moaning. The tables are eventually turned as the conversation fades into the background and the mix by itself takes center stage for several minutes. In this extended passage, more layers are added and the melody is broadened. The mix is quickly scaled back to its original thinness as soon as the next clear call is captured. This new conversation between a man and a woman proves rather uninteresting and one-sided, and when it ends, so does this section of the performance.

In Scanner's ambient settings, the conversations – so personal to the people on both ends – become anonymously impersonal. The talk of

constant melodic and timbral variation (such as pitch inflections). By isolating individual phrases from the original blues recordings, Moby freezes that process, giving us a single phrase that is never varied as it was in the original performance. Deprived of those variations, the sampled phrase becomes just as static as the instrumental and rhythmic layers in the electronic mix. In other words, it has become part of the machine.

46 Scanner, *Sulphur* (sub rosa vista 2 sr 95). The performance was recorded at the Purcell Room at the South Bank Centre on 11 March 1995.

babies, jealousy, buying milk, and illness dissolves into just that – talk. The scanner, no matter how precise, cannot pick up the personalities and emotions fueling those voices, those human elements becoming mere chaff. This voiding is what happens when human interaction is entrusted to technology, when it is thrown into the airwaves. The hollow chatter becomes even more hollow when backed up by the vacuous electronic accompaniment. Thrown into this mix, the callers themselves soon become vacuous electronic sounds. Scanner's works not only drain the humanity out of voices, they also rip away our "illusion of privacy," the belief that there are moments and spaces in which we are alone.[47] With technological eyes and ears around every corner, that private space has shrunk, if not disappeared. We may not have to worry about Big Brother, but a nosy techno musician armed with a scanner is worrisome enough.

Warnings about dehumanization and lack of privacy have become modern-day clichés. What gives them some urgency in Scanner's recordings is the act of theft. With Scanner and other theft musicians, the means of borrowing becomes central to the cultural critique. Theft rattles listeners and stirs anxieties about technology. It particularly arouses an age-old fear that machines can rob us of personal qualities, a fear as old as the beliefs that the camera can steal a soul or the phonograph a voice. In today's world, that fear hovers around the computer, particularly the figure of the hacker, who has become the bogeyman of the digital age. Sneaking through the Internet labyrinth, these phantoms – known, if at all, by computer or science fiction names – can ransack the data of our lives. With his own technological moniker, Scanner calls to mind a hacker. Like one of them, he turns technology against us and preys on us from afar, an unknown presence that listens to our personal conversations. Hackers, however, do not drag us into the crime. Scanner makes us listen to this theft, to partake of it. Implicated in the thievery, we may begin to see privacy and individuality as "illusions."

"John Oswald" is not the name of a hacker but that of a real person. Appropriately, Oswald deals not with anonymous figures in his works but with real people – that is, people we know, or know of, like Michael Jackson and Dolly Parton. But are these people, pop culture celebrities, more real than the nameless cell-phone users? The question is irrelevant. As interpreted in theft works, both are individuals. The two just happen to sit on different sides of the mass media: the private people who place their voices in supposedly private airwaves and the public personalities who huckster in the very public airwaves. Whatever side they occupy, these people suffer the same fate: their individuality is effaced.

---

[47] "Scanner: Scanning for realism, and those real juicy bits!"

Oswald's *Plunderphonic* CD is an affair of individuals. On the back cover, the titles of the tracks share equal billing with the composers and/or performers of the sampled recordings, a diverse group ranging from Anton Webern to Cecil Taylor. For many listeners, these atonal celebrities take a back seat to the roster of pop stars, which includes Jackson, Parton, Bing Crosby, James Brown, and Elvis Presley. Those listeners, though, won't hear these stars as they have heard them so many times before. Oswald puts them under a new light, in which we perceive them as media packages, nothing more than sounds and images assembled together and sold to the public. By "plundering" and transforming these valuable commodities, he undoes the music-business glue and rearranges the pieces, so that we hear one bit of a hit tune here and another bit there. What we hear is how artificial the individuality of Michael Jackson the pop star is, so artificial that an unknown Toronto musician can easily disassemble it and either make a new individual from the different pieces or erase that person altogether.

Theft is again crucial to this erosion of individuality. As with Scanner's works, the unauthorized use of a voice suggests violation. Oswald does not steal Jackson's privacy – the tabloids have already done that – rather he takes the star's most distinct and profitable qualities, his sound and image. With that theft, the old superstitions about recordings and cameras stealing a person's essence resurface. Through sampling, Oswald has taken the voice of a star, a voice that he now controls and with which he can do whatever he wants. The one-of-a-kind voice defines the star performer, is how we know him or her. The star in many ways is that voice. By controlling the voice, Oswald controls the essence of that performer. His "plundering" focuses on essential qualities of these individuals, including voice and gender. His "revised performance" of Parton's "The Great Pretender," for instance, revises the singer's gender by slowing down the speed of her voice until it becomes "a handsome, slightly more elegiac tenor."[48] At the end of the song, Parton the country diva and the newly created male Parton sing side by side.[49] The CD cover photograph of Jackson performs another gender revision by grafting Jackson's head onto the body of a naked woman, giving us a new Jackson, one to compete with Michael's numerous surgical revisions of himself.

With "DAB," Oswald surgically alters Jackson's voice and then removes him from his own song. To appreciate that procedure, the listener should keep in mind Stockhausen's *Gesang*, which Oswald asks

[48] Oswald, "Neither a borrower nor a sampler prosecute," 14.
[49] The gender switch can also be heard as a comment on Parton's cover version of this song, which was originally recorded by the Platters in 1955. It could also poke fun at the artificiality of Parton's gender persona. Her big hair and breasts and her outrageous outfits call to mind a drag queen, whose "covered" voice has finally been released.

us to do by listing the piece as a reference point to the song in the liner notes. There are some strong similarities. Both Stockhausen and Oswald work with the very familiar, be it the *Benedicite* derived from the story of the youths thrown into the fiery furnace or a recent chart topper. Both composers play off this familiar material against the foreign electronic surroundings, constantly moving between "a general similarity between the source material and abstraction."[50] Part of that abstraction involves diffusing the vocal parts into a series of phonemes. There is, however, one key difference between the two: Stockhausen's *Jüngling* lives, whereas Jackson disappears. In *Gesang*, the boy, like the Biblical youths, withstands the electronic fire, his voice sounding until the very end of the work. In "DAB," that fire consumes Jackson, leaving behind almost no trace of him.

This incineration occurs over the course of three formal sections, which Oswald calls "Revised, Improvised, and Homogenized."[51] "Revised" is a rather understated way to describe the extensive transformations of "Bad" that open the work. The term also fails to capture the prankish spirit of those changes. Most mischievous is the prominent bass line, which has been "re-ordered." No club dancers are going to be able to follow this new order, as the one-measure groove that supported the original now goes herky-jerky (see Ex. 5.1).[52] The pitches have been scrambled and the meter constantly changes, hopping between regular and irregular patterns. The vocal part has also been "revised." Oswald statically repeats isolated words, such as the opening pounding of "bad," or scrambles the words and pitches to form new melodic lines. These rewrites prove nonsensical and laughable. For instance, Jackson's taunt "your butt is mine" becomes "your butt is love" (Ex. 5.1).

The bass and vocal parts have each been "re-ordered" but that doesn't mean that they follow the same order. The two start off relatively connected – the pickup note in the vocal phrase occurs at the end of each measure – but they diverge increasingly. According to Oswald, "this lack of synchronization was intentional."[53] As mentioned earlier, the alterations comment on the illusory perfection of multi-track recordings which suggest a full ensemble playing together rather than a compilation of independently recorded parts. Oswald takes apart that mix and gives us the individual parts, which are now very much independent, as

---

[50] John Oswald, "Bad relations," 10.

[51] The following details about "DAB" have been taken from Oswald, "Bad relations," 9. Another discussion of "DAB" can be found in Holm-Hudson, "Quotation and context," 20–23.

[52] The groove could be heard as a two-measure unit, in which the second measure is a rhythmic variant of the first, particularly in the use of an eighth-note rest to begin the measure.

[53] Oswald, "Bad relations," 9.

Ex. 5.1

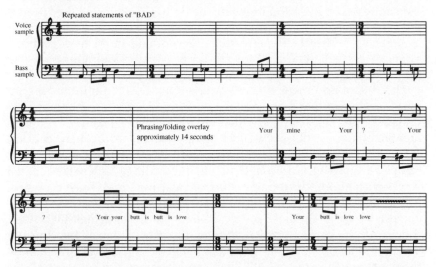

Adapted from transcription in Kevin Holm-Hudson, "Quotation and Context:Sampling and John Oswald s Plunderphonics,"
Leonardo Music Journal 7 (1997), 20.

they sound in new, often fractious, relationships. Instead of all of these parts being coordinated so as to support and highlight Jackson, he is now just one in a frenzy of parts.

The next section, "Improvised," discombobulates the studio mix even more. The improvisation is not done by Oswald but by a machine. Oswald sets up a CD player search function within a narrow range in the original and has the device shuffle between minuscule bits, less than a second in length. This mechanical flight of invention results in a ricochet of fragments, most of them vocal, which Oswald makes even more clamorous by double-tracking those fragments. The act of improvisation, especially when it is based on chance, and the resulting sonic fracas strike even deeper at the ideals of studio smoothness. As Oswald claims, "perfection has been messed with by improvisation."[54]

The identity of Michael Jackson has also been "messed with." As described above, the individuality of superstar performers like Jackson rests upon distinct qualities, such as voice and image. That voice possesses a uniqueness that by itself identifies the musician, no matter how much the tunes or styles change. For Jackson, it is the high pitch "whews," the soulful and tremulous falsetto, and percussive exhalations that make the star. Those sounds are him, or, to turn things around, he is those sounds. Oswald elaborates upon that point in *Plexure*. That recording operates on the premise that all a listener needs to

[54] Ibid., 10.

recognize a performer or song is less than a second of the timbre of either one (an observation ironically made while exploring the "threshold of recognizability").[55] Timbre – the unique sound – is how we know a musician.[56] Therefore, performers are nothing more than timbre – so much so that they can be reduced to minuscule amounts of that property.

This line of argument is also borne out in "DAB." Both the "improvised" section of that piece, and the opening "revised" part concentrate on speck samples, most of which bear the distinct Jackson vocalisms mentioned above. "Dabs" of Jackson are all we need. There is a key difference, though, between *Plexure* and "DAB." The former amasses samples from over a thousand separate recordings, whereas the latter works with hundreds of fragments from just one tune. Given the use of a single source, it might be expected that the individual parts in "DAB" could add up to a whole roughly similar to the original. Of course, they never do, because Oswald has so impishly "revised" the song. Or maybe, as "DAB" suggests, the parts are the whole, as they are all that there is for us to know of both "Bad" and Jackson. The latter is nothing more than a group of distinct sounds.

Going further in this dismantling of the star's individuality, "DAB" presents Jackson as nothing more than a sound in general. In "Improvised," the vocal sounds are exactly repeated. That repetition strips the ecstatic vocalizations of any connection with the spontaneity of live performance. They have become an element that can be isolated and endlessly reproduced. In other words, Jackson's voice proves no different from a drum or bass sample. It too can be used here and there and repeated for as long as needed. Oswald never handles the vocal samples in such a regular fashion (nothing is handled in such a way), but he does convey that the voice is only one sound in the mix. It is a sound moreover with which he (or a randomly searching CD player) can improvise, just like an instrumental sample. His improvisation also further eclipses Jackson's presence. Only Jackson supposedly possesses his voice, can use it as he wants. No one else should be able to improvise with it, to handle that distinct and personal timbre so freely. Yet Oswald does play with it, just as he does with the bass line. Not only does the very act of improvisation efface Jackson's individuality but so do the results. The improvised section builds to a climax of density, in which vocal and instrumental fragments are piled on top of each other.

---

[55] Norman Igma, "Recipes for plunderphonics: an interview with John Oswald," *Musicworks* 47 (1990), 4; and Duguid, "Interview with John Oswald."

[56] A discussion of sampling and timbre can be found in Holm-Hudson, "Quotation and context," 20–24.

So congested is the mix that Jackson's voice becomes almost lost in the chaos; only scraps of it can be heard.

The next step would be to erase the distinctive qualities of Jackson's voice, in other words, to remove Jackson from his own sound. The final "Homogenized" section takes that step. It stands apart from the previous two sections in several ways. Most noticeably, it is not harried by the incessant bass and drum tracks.[57] In this "rhythmically featureless mix" float streams of sound. Those streams are expanded versions of the brief fragments heard earlier, some swollen up to twenty seconds in length. The samples have not only been extended but also blended so that they lose all color and become uniform, hollow sounds. Some of the streams begin with recognizable vocal residue, but those traces are soon purified, made as vacuous as the other sonic clouds. By this point in the song, all traces of Jackson have been effaced, even in his own voice. This gradual depletion reverses the media process that builds upon the one-of-a-kind voice to create the person, or the phenomenon, that we know as Michael Jackson. Moreover, Oswald has turned the studio and recording technologies used to create Jackson against the star, enlisting them now to erase his presence. With "DAB," "very popular music meets its extremities," which, in this case, is a Michael Jackson song that ends without Michael Jackson.[58]

Like Oswald, the Tape-beatles draw upon individuals from the mass media, not stars but the generic voices encountered every day on radio and television. Although nameless, those voices emerge as individuals. In the 1990 *Music with Sound* CD, many of the voices grasp at individuality by claiming an "I" and declaring their desires in sentences beginning with such phrases as "I want" or "I believe." Not only do we hear their desires, we also hear their personal distinct sounds. As in Scanner's works, the sounds of the voices are often not transformed, giving us the real person and not some Oswald "Pretender."[59]

The Tape-beatles, however, do not keep the voices as pristine as Scanner does. They may not alter the sound of the voices, but they do fragment them and rearrange the pieces. More intriguingly, these anonymous "I's" find themselves in new surroundings, having been extracted from their original sources and replanted in collages littered with other mass media debris. Such transplantations offer a means of exploring what happens to individuals in the media din. It is a question that the group has addressed in both writings and music. Member Ralph

---

[57] This stillness has been heard earlier in the "vowel composite field" that closes off the first section of the piece. That "field" blends Jackson's voice into cloudy sounds and prefigures the final "Homogenized" section.

[58] Oswald, "Bad relations," 10.

[59] The voices are occasionally distorted, as in the tracks " . . . of rebellion" and "XT92-007."

Johnson has described how the media "creates an 'empty affect'" around texts and voices that "saps" them of any "original feeling."[60] Several of the group's recordings simulate this "empty affect," an emptiness that engulfs the lone individuals thrown into the collage.

Such is the case with three successive tracks from *Music with Sound*: "Stress," "Coma," and "Creditwise." "Stress" samples from an uncredited source the voices of everyday people describing how work and personal pressures have riven their lives, to the point that one woman cannot "go on living" and another has even been "ready to kill." "Coma" has us ready to laugh. This track consists of what appears to be a thirty-one-second pilfer from a soap opera, a formulaic scene in which a tearful woman is about to make a bedside confession to a comatose loved one. Her confession turns out to be concerns about her credit rating, as an abrupt cut flips the channel from the soap opera to a commercial about credit. In "Creditwise," we hear more personal anxieties, as one actor worries how he will "pay the bills" and another frets over being able to afford "sharp-looking ski clothes." Their salvation is credit, which will allow them to "have more and enjoy more."

Of the individuals in these three tracks, those in "Stress" would appear to stand apart. They are everyday people expressing real concerns, not creatures of melodrama or shill. "Stress," however, blots out that genuineness by backing up these speakers with a cheap Latin dance track, which harries them back into the rat race, now a demented conga line. With this Latin bombast, the Tape-beatles are not laughing at these obviously troubled individuals but rather what can be made of their anguish. "Stress" makes it not too hard to imagine these confessions, like the fake ones in "Creditwise," ending up in a commercial, perhaps one for a pain reliever. The dance track may be too crass for a commercial, but it is not that far off the mark. After all, no advertisement would ever just let these people speak by themselves. Something has to be added to exaggerate the pain and pressure from which the product will deliver them. Hearing the testimonies in "Stress" alongside the canned ones in "Coma" and "Creditwise" makes such commercialization seem not too unlikely. In this company and with the banal Latin backdrop, the pained voices come across as just as vacant as those of soap opera characters and advertisement lackeys. With a few new sounds, the "empty affect" of the mass media can be put into action, draining the personal from personal confessions.

It is not just the people in the media who lose their individuality; none of us can escape its unrelenting blast. As the Tape-beatles and Negativland describe it, the media is a one-way flow at the end of

[60] Ralph Johnson, "Plagiarism from my perspective," *Photostatic Magazine* 31 (May 1988) http://soli.inav.net/~psrf/CVS/Plagiat3.html (28 July 1999).

which we have been reduced to "sponges," helplessly soaking up its messages.[61] The two groups and the other artists discussed here offer a means of resisting that fate and of regaining one's individuality. Rather than absorbing the media, they "steal" from it, selecting what they want, not what is forced upon them, and, even more subversively, they transform the goods, turning them into their own products.

This thievery and re-branding remind us that quotation, be it of commercials or Bach, can serve as a way of challenging authority and of asserting individuality. Adorno, on the other hand, argued that quotation courts authority, describing it along the lines of an academic citation: "As in all other areas of human knowledge, the quotation represents authority."[62] There is, however, a key difference between academic and musical quotation. Academic writers may quote from sources but they never (or, obviously, should never) alter them, while composers do (or should do). That act represents a means of exerting control over the authority of past masters by showing how the composer can fit their music into his or her own piece. Rarely does a composer attempt to knock those masters off their pedestal and claim him- or herself the superior artist, but quotation still involves the composer asserting his or her presence by manipulating past works. Theft artists, in contrast, do attempt to topple authority, not past masters but the media and giant corporations. Their stealing and transforming similarly proclaim their creative presence, an avowal that is crucial in resisting the passivity of media consumption. Some of these musicians have described their molding of media bits as "a liberation" and "empowering," hardly the words of "sponges."[63]

Also "empowering" is the act of throwing these altered chunks back into the media by releasing them on CD or on the Internet. This redirection changes the one-way flow into a two-way process. Traveling against the current, these bits can "jam" the media. In the early 1980s, Negativland coined the term "culture jamming" to describe how their recordings and performances disrupt media messages, just as radio operators block signals with static and other noises.[64] To large corporations, this cultural static may be merely annoying and easy to tune out, but it has proven disruptive, to such an extent that lawyers have been called in to stop it.

Some listeners, in contrast, have tuned in this static and have heard not noise but a critique of the media. By turning the dial to these dissident channels and realizing how the media has manipulated them, they are

---

[61] Negativland, "Fair use," 92; and "Plagiarism®: interview with the Tape-beatles," 219.
[62] Adorno, *The Philosophy of Modern Music*, 48.
[63] Negativland, "Fair use," 92; and "Plagiarism®: interview with the Tape-beatles," 219.
[64] "Negativland bio."

in a position to be "liberated" and "empowered." As one member of the Tape-beatles has claimed: "where I think we do some good is by pointing out to our listeners that it's possible (at the very least) to think about our society and its mechanisms in a different way, and thereby not wholly succumb to its flickering promise of comfort and prosperity, and make some effort to enrich our internal lives, as well as external lives."[65] Ironically, this "enrichment" comes by listening to the group depict how the media empties our lives. It is the media, though, that ultimately suffers the "empty affect." After listening to the skewing of media debris by the Tape-beatles and Negativland, it is almost impossible to hear radio and television in the same way, so skillfully have the groups laid bare the artificiality and manipulation of the two.

Quotation as resistance. That is a new way of thinking of the gesture. Quotation as a means of connecting with the past, of bridging the gap between high and low: these are some of the roles it has been recognized as playing. To this repertory, we need to add resistance, for that role expands our understanding of quotation as a cultural agent. Specifically, it lets us see how borrowing has been enlisted in a present-day dissent against the media, which one "jammer" has called "the most significant social movement" of the early twenty-first century.[66]

That there is such a movement and that quotation drives it may come as a surprise to some. Many artists and cultural critics, though, have long been aware of this fight. Indeed, several of them are the ones throwing the bombs. Moreover, as they would tell you, the conflict and the weapons are not so new. Similar tactics were used by the Situationist International (SI), an artistic movement active between 1957 and 1972.[67] The SI targeted, among other things, the growing commodification and automation in modern life and how those forces alienated people not only from "the goods they produce and consume, but also from their own experiences, emotions, creativity, and desires."[68] The group developed artistic strategies to combat these developments and to destabilize ruling economics and political systems. One such strategy was *détournement*, or the diversion of mass media forms from their original meanings. Some SI artists, for instance, would "steal," or reuse, pre-existing films or comic strips and add new dialogue to them that propagated their aims.

---

[65] "Steev Hise interviews the Tape-beatles for Synergy," http://soli.inav.net/~psrf/Tb/interview2.html (28 July 1999).

[66] Kalle Lasn, *Culture Jam: the Uncooling of America*™ (New York: Eagle Brook, 1999), xi.

[67] For accounts of the SI, see *On the Passage of a Few People through a Rather Brief Moment in Time: the Situationist International: 1957–1972*, ed. Elisabeth Sussman (Boston: The Institute of Contemporary Art, 1989); Sadie Plant, *The Most Radical Gesture: the Situationist International in a Postmodern Age* (London: Routledge, 1992).

[68] Plant, *The Most Radical Gesture*, 1.

As heard in the works of the Tape-beatles and Negativland, *détournement* lives on. Indeed, the SI has given birth to the legion of present-day "culture jammers," though, unlike the SI, which published manifestos and held conferences, these "jammers" are not an organized movement.[69] The name harbors a disparate group of artists and radicals, loosely connected by an opposition to the media and corporate culture. "Jamming" is above all a movement of individuals. Not only is it populated by isolated artists and groups; it also asserts individuality. The fundamental stance of the movement, as described above, is to stand apart from the media, to take what you want from it, and to turn those media materials into your own products.

"Jammers," however, are not the only ones who hold that position. Some popular recording artists have recently begun talking like "jammers." Beck, a musician who has taken sampling mixes up the album charts, has remarked: "it's a trap to just be solely reactive to these things – the Backstreet Boys, the latest blockbuster film. It's more empowering to take these elements, transfigure them, and create something new. That's what I'm trying to do."[70] Beck's comments can be seen as another example of a mainstream performer drawing upon the ideas and sounds of a fringe scene. By using "jamming" rhetoric, he assumes an outsider status, placing himself on the fringe far away from the Backstreet Boys. To be sure, Beck does not fit the definition of a mainstream artist, and his works are far from formulaic pop; however, from the perspective of the charts, he is much closer to the Backstreet Boys than to Negativland.[71] Beck's putting on the airs of a "culture jammer" does not speak so much of posturing as of how the ideas of "jamming" are emerging from the underground.[72]

[69] For an account of "culture jamming," see Mark Dery, *Culture Jamming: Culture Jamming, Hacking, Slashing and Sniping in the Empire of Signs* (Westfield, NJ: Open Magazine Pamphlet Series, 1993).

[70] Quoted in T'cha Dunlevy, "Pop for the post-ironic age," *Vancouver Sun*, 27 April 2000, sect. C, p. 13.

[71] For a discussion of how many artists try to appear to be "underground" and how the media has made such a scene no longer possible, see Hal Niedzviecki, *We Want Some Too: Underground Desire and the Reinvention of Mass Culture* (Toronto: Penguin, 2000), 79–115.

[72] In the ties made with the "culture jamming" fringe, Beck and his recording company have only ended up being tied in knots of hypocrisy. In 1998, the company Illegal Art released a CD entitled "Deconstructing Beck" that featured the plundering of Beck recordings by a group of "culture jamming" artists, who were undoubtedly motivated by some of the same ideas of "empowerment" and fighting media passivity that were espoused by Beck. Beck's attorneys threatened legal action. It is not clear what Beck himself thought or what steps he would like to have been taken. In a different light, the CD and Beck's own recordings reveal two different cases of how sampling musicians have focused on individuality. In the above quotation, Beck suggests that the combination and transformation of samples "empowers" him, gives him an identity. In

185

How far they will make it out of those depths is not clear. But as seen in the comments of Beck and the many press reports and books on "culture jamming," these ideas have begun to grip the public imagination.[73] If that grip gets tighter, "jamming" has the potential to broaden the scope of borrowing in popular styles. Inspired by these ideas, many musicians could draw more upon media elements and take a critical stance towards the media. For some musicians, borrowing could become, as it has for "culture jammers," more than a practice. It could become an outlook, a way of defining oneself and how one relates to the surrounding media world. It is borrowing that "empowers" Beck, making him a "creator" and allowing him to assert his presence in the empty impersonal space of the media.

Beck may sound like a "culture jammer" with his talk of "empowerment," but he never uses words like theft, plunder, or plagiarism. That omission reveals how more mainstream artists ultimately keep a distance from the fringe, adopting some of its attitudes but not its most radical positions. It also raises the question of what will happen to theft if "culture jamming" ideas become more and more popular. Will there be a surge of illegal borrowings and a rush of lawsuits against musicians? If the present situation is any indication, the answer appears to be no. There is already much unauthorized use of samples – by musicians ranging from major pop acts to kids at home computers – and, given the size of the practice, not much legal action taken against it. Looking at press reports, sampling theft is no longer the hot-button issue it once was. How could it be when recording companies face the new threat of free Internet distribution of songs? Maybe those companies have finally distinguished between quotation and piracy (which, to them, free Internet distribution is), or at least have viewed the latter as the greater danger to their profits.[74]

Undoubtedly, though, there will still be prosecution of unauthorized sampling. Just as there will be bandying of theft by "culture jammers." For them, illegality is crucial to their use of sampling, and that aura must not be allowed to disappear. Indeed, it has not disappeared, and

deconstructing Beck – an artist who, as depicted in the CD, has made himself up from an array of samples of other artists' music – the "jammer" recording is taking apart what he put together. For a different view of this CD and Beck's music in general, see Niedzviecki, *We Want Some Too*, 139–42.

[73] In particular, see Niedzviecki, *We Want Some Too*, and Lasn, *Culture Jam: the Uncooling of America*.

[74] Sampling and internet file-sharing have merged, particularly in the practice of mash-ups, which consist of creating mixes that draw upon samples taken on-line, usually from copyrighted sources. In a typical mash-up, the vocals of one song are combined with the rhythm tracks of another. These mixes abound on the net and have appeared in clubs. On the practice, see Neil Strauss, "Spreading by the Web, pop's bootleg remix," *New York Times*, 9 May 2002, 1.

many "jammers" will not allow it do so, as they continually raise the stakes with their quotations. Recently, five companies refused to press Negativland's 1998 CD *Over the Edge, Volume 3: The Weatherman's Dumb Stupid Come Out Line* partly because of the fear of legal action over the use of some samples.[75] But theft is not just a means of stirring controversy for these musicians, it plays a major role in their music. The cultural commentary on the media and its effacement of individuality is built largely upon that act. Theft also enters into the dynamics of their borrowings, an act that pushes quotation to extremes and sways the relationship between the original and transformation. With their samplings, these musicians have shaped a new approach to borrowing befitting our media environment: creative theft.

[75] See Niedzviecki, *We Want Some Too*, 136.

6

Covered up: borrowing in Sandra Bernhard's *Without You I'm Nothing*

Composer John Oswald has remarked: "Cover versions of popular songs are very perverse things."[1] Cover versions, or cover songs, as they are better known, are the performance by one musician of a song written or made famous by another artist. To Oswald, such renditions are "perverse" in that they reject what he considers to be the defining element of a popular song: the original performer's distinct sound. It is that sound, and not a memorable tune or rhythm, that attracts Oswald. "DAB," for instance, is more about Jackson's sound – the falsetto, the whoops, the breathiness – than anything else in "Bad," including the bass line that Oswald scrambles. Only that sound will do.

Comedienne Sandra Bernhard also finds cover songs perverse, but in very different ways from Oswald. That is what she makes of such songs in her 1990 film *Without You I'm Nothing*, which strings together a series of episodes in which Bernhard performs songs intimately connected with other artists.[2] Many of her performances could be considered perverse in the ways she steers the original songs in sexual directions, ones usually considered prurient. Dressed as Dionne Warwick, she interrupts a Bacharach medley with asides about oral sex, bisexuality, and drag queens. Other renditions come across as perverse for being so odd. To a slow folksy version of Prince's "Little Red Corvette," a loinclothed Apollo and a chorus of hippie girls dance around Bernhard wrapped in the American flag. Unlike Oswald, Bernhard shows no interest in the unique sounds of the original performers. She always sounds like herself. Nor does she focus much on the tunes and rhythms of the borrowed songs, meaning that she does not involve herself in manipulating those elements in the highly personal and free ways that many popular music and jazz performers do. To be blunt, Bernhard lacks the musical imagination and vocal technique for such elaborate reworkings, though her self-consciously awkward singing does intriguingly contort

---

[1] Duguid, "Interview with John Oswald."
[2] John Boskovitch, dir., *Without You I'm Nothing*, M.C.E.G. Productions, 1990.

these songs. But she turns a rich comedic and theatrical imagination on those tunes, drawing upon elements other than pitch and rhythm. In her high-fashion impersonations of these performers, image – the unique look rather than sound – yields ample material. Bernhard works with not only the looks and clothes of the stars but also the cultural associations of their images, particularly, as the above examples illustrate, the makeup and outfits of sexuality, gender, and race worn by those celebrities.

Just as Oswald transforms the distinct voices of pop stars, Bernhard molds the image and cultural elements surrounding those voices. According to Oswald, transformation – the ability to make "something new" out of something old – is what places his plunderphonics in a tradition of musical borrowing as "old as music itself," one including everything from the parody Mass to Stravinsky.[3] That tradition apparently does not include cover songs, which Oswald shrugs off as perversities. Yet cover songs, especially in creative and perverse hands, thrive on transformation, as demonstrated in the singular reconceptions of Cole Porter songs in the multi-artist compilation *Red Hot and Blue* CD.[4] Assuredly, there are the stereotyped "cover bands" that mimic Top 40 hits and thrive in hotel lounges and third-rate clubs. Bernhard ironically stages her act in such a club, a fictitious Parisian Room in Los Angeles. Her cover fare, however, rises well above the lounge circuit, reminding us how provoking such fare can be.

If we were looking only for examples of cover songs, then we could admittedly spend our time better elsewhere, say in the *Red Hot and Blue* CD. What is so fascinating about Bernhard's work is that it uses borrowings to comment on the act of borrowing.[5] That commentary turns around questions of who, how, and what. Who can borrow? Specifically,

---

[3] Oswald, "Neither a borrower nor a sampler prosecute," 12.

[4] For a discussion of the Porter covers, see Katherine Bergeron, "Uncovering Cole," *repercussions* 4/2 (1995), 10–29.

[5] For such a prominent facet of the film, borrowing has surprisingly not received much attention in the critical literature on the work. That literature has been produced within the larger field of cultural studies and focuses on issues of sexuality, race, and gender in the film. The following works discuss the film and will be referred to in this essay: Lauren Berlant and Elizabeth Freeman, "Queer nationality," *boundary* 2/19 (Spring 1992), 149–80; Cynthia Fuchs, " 'Hard to believe': reality anxieties in *Without You I'm Nothing, Paris Is Burning*, and 'Dunyementaries,' " in Chris Holmlund and Cynthia Fuchs, eds., *Between the Sheets, in the Streets: Queer, Lesbian, Gay Documentary* (Minneapolis and London: University of Minnesota, 1997), 190–206; bell hooks, *Black Looks: Race and Representation* (Boston: South End Press, 1992), 37–39; Tania Modleski, "The white Negress and the heavy-duty dyke" in Diana Heller, ed., *Cross Purposes: Lesbians, Feminists, and the Limits of Alliance* (Bloomington and Indianapolis: Indiana University Press, 1997), 64–82; Z. Isiling Nataf, "Black lesbian spectatorship and pleasure in popular cinema," in Paul Burston and Colin Richardson, eds., *A Queer Romance: Lesbians, Gay Men and Popular Culture* (London and New York: Routledge, 1995), 57–80;

who is entitled to borrow from a cultural tradition – someone on the inside or someone on the outside of that tradition? That question comes up in Bernhard's parodies of white musicians appropriating black styles and songs. Cross-cultural borrowing is obviously a vexing issue, and, not surprisingly, Bernhard arrives at several, and often contradictory, responses to her query. Those responses also return us to the relationship between whiteness and blackness, offering us another opportunity to see how borrowing can shape that relationship.

How to borrow? This study has answered that question in many different ways. Particular attention has been paid to how borrowing lends itself to certain sentiments or rhetorical practices, such as nostalgia and signifying. To that group can be added camp. As discussed here, camp forms a unique style of borrowing, one that takes the dated and often empty debris of popular culture, be it a once-trendy hairstyle or a Bacharach tune, and gives it new life with jolts of irony. These flashes of wit illuminate a distinct approach to borrowing while offering new insights into topics addressed earlier, particularly the uses that can be made of popular culture materials and the relationship between past and present, which, in the brightly-lit makeup mirror of camp, become the tragically out-of-fashion and the mercilessly in-fashion.

The notion of "what" takes a unique form in *Without You I'm Nothing*. The film poses a seldom-asked question: what is the effect of constant borrowing, like that practiced by Bernhard? Borrowing is an act freighted with anxieties about inspiration, particularly the specters of creative desperation and sterility. Rarely, though, are those fears voiced in a work, especially in the dramatic way that they are by Bernhard. At the climax of the film, those anxieties lead to a breakdown that brings both the show and the stream of cover songs to a sudden halt. During these uneasy moments, we are left to ask, as Bernhard seemingly does of herself: "without" the songs and images of other musicians is she "nothing?"

Black and white

Without You I'm Nothing began as a one-woman stage show in New York City during the summer of 1988. In leaping from stage to screen, most shows don't jump that far, settling for a mere filming of a theatrical

Elspeth Probyn, *Sexing the Self: Gendered Positions in Cultural Studies* (London and New York: Routledge, 1993), 150–64; Marlon Riggs, "Cultural healing: an interview with Marlon Riggs," *Afterimage* (March 1991), 8–11; Pamela Robertson, "Mae West's maids: race, 'authenticity,' and the discourse of camp," in Fabio Cleto, ed., *Camp: Queer Aesthetics and the Performing Subject – A Reader* (Edinburgh: Edinburgh University Press, 1999), 403–05; Jean Walton, "Sandra Bernhard: lesbian postmodern or modern postlesbian," in Laura Dorn, ed., *The Lesbian Postmodern* (New York: Columbia University Press, 1994), 244–61.

event that may occasionally break away for offstage shots. Bernhard and director/co-writer John Boskovitch jumped much further. What kind of film they produced is not exactly clear. It does present bits of a Bernhard show performed in front of an audience, yet, at the same time, it has the trappings of a documentary, as Bernhard's manager and friends give us behind-the-scenes scoops on her professional and personal lives. Compounding matters, the show we are seeing is not the New York production, although parts of it are used, but instead a new stage show written for the screen. According to the manager, what we are seeing is Bernhard's next step after her "smash" hit New York run. In yet another twist, this new show is part of a fictional drama about Bernhard's career, about where she has been and where she is going.

The film opens with Bernhard returning to her "roots," a black club – the Parisian Room – in Los Angeles.[6] According to her manager, Bernhard had grown "too grand" after her New York success. The only way to "rein her in" was to put her back in the unglamorous orbit of "upscale supper clubs." Such clubs do not usually present the sort of lavish show put on by Bernhard, which consists of a series of elaborate musical numbers. In these sets, Bernhard, accompanied by a group of black musicians, performs songs made famous by other performers, including Nina Simone, Diana Ross, and Hank Williams, while often dressing as the performers, particularly the black female artists. The songs become backdrops for monologues that veer into all sorts of topics, including safe sex with Warren Beatty, Andy Warhol's estate auction, and Bernhard's vision of America. A description of the individual numbers can be found in Table 6.1, which lists both the borrowed music and scenarios.

Bernhard may have been a success in New York, but she is bombing in Los Angeles. The black audience gathered at the club cannot believe her act, especially her attempts to look like such stars as Ross and Simone.[7] Her self-indulgent stage chatter about her career and white celebrity

---

[6] It is important to keep in mind that the film presents us with two Bernhards: the one on stage and the one behind the camera. It is the former – the cover version of Bernhard, as it were – that engages us in that fictional drama with her singing, monologues, and personal confessions. Never seen but always there is the "original" Bernhard, the woman who co-wrote the film. She has created the stage show and the woman starring in it. Above all, she has conceived of the cover songs and reflections on borrowing that make that show so captivating.

[7] Occasionally some white clubgoers, in particular an older couple, can be spotted in the audience. During the Hank Williams tune, the camera pans back and reveals an audience consisting largely of white clubgoers dressed in cowboy hats and western wear. As opposed to the black audience in the other scenes, this one seems to enjoy Bernhard's performance, seeming not to mind a Jewish performer's kitschy version of a country classic thrown together with her tribute to Andy Warhol. Some white clubgoers can also be spotted in the final striptease.

Table 6.1 *Cover song episodes in* Without You I'm Nothing

Cover Song	Description of Episode
"Four Women"	Bernhard appears in Afro-centric drag and tries to convey the pain of three black women.
"Me and Mrs. Jones"	Bernhard plays the part of a black lounge singer, who has a special female friend and also gets along "so well" with her Jewish piano player.
Bacharach Medley	Bernhard plays the part of a young secretary who has just arrived in San Francisco. Only one day on the job, she has a date with the boss, the man of her dreams whom she will marry.
"You Make Me Feel (Mighty Real)"	Bernhard takes us back to the 1970s with the tale of a young straight guy who is led into a gay disco by a friend. Thanks to poppers and a black male "angel," he discovers a "new world." The episode ends with a farewell to Warhol and other members of the Studio 54 gang.
"I'm So Lonesome I Could Cry" and "On Broadway"	Bernhard's reflections on the Warhol Estate Auction and her own career.
"I Never Meant to Hurt You"	Bernhard looks back at her relationship with Joe.
Diana Ross Medley	Bernhard tells of a passionate night with Warren Beatty, during which she "stops in the name of love" to practice safe sex.
"Do You Wanna Funk"	Through a historical and multicultural pageant, Bernhard pays tribute to the all-powerful funk.
"Little Red Corvette"	Bernhard first performs a slow folk version of the song, replete with allegorical ballet. The episode winds up with her striptease to the original recording.

friends only exasperates them all the more. The audience talks during her sets, scoffs at her, and slowly walks out. Meanwhile, outside the club, a young black woman named Roxanne goes about her daily routine, scenes from which are presented in a series of non-speaking episodes between the stage numbers. The film draws several connections between Roxanne and Bernhard; for instance, they are shown cutting a lock of hair in a similar way in two separate scenes. What exactly the relationship is between these two women is a question that has preoccupied many writers on the film. Different interpretations abound: Roxanne is Bernhard's black double; she is the projection of Bernhard's fantasy to be black; she is the object of Bernhard's sexual desires; or she is a bridge between black and white.[8] The last scene of the film adds to the enigma. Bernhard's show winds up with a striptease, after which all of the audience has left – all but Roxanne, who, unknown to us, has entered the club. As Bernhard nervously looks to her, Roxanne writes in lipstick on the tablecloth: "Fuck Sandra Bernhard" (the ultimate statement from a possible lipstick lesbian). She then walks out of the club, and out of the film, into sheaths of white light, leaving us even more confused as to who she is and, moreover, what she meant with her lipstick curse.

What that curse does is cleave Roxanne and Bernhard apart. It ends any fantasies of a black double or of being black. Bernhard is aware that such fantasies of taking on another identity are endemic in, or emblematic of, American society. In a society dominated by the mass media, it is all too easy for a celebrity to recreate him- or herself as an image, even one that clashes with his or her own background. As an example of such media reincarnation, Bernhard upholds the Jewish Ralph Lifshitz, who took on a new life as Ralph Lauren, WASP couturier. To Bernhard, those who have best realized this fantasy, and have most profited from it, are the white musicians who draw upon black styles and looks. They may not attempt to pass as black, but they come close to it by taking on such sounds and images. The racial and sexual lines that these figures have blurred, Bernhard rips apart. She makes us aware of a gap between, to use two words that appear prominently in the film, the "real" and the "phony."

Cover songs offer a perfect tool with which to expose that gap.[9] Like all borrowing practices, they create a division between the original and the transformation. In cover songs, the original and new versions run the risk of devolving into the "real" and the "phony," the song that everybody knows and the imitation of that song. Talented musicians can redeem the "phony" by giving their covers some essence of individuality. Bernhard has no interest in saving the fake. Quite the contrary, her covers strive to be "phonies." She does what even the most

---

[8] For different views on this relationship, see Berlant and Freeman, "Queer nationality," 173; Fuchs, "'Hard to believe,'" 202–03; hooks, *Black Looks*, 38; Modleski, "The white Negress and the heavy-duty dyke," 73; Probyn, *Sexing the Self: Gendered Positions in Cultural Studies*, 151–56; Walton, "Sandra Bernhard: lesbian postmodern or modern postlesbian," 255–58.

[9] For a discussion of the critical potential of that gap, see Mary Hunter, "What have they done to my song?: work, performance, and meaning – introduction," *repercussions* 4/2 (1995), 7–9.

uninspired cover band would never do, that is, attempt to look like the original performer. Such a masquerade sinks a performance into a realm below cover songs, into that of Elvis impersonators and Beatlemania. Bernhard, though, satirically swerves away from that dead end. She uses touches of fakery to clear creative distance from the original just as other musicians use touches of melodic and rhythmic ingenuity. With the self-aware "bad" singing, awkward movements, and far-from-believable masquerades, her versions are clearly fakes – that is, fake cover songs, not just cover song fakes.

Those fakes, though, are "real" borrowings, in that, like a compelling borrowing, they open up an engaging space between the original and the transformation. That space lays out a playground for Bernhard's bounding wit. In that gap, she butts together different cultural elements. Many of her cover songs deal with the relationship between whiteness and blackness. She focuses on how white musicians have "stolen" black styles and images. Bernhard, of course, is not the first to make that accusation, but she is one of the first to depict these appropriations as hollow and often ludicrous – in other words, as fakes.[10] Indeed, she appears absurd after the charge of theft has been leveled. Her manager makes the farcical claim that Nina Simone, Diana Ross, and other black female performers have "stolen" from Bernhard, only to be answered by Bernhard appearing dressed up as Diana Ross and singing Supremes songs.

Elsewhere, Bernhard goes so far as to point the finger at one partic-ular thief: Madonna. Sharing the bill with her at the Parisian Room is Shoshana, a Madonna knockoff. Characteristically using a fake Madonna to comment on the real one's fakery, Bernhard points to how Madonna has routinely siphoned off black fashions and idioms. In the film, Shoshana appears in a black club and dances, or more accu-rately strips, to clunky rhythmic grooves that sound like those from Madonna hits. The audience appears mildly more interested in her than in Bernhard; at least one man reaches for her cast-off clothes. In either case, the audience reaction is crucial to Bernhard's commentary. She not only makes the charge of theft but also has a jury of black club-goers deliver the verdict. Their looks of boredom and discontent make clear what they think of such appropriations. Those looks further bol-ster Bernhard's case against Madonna, who often surrounds herself with black musicians and actors in her videos, as if to make herself black by association and to suggest that these performers approve of her borrow-ings. In the "Like A Prayer" video, for instance, Madonna runs into the

---

[10] For a discussion of the appropriation of black styles by white artists seeking hipness, see Andrew Ross, "Hip and the long front of color," in *No Respect: Intellectuals and Popular Culture* (New York and London: Routledge, 1989), 65–101.

embrace of a black gospel choir. In the Parisian Room, however, she, or her double, runs into a black wall of scorn.

Bernhard too runs into that wall. The audience is especially contemptuous of her opening number, Nina Simone's "Four Women." Written by Simone during the Civil Rights era, the song tells the tales of a quartet of black women. They include Aunt Sarah, a laborer who suffers in silence; Siffronia, the bi-racial child abandoned by her white father and caught between "two worlds"; Sweet Thing, a young light-skinned prostitute; and Peaches, a not-so-sweet woman who is ready "to kill the first mother [she] sees." Performed as a showstopper, the song is all Simone's. Very few other musicians have covered the tune, realizing how difficult it is to shake it from her grip. Apparently no white singers have performed it – that is, until Bernhard takes the stage at the Parisian Room.

From the opening lines, it is clear that she has no business performing this song. "My skin is black . . . my hair is woolly," she sings as the camera gives very tight shots of her pale skin and straight hair. Actually, we never see her hair, for it is covered up by a large turban that caps an outrageous Afrocentric outfit with a bulbous gourd-like middle that is so big it could hold four women. The outfit looks even more absurd when Bernhard starts to do some sort of African-American inspired dance, which consists of a series of sluggish swoops and terse twitches. The closer Bernhard attempts to get to blackness – song, clothes, and dance – the further removed she becomes. Of course, her appropriation aims to create distance between whiteness and blackness. That gap may explain Bernhard's decision to drop one of the "four women." Never heard from is Siffronia, the child who blends both races. In Bernhard's performance, there is no blending, only distance.

Bernhard also uses her voice to widen that gulf. There is, of course, already a large gap between her voice and Simone's; however, Bernhard uses adroit touches to make the gap even more spacious. The original Simone recording displays the wealth of timbres that the singer utilized. In "Four Women," she creates a distinct vocal portrait of each character, quite a feat given that the separate choruses for all the portraits use largely the same melody, a short phrase only a fourth in range. Moreover, the phrase is shaded differently each time it occurs, even within an individual chorus. When it comes time for Peaches, Simone spits out, to quote the lyrics, "bitter" and "rough" tones that only get more and more so. With the big finale – "What do they call me? They call me Peaches" – her voice, straining in the upper half of the octave range of the song, becomes a rancid holler.

In her cover version, Bernhard sticks very closely to the pitches of the melody. That fidelity is unthinkable to most jazz vocalists, as heard in the melodic and stylistic freedoms taken by the African-American singers

René Marie and Nnenna Freelon in their recent versions of the song.[11] Also unthinkable is Bernhard's lack of timbral change, which amounts to the major difference between her performance and Simone's. She uses the same pure, light voice for all three women. It is a dulcet voice that moves from pitch to pitch with exactitude, unlike Simone's free swerves. With Peaches, Bernhard tries to convey the character's rage through defiant gesticulations, but her voice, no matter how angry she attempts to sound, remains impervious, or perhaps oblivious, to the "bitterness" in the text. Whereas Simone's tone grows "rougher," Bernhard's becomes lighter, especially on the bristling words "rough" and "slaves." This inversion of Simone's performance reveals how perceptively Bernhard keys her changes to defining aspects of the original, focusing on one specific gesture to suggest how hopelessly out of touch she is from that performance. But she is up for the big finish, throwing out her arms and belting out the final lines with an earnest tone, one not bearing any of Simone's sardonic touches. Taken by her performance, Bernhard smiles and looks upward, waiting for the applause. It never comes.

Throughout her performance, Bernhard masquerades not only as black but also as white, that is, the white performer appropriating black styles. The next scene features such a performer: Shoshana/Madonna. Seeing her bowdlerize black idioms provides a context for Bernhard's covers (a fake pointing to another fake). The scene after Shoshana/Madonna offers another context. Bernhard appears on stage singing Israeli folk songs and telling us about growing up in a Jewish family.[12] It is one of a few scenes that make clear that the "real" Bernhard is Jewish. That "real" performer obviously enjoys playing the parts of fakes, including white (a "big, blond girl" named Babe Jensen), black (the nightclub singer in the "Me and Mrs. Jones" number), and, of course, white playing black.

Through these parts, Bernhard creates a triply divided racial terrain: Jewish, white, and black. How she positions herself in that terrain can be better appreciated by turning back to the many early twentieth-century Jewish performers, notably Al Jolson and Sophie Tucker, who borrowed black idioms, often doing so in blackface.[13] Those performers drew upon

---

[11] See Nnenna Freelon, "Maiden Voyage" (Concord, 1998), and René Marie, "How Can I Keep From Singing" (Maxjazz, 2000).

[12] In this context, the Shoshana character also takes on a new significance. The name "Shoshana" not only evokes Madonna but is the Hebrew word for a rose.

[13] It is not clear if Bernhard is aware of this practice. Her popular culture radar only scans back as far as the 1960s. She does mention close ties between African-American and Jewish performers, such as Nina Simone and Shelley Winters offering an integrated concert in the South during the Civil Rights period. While playing the part of a black cocktail lounge singer, she mentions her "Jewish piano player" and quips "you know how well we people get along." In none of these references does Bernhard mention

black styles as a way of moving through the racial spectrum of American society. Contemporary racial views placed Jews in a middle ground between white and black. By appropriating black styles, they could dip toward the black end of that pole and then rebound toward the opposite white end. For instance, the exteriorizing and mocking of blackness distanced them from that racial area by demonstrating their ability to control it, a control previously assumed only by whites. Their use of the captivating sounds and rhythms of African-American styles also won them celebrity and allowed them, through their music, to enter white Americans' households. As Michael Rogin has discussed in his account of *The Jazz Singer* (1927), the Al Jolson character employs blackface and (so-called) jazz as a means of moving away from his father's world as a Jewish cantor and into the spotlight of being a national star. His arrival in white America is confirmed when he wins the heart of, and marries, a Gentile woman.[14]

Over sixty years later, Bernhard is told to "fuck" off by a black woman and scorned by an African-American audience in a black supper club. How things have changed. In *Without You I'm Nothing*, blackness has a presence, an angry one. We see black clubgoers and musicians. They are not only seen but also heard, as the film shows them deriding the appropriations of their culture. Through that disdain, *Without You I'm Nothing* acknowledges blackness as a source of rich musical traditions, a recognition never made by the Jolson film. Bernhard's film also acknowledges whiteness. In *The Jazz Singer*, whiteness, as is often the case, is undefined, a racial category that claims dominance by appearing to be natural, beyond definition.[15] Bernhard, however, exteriorizes whiteness, putting it on just as Jolson puts on his face paint. Instead of makeup, she uses her awkward singing and unbelievably bad renditions of African-American idioms. Through those performances, whiteness emerges not as a source

Jewish performers drawing upon black styles, in the way that she does, and Jolson and Tucker did well before her.

[14] This discussion of *The Jazz Singer* and the dynamics of racial borrowings by Jewish performers draws from Michael Rogin, *Blackface, White Noise: Jewish Immigrants in the Hollywood Melting Pot* (Berkeley: University of California Press, 1996), 73–120. In his study of nineteenth-century blackface, Eric Lott has described how racial masquerade contained strong currents of homoerotic desire by white men for black men, a desire that was at that time safely disavowed through the mockery and violence of minstrelsy. Eric Lott, "Love and theft: the racial unconscious of blackface minstrelsy," *Representations* 39 (1992), 23–50. It could be argued that appropriation provides Bernhard with a means of pursuing an erotic interest in black women by allowing her to mingle with Diana Ross, Nina Simone, and maybe even Roxanne. For a discussion of how Bernhard's appropriations provide a means of exploring and later disavowing a desire for black women, see Modleski, "The white Negress and the heavy-duty dyke," 69–76.

[15] For a discussion of how whiteness can place itself beyond representation, see Richard Dyer, "White," *Screen* 29/4 (1988), 44–64. Ideas about representations of whiteness and blackness are explored further in Dyer, *White* (New York: Routledge, 1997).

of creative energies but rather as parasitic, dependent on the energies of black culture.[16]

Bernhard not only has us see blackness and whiteness in ways different from those offered by *The Jazz Singer* but she also offers a contrasting perspective on Jewishness and its relationship to those two races. She does not slide along the pole connecting blackness and whiteness, as the Jolson character does; if anything, her film pushes the races further apart. Through her borrowings, Bernhard stands at a remove from blackness and whiteness. She has reclaimed the murky racial middle ground in which early twentieth-century views sequestered Jews. For her, it is a privileged position, one from which she can observe and comment upon the interaction between two races that, just as in the days of *The Jazz Singer*, still shapes American society.

Bernhard's borrowing of both black and white elements raises a question that surfaces throughout the film: should a borrower be on the inside or the outside of the borrowed tradition or style? It is a crucial question, especially where different racial and cultural groups are involved. Much recent cultural studies literature has focused on cross-cultural borrowings. Those studies have challenged the legitimacy of the outsider by pointing out how such appropriations have often been fed by racial fantasies and have given no voice to the original tradition.[17] Bernhard casts similar doubts on the appropriations of white pop stars, viewing them as thieves. The extent to which these white stars are outsiders is revealed by putting them on the inside, that is, in the Parisian Room, where they come across as ludicrous and meet with disdain from the black club-goers. With that relocation, Bernhard implies that one can borrow only from the inside of a tradition.

What then is one to make of the music in the first two scenes, in which a black pianist appropriates Bach? The opening credit sequence pans the centuries and races by having a shot of a white eighteenth-century man playing the Prelude from Bach's B♭ Major Partita on the harpsichord segue into one with a black woman at the piano picking up the piece where he left off and concluding it. Immediately afterwards, the background music for a dressing room monologue by Bernhard features a line from the Prelude being touched up as a blues lick by a pianist, presumably the same black female pianist (Vanessa Burch) whom we see throughout the film. It is a brief moment and the only example of black appropriating white in the film, but that moment receives no

---

[16] This view of whiteness is also explored by Dyer in "White."

[17] A large number of studies have dealt with these issues. Two notable ones are Marianne Torgovnick, *Gone Primitive: Savage Intellects, Modern Lives* (Chicago: University of Chicago Press, 1990), and Hal Foster, " 'Primitive' scenes," *Critical Inquiry* 20 (1993), 69–102.

commentary, suggesting that the film nods in approval, or at least looks the other way, at such appropriations.

One way out of this contradiction is a line of defense that borrowers have long used: the ability to transform. As far back as Seneca, the taint of unoriginality raised by the act has been dispersed by prizing the creative uses made of borrowed materials.[18] In our time, that defense has been used increasingly to justify the crossing of legal or cultural lines. The "culture jammers" justify their march across copyright by flaunting their creative transformations. *Without You I'm Nothing* upholds the ability to transform as a talent that sanctions borrowing from the outside of a tradition, especially across racial lines.[19] The fleeting bit of bluesy Bach is not much upon which to make that case, but it should be noted that it sounds more altered, and much more inspired, than what Shoshana creates. She can only imitate black styles, not transform them, and, in the end, produces nothing more than cheap fakes. Bernhard, on the other hand, can transform African-American styles, as well as the white cheap fake versions of those idioms. That ability apparently gives her leeway in borrowing, allowing her to draw upon both black and white materials. From those sources, she creates her own wonderfully "bad" performances and lambent monologues. Her cover songs clearly do not belong in the black Parisian Room, nor would they ever find a home in a white mainstream club. They thrive in her world, one very much apart from those two realms.

The ability to transform, though, has not given Bernhard complete impunity in the fraught realm of racial appropriation. As several writers have pointed out, she implicates herself in some of the same practices of appropriation that she critiques.[20] For instance, she proves to be in some ways no different from the white musicians who borrow black idioms in an attempt to be hip or outside the mainstream. One major difference is that she is trying to out-hip these musicians, to put herself even more on the outside by mocking those who have already tried the same thing. As with the white hipsters, that move is done through ties with blackness. Bernhard never tries to dress or sound black (at least not in any sort of realistic way); rather, she tries to raise a black voice

---

[18] For an engaging discussion of views of borrowing by Seneca and Swift as relevant to Handel, see John T. Winemiller, "Recontextualizing Handel's borrowings," *Journal of Musicology* 15 (1997), 444–70.

[19] There are other factors at play here. Bernhard's film also points to issues of inequality in cross-racial borrowing by contrasting the superstar Madonna (through her double Shoshana) with the anonymous black musicians in the club. As the contrast makes clear, the former has profited tremendously from her appropriations, whereas the forgers of the original style have not enjoyed anywhere near the same level of financial success.

[20] In particular, see hooks, *Black Looks: Race and Representation*, 37–39; and Riggs, "Cultural healing," 10–11.

of scorn. The crowd at the Parisian Room expresses indignity at seeing their culture ripped off and bastardized. That audience, however, is, to use the logic of the film, "fake," meaning that they are actors involved in Bernhard's film rather than off-the-street clubgoers giving us their views on white appropriations of black idioms. As is so often the case in such appropriations, blackness lacks a voice.[21] The clubgoers are saying what Bernhard wants them to say, or, more accurately, what she feels black people want to say.[22] Through them, Bernhard, like the white rap star talking about his posse, distances herself from the white mainstream. In many ways, she attempts to become part of the audience at the Parisian Room, the only problem being that they have always been part of her.[23]

Camp

Bernhard's cover songs can also be viewed from another perspective: camp. If there is one word that captures *Without You I'm Nothing* – and it has been used to do so many times – it is camp. Camp, though, is so difficult to capture itself, an admission that amounts to a pro-forma preamble in most scholarly discussions of the concept, including Susan Sontag's classic 1964 essay.[24] Defining camp is like putting perfume back in the bottle once it has been sprayed. All we can do is take in the scent. *Without You I'm Nothing* bears that scent, being infused with arch touches of camp. It, for instance, abounds in artifice – in particular it bounds from one extravagant number to another. Many of these

---

[21] As Riggs comments, "Bernhard can never speak for the black woman. She can read the black woman's contempt within her eyes and then verbalize it with a 'fuck you,' but Bernhard cannot, in all of her appropriation, articulate the experience of black people. That's where movies from Hollywood continually fail. They can never articulate black subjectivity, because they're so clearly and obviously made through white eyes." Riggs, "Cultural healing," 10–11.

[22] As with the Bach blues lick, some of the sonic scraps in the film convey black creativity and viewpoints. During the scene in which Roxanne is doing her hair in front of the mirror, a recording of NWA's "Compton's N The House" can be heard. In that song, NWA inveighs against other musicians, black and white, who are trying to pretend they are gangsta rappers from Compton – that is, they are protesting against whites and blacks trying to take advantage of a socially outsider black idiom and style. The rap song could be seen as a black voice being raised against appropriation; however, it ultimately remains a voice brought in to the film (appropriated) by Bernhard.

[23] Also placing her outside of the mainstream are her occasional lines about desiring women.

[24] Susan Sontag, "Notes on 'camp'," *Partisan Review* 31 (1964), 515–30. Sontag's essay is part of a collection of numerous essays dealing with camp collected in *Camp: Queer Aesthetics and the Performing Subject*. Another important collection is David Bergman, ed., *Camp Grounds: Style and Homosexuality* (Amherst: University of Massachusetts Press, 1993). Many of the approaches to camp taken in this essay have been shaped by views offered in the numerous pieces in these two collections.

decorate songs from periods with distinct stylistic profiles, such as the 70s Disco number ruled by leathermen or the Motown performance crowned with bouffants and regaled in satin. Sontag remarked that "camp is a woman walking around in a dress made of three million feathers." That dress flaunts both the emphasis on style and the "spirit of exaggeration" so central to camp.[25] Bernhard may not wear feathers, but her dresses, many of them created by top designers, brim with high style and threaten to steal the show. Moreover, some of those outfits, like the mass of chiffon and lace in the backup singers' dresses, take certain looks to absurd extremes. Such excess only serves to heighten the artifice of the show by drawing attention to the thin yet so rich layer of style that drapes it.

If her fashion goes over the top, so does Bernhard's emotional delivery. She thrives on melodrama, her speaking voice pitched between extremes of sadness, defiance, and tenderness, almost none of which ring true. These mock emotions cake especially those sections in which Bernhard shares her deepest feelings, which become nothing but style, sequins of sadness, bobbles of joy. *Without You I'm Nothing* also sinks into what Sontag called the "failed seriousness" of camp.[26] In that state, there is an intense effort to achieve some new quality – say, deep emotions or a glamorous look – but that effort falls well short, producing either cheap melodrama or a grotesque imitation. What is left is excess, the push of the effort that never stood a chance, and the spill of melodrama and grotesqueries resulting from it. *Without You I'm Nothing* mounts numerous such failures. Indeed, the film is a record of one colossal failure: Bernhard's nightclub act. As seen in the performance of "Four Women," Bernhard appears to take her cover rendition of that song seriously, believing that she can convey, even share in, the anguish of the black women depicted. In her biggest delusion, she expects rapturous applause from the black audience. They don't clap, but we might, as we can savor the excess of her doomed efforts, enjoying the bad taste, artifice, delusion, and missteps.

Bernhard does not so much create failures as transform the already failed. Camp feeds upon outdated pieces of popular culture, which, in its grasp, are held up as failures. These pieces – songs, dresses, and advertisements – have failed in that they no longer hold the original meanings and sense of contemporaneity that they once did. The glow of novelty, fashion, and celebrity that made them appear so natural – that is, so much a part of their time – have long faded, leaving behind the passé. In these relics, those animating qualities no longer appear as intrinsic to the original but rather as empty embellishments, or excess. In relishing such failure and excess, camp does not merely make fun of

---

[25] Sontag, "Notes on 'camp'," 59.   [26] Ibid., 62.

the out-of-fashion. On the contrary, it alters those pieces and gives them new meanings, which, as in Bernhard's film, comment on both the past that they once commanded and the present in which they are so out of place.

The intermingling of past and present is one way in which camp serves as a strategy of borrowing. The practice has never been explicitly viewed from that angle. Discussions of camp split over whether it is more a mode of perception or of production. Sontag, for instance, favored the former, which she called "pure camp." In that form, the "camp eye" or "camp taste" could discern the potential of a "failed" object. She found "deliberate camp," or the act of "camping" something, less "favorable," perhaps because it rewarded the figure creating camp displays rather than the critic possessing the perceptive "eye" and "taste."[27] As Bernhard and countless drag queens (a group not once mentioned by Sontag) demonstrate, the latter approach can captivate even the most discerning taste. In Bernhard's "deliberate" hands, camp captivatingly performs the transformations and recontextualizations emblematic of borrowing.

Viewing camp as such returns us to the question of whether borrowing should take place from outside or from within a tradition or category. In regard to racial appropriation, Bernhard offers a mixed reply to that question. With camp, there is no such ambiguity. It is created from the outside. The best practitioners stand apart from the dated popular culture materials that they exploit, separated not only by time but also by sexuality and gender, as demonstrated by the mistresses of the style, drag queens. They are also removed from that debris by wit and taste. In many ways, camp has an air of elitism about it. As Andrew Ross has argued, some 1960s intellectuals and artists, including Sontag, adopted camp as a rear-guard defense against the challenges made by the pop art elevation of the mundane, a challenge to their ability to patrol the "boundaries of taste."[28] Camp allowed them to interact with popular culture while maintaining a distance from it through their flaunted cleverness.

Bernhard has plenty of wit to flaunt, which she also directs at popular culture. Although she does not seek an elitist enclave from which to satirize popular culture, she still stands at a remove. Popular figures may influence Bernhard's world, but that is not to say that she is part of theirs.[29] As her monologue and borrowings make clear, she is too much aware of, to use again two tokens of camp, the failures and excesses of

---

[27] Ibid., 58–59. See also Andrew Ross, "Uses of camp," in *Camp: Queer Aesthetics and the Performing Subject*, 316.

[28] Ross, "Uses of camp," 318–22.

[29] At the time of the film, Bernhard was pretty much on the outside of mainstream popular culture. However, during the 1990s she made her way closer to the mainstream, if not actually crossing over into it.

popular culture, its one-hit wonders and formulaic pap. Such awareness, and especially the ability to act upon it, is lacking within that culture – at least it is not displayed by Madonna and other entertainers depicted in the film. Like her take on racial appropriation, that critical perspective places Bernhard on the outside of the scrutinized cultural area, a position from which she can borrow and transform elements from that world. For Bernhard's brand of borrowing as cultural criticism, the outside is the only viable location. The closer one gets to the inside, the more diluted that criticism becomes, as in Bernhard's racial masquerades, where she steps into the same stances that she critiques white musicians for taking.

For Bernhard, camp serves as an incisive form of cultural criticism, a way of digging in the knife with a laugh. That comic incision can be heard in the segment built around the songs of Burt Bacharach. That episode opens with Bernhard sitting in a chair and, after a pensive pause, stating: "You know what I'm in the mood for?... A little bit of Burt." That line unleashes a chain reaction of Bacharach particles. First, we see Bernhard dressed up as Dionne Warwick. It is not a close likeness – the hairdo by itself pretty much makes the connection – but then again it is not the outrageously ludicrous imitation seen in the Simone number.[30] However, like that outfit, the dress, a silver sparkling miniskirt cut much shorter than Warwick, or most women, would ever wear, places us once again in a scene dominated by fashion, a scene enhanced by the white chiffon and sequin dresses of the backup singers. Dressed all in white and playing white instruments (including the piano), the musicians serve as the perfect accessory. Only a few notes of Bacharach have sounded, but they were enough to create this world of artifice. Full of white fluff, the stage and the music become pure confection. No wonder that Bernhard, after hearing those initial notes, exclaims "Delicious."

She takes a bigger bite of Burt by singing a few phrases from the song "A House is Not a Home." That tune appeared in a 1964 film of the same name, which tells of a woman in a whorehouse looking for a husband,

---

[30] Blackness – that is, Bernhard's attempt to appear as a famous black woman – is not emphasized in this episode. The downplaying of this theme may have to do with the low profile of Warwick's own blackness in the Bacharach 1960s hit rush. In her performances of Bacharach songs, race was not emphasized to the same degree that it was in the public personas of the other black performers evoked in the film, namely Simone and Ross. Another reason for the lack of emphasis on race may be that the Bacharach–Warwick hits do not fall neatly into the category of white appropriations of blackness that are satirized by Bernhard. These were songs by a Jewish composer sung by a black performer. This is the type of collaboration that Bernhard praises elsewhere (the Simone and Shelley Winters concert, the black nightclub singer and Jewish piano player in another segment) and emulates in her own identification with blackness. Surprisingly she does not play up that connection. In fact, Bacharach's Jewishness is never once even mentioned.

the man who will make her house (the whorehouse?) a home.[31] The film is sopping melodrama, and so is the song, full of impassioned, stand-and-deliver phrases. In other words, it is the perfect song for Bernhard, who not surprisingly plays up the melodrama. Singing from her chair, she begins with the second line of the lyrics – "But a chair is not a house" – only to have the "house" come falling down around her with a large crash from the band. That crash exaggerates the melodramatic windup endings to the phrases in the original. After the crash, Bernhard concludes the second line in another melodramatic style, the tearful ballad. In a little over a minute, Bacharach has received a thorough camp makeover, becoming artifice and melodramatic excess.

From her recollections of 1960s Bacharach, Bernhard abruptly switches into the present. She mentions a controversial 1986 *Newsweek* article that stated that a single woman over the age of thirty-five was more likely to be killed in Europe by a terrorist than to be married. That article roiled many feminists, including Susan Faludi, who, in a celebrated 1991 book, saw it as part of a "backlash" against American women.[32] Like Faludi, Bernhard attacks this scaremongering statistic, but with much different weapons. Where Faludi marshals her own barrage of statistics, Bernhard throws down Bacharach songs. Behind the smoke screens of artifice and melodrama, that attack is built on establishing a link between past and present. In particular, she has us see the present through the passé.

The Bacharach chiffon and mawkishness are two of the "delicious" tastes of the *démodé* enjoyed by camp. Bernhard shows other ways in which those songs have "failed" to maintain their vibrancy in the present. For the rest of the segment, she goes off on an extended monologue accompanied by a series of Bacharach tunes played by the band and back-up singers.[33] This medley features lite jazz piano solos, whispering textless vocal phrases, and a mellow flugelhorn solo. In other words, this accompaniment is background music of another sort, namely easy-listening music. That has been the fate of Bacharach's hits in the present. As heard in elevators everywhere, his catchy rhythms and sparkling melodies have become sonic gauze used to patch over silence.[34]

---

[31] The film stars Shelley Winters and was directed by Russell Rouse.

[32] Susan Faludi, *Backlash: the Undeclared War Against American Women* (New York: Crown Publishers, 1991), 100.

[33] The songs include "A House is Not a Home," "This Girl's In Love," "The Look of Love," and "I Say a Little Prayer for You."

[34] Bacharach songs took also on new life in the 1990s as emblems of an overly slick sophistication, a gloss seen in the Austin Powers movies mentioned below (see note 37) and the prominent appearance of the songs in the lounge music revival. On the 1990s Bacharach revival, see Geoffrey O'Brien, "Resurrecting Burt Bacharach," *The New York Review of Books* 46 (6 May 1999), 46–52.

In Bernhard's number, this background music is not so innocuous. One should listen to it, or listen to what is not there. The unstated lyrics of the chosen songs all tell a tale of women desperate to find or to hold on to a man, and most likely never being able to do so. For the woman in "I Say a Little Prayer for You," her daily supplication is to have her "darling" say "I love you," whereas the protagonist in "The Look of Love" pleads "don't ever go...don't ever go...I love you so." With these melodramatic cries, that tale comes across as dated. Or is it? The *Newsweek* article suggests not. Bernhard, though, wants us to see that it is very much of the past, or should be, and does so by throwing more dross on the campfire. Her monologue works over another hackneyed tale, that of the young beautiful woman who effortlessly falls in love with and marries a rich successful man. She plays the part of a secretary arriving in San Francisco, who after one day on the job dates and falls in love with the boss, the man she will wed. Scorning the *Newsweek* article, she gushes: "I'll never be a statistic, not me...I'm under 35 and I'm going to be married." Her story is as thick with clichés as the evoked cliché San Francisco fog, all of which are enhanced by Bernhard's overdone gestures and expressions. With these two formulaic stories – desperate, lonely woman and marriage at first sight – running side by side, it appears as if one may cancel out the other. On the contrary, the two just add up to one big blob of cliché, so big and so vapid that within it there is no such thing as a contradiction. Once again we can enjoy excess, watching that blob grow bigger and bigger until it appears ready to burst.

Adding to that mass is a junk heap of cosmetic and domestic products. Our young secretary has found her man because she has purchased all the right makeup, fashions, and furniture. She keeps rattling off the brand names of such goods and bits from their advertisements. Full of banal talk of beauty and love, those advertisements have promised her success, assurances – like that of the perfect husband – which she has never doubted. By intermingling those promises with the fears and dreams offered by the two romantic tales, Bernhard shows how those advertisements feed off the hopes and anxieties of women.[35] A similar point was made in Naomi Wolf's 1991 book *The Beauty Myth*, which described how women have been harried by commercial ideals of beauty, some falling prey to eating disorders.[36] Bernhard avoids such grim news,

---

[35] Bacharach and David did write a song critiquing the empty promises of consumer society, a critique made in their characteristically smooth (and consumer-friendly) style. The song, "Paper Maché," was not much of a hit, making it as far as number 43 on the top 100 in 1970.

[36] Naomi Wolf, *The Beauty Myth: How Images of Beauty are Used Against Women* (New York: William Morrow, 1991).

but she still makes her point by depicting a young woman unable to live her life without the allure of such products, a life that becomes just as hollow as that allure.

The links with both Faludi and Wolf make clear how involved Bernhard's borrowings are in the cultural arena of the time. Appearing within a two-year period, the works of all three women put forth and honed ideas that, as is clear from the success of the two authors, gripped the public imagination. The public may not have gripped Bernhard's film with the same intensity, but that has probably more to do with its unique offbeat approach. Whereas Faludi and Wolf chop away at cultural "myths" with precise arguments, Bernhard swells them to ludicrous extremes through camp exaggeration. Camp also provides her with a line of attack unthinkable to the two steely-eyed writers. In particular, the celebration of the out-of-fashion makes us aware of how dated these views of women are, or again how dated they should be in the present day. When such views are wrapped up in the superficial excess of 1960s hits – the chiffon, the hairdos – there is no taking them seriously. In such guises, they belong to a past as distant as the slick songs and fashions of Bacharach.[37]

No matter how you compare Bernhard to Faludi and Wolf, there is no denying that Bernhard puts on a bigger finale. The two writers end with impassioned calls to action, while Bernhard winds up with a glitzy display of bad taste. After the announcement of her wedding, she returns to the opening song "A House is Not a Home." However, with her husband, that house is now a home, leading Bernhard to rewrite the lyrics accordingly. This happy ending is made even emptier than the melodramatic conclusion of the original. Bacharach's Broadway-belting finale becomes a celebratory romp, as the tempo picks up and Bernhard punctuates the short phrases ("This house is now a home") with crass "wow's" and leg kicks (while sitting in the chair from the opening). What could cap off this flurry of vulgarity? Nothing less than Sandra being circled by muscular go-go boys in white-sequin hot shorts, clearly branded as gay. Needless to say these figures never appear in any of the lonely-lady Bacharach songs – women could never objectify men in that world, nor did men stray from heterosexuality and don sequins. The dancers visually rewrite the Bacharach songs, showing us a woman who can indulge her erotic whims and see other erotic possibilities. As

---

[37] Bernhard was not alone in the 1990s in reworking Bacharach's 1960s songs and the gender relationships constructed around them. Two of the Austin Powers films starring Mike Myers (*Austin Powers: International Man of Mystery* and *Austin Powers 2: the Spy Who Shagged Me*) drew a connection between Bacharach and the ultra-stylish, sophisticated 1960s playboy, a figure that the film upholds as ludicrously out of date, just as Bernhard does Bacharach's desperate women.

Bernhard mentions earlier in the episode, contemporary women simply want their "options" left open. Sitting at home in 1990, Bernhard, with or without a husband, has her "options," including watching sexy gay male dancers.[38]

Abjection and triumph

At the end of her show at the Parisian Room, Bernhard is alone. She stands by herself on stage, wrapped in, of all things, the American flag. There are no backup musicians. Nor are there any celebrity images, like those of Dionne or Nina, to keep her company on stage. Bernhard alone is a surprising sight. Even more surprising is the declaration that she makes. Promising to "cut the fame shit out for just this moment," she admits to being "a total phony and a fraud." The club audience finds that remark overdue, as Bernhard acknowledges what they have long realized: she is not the big-name New York star that she makes herself out to be; far from it, she is a failure, one caught up in her own "fame shit." Underneath this declaration can be detected anxiety, not about being a star but about being a borrower. What makes these doubts more apparent is the fact that Bernhard has stopped borrowing. As promised, she has "cut the fame shit out," meaning that she is no longer borrowing and dressing up celebrity images but rather appearing as herself.

Why she has stopped doing so may have to do with anxieties over what to make of an artist who continually borrows, especially one who draws upon the images of other people. Throughout the film, Bernhard has posed questions about the act of borrowing. Now, however, the questions are turned inward. She calls herself a "fraud" and a "phony," names that at once raise and respond to the question posed above. These are the same words that have been used to discredit borrowers like Madonna/Shoshana and celebrities who adopt images, such as Ralph Lifshitz/Lauren. With those labels, she casts doubts upon her own borrowing. Putting on celebrity personas makes her a "phony," no different from the white hipster who draws upon blackness to assume presence and vitality. Bernhard has drawn upon not only blackness but also celebrity to give herself a creative presence. When she "cuts out" using "fame," she loses that presence, possessing none of the verve that she had in the preceding string of masquerade cover songs. Indeed, in comparison with her Simone and Warwick recreations, she comes across as almost nothing in the final scene. Perhaps that is what she alludes

---

[38] Throughout the segment, Bernhard breaks away from the cliché script to mention other "options," including oral sex and bisexuality.

to when she tells the audience "without me" – only to falter and begin again – "without you I'm nothing." That "you" may very well be the audience but it could also be the celebrity images upon which she has drawn.

Bernhard's breakdown stems from doubts that come with the act of borrowing. That practice has long raised anxieties of creative desperation and, in the case of Bernhard, of self-erasure; any borrower has had to contend with such fears in one form or another. It is rare, though, that they are voiced so openly and dramatically. In *Without You I'm Nothing*, those anxieties form part of a compelling drama of abjection, one in which Bernhard repeatedly humiliates herself, revealing herself to be a failure in both show business and life. At the Parisian Room, the audience openly derides her. Outside the club, as she embarrassingly tells the crowd, she has had a disastrous relationship with her boyfriend Joe, in which she stooped from one low to the next. Her abjection culminates with the venting of anxieties over borrowing, her creative *métier*, and the admission of being "nothing."[39]

As much as Bernhard knocks herself down, she just as often picks herself up again. Ironically, she does so through the mode of camp borrowing that she has practiced all evening. As Wayne Koestenbaum has noted in his study of opera queens, camp offers a way of "reversing one's abjection." Camp amounts to something like the blind leading the blind, or, in this case, the abject borrowing the abject. With that practice, the borrower – be it the homosexual opera queen or the bisexual show business wannabe Bernhard – is often a figure scoffed at by society. The borrowed material has often similarly been mocked and cast aside, scraps of popular culture that once briefly captured fashion but soon plummeted into the pitifully out-of-fashion. Through camp, the abject figure can place him- or herself above those depths by recognizing the abjection of such pieces. Moreover, he or she can see the camp potential of the scraps and display the "power to fill [those] degraded artifacts to the brim with meanings."[40]

Koestenbaum depicts camp as a mode of perception, not borrowing, a private act in which the opera queen luxuriates in the pleasure of finding the "sublime" in the untouched ephemera of opera stardom.[41]

---

[39] Bernhard's rejection of borrowing, her creative gift and *modus operandi*, accords with the type of loss that plays a role in what Julia Kristeva refers to as the "abjection of self." That loss occurs at the "foundations" of one's "being" and forces the subject to see the abject in him- or herself, as Bernhard does by calling herself a "phony." Kristeva, *Powers of Horror: an Essay on Abjection*, trans. Leon S. Roudiez (New York: Columbia University Press, 1982), 8.

[40] Wayne Koestenbaum, *The Queen's Throat: Opera, Homosexuality, and the Mystery of Desire* (New York: Poseidon Press, 1993), 117.

[41] Ibid., 117.

Bernhard's film, on the other hand, approaches camp as a very public practice of borrowing. In that light, it expands the scope of abjection and release described by Koestenbaum. The act of borrowing stirs creative doubts that further drive Bernhard down into her personal depths. At the same time, though, borrowing elevates her above the abject. She not only displays the power to recognize the depletion and camp potential of an item but she also wields more power by transforming that item, making it something new and usually even more abject. Once again borrowing emerges as a means of empowerment. The "culture jammers" in chapter five enlisted sampling to resist the passivity forced upon them by the mass media and to fight back against that pervasive force. Bernhard draws upon cover songs to raise herself out of "nothingness" and to "take apart American pop culture."[42]

Perhaps nowhere is her power as a borrower more forcefully displayed than in the cover performance of Prince's "Little Red Corvette" that closes the final scene. The performance stands out as Bernhard's most extensive and imaginative reconception of a borrowed song and, as such, it quickly scatters any doubts that she or we may have had about her borrowing. Indeed, she must have regained her confidence, for, by choosing Prince, she has resumed playing with "fame shit." The star that she has picked for the finale is unlike any of those who have been put on display in the previous scenes. As the name says, Prince is royalty. To Bernhard, he is much more, as she makes clear in a long tribute. She holds him up as a pop culture oracle, a voice that presents us with "the sign of the times." Not just the mouthpiece of the gods, he is a god, having attained that apogee of celebrity: divinity. The "purple paisley god," as Bernhard calls him, resides in the heavens, sitting underneath a "cherry moon." Bernhard elevates Prince just to knock him down. The more imposing the subject, the more impressive her ability to transform him and make him part of her creative world. Who else but the most talented borrower could dethrone a prince, twist the words of an oracle, and make a god in her own image?

Like Oswald's sampling of Jackson, Bernhard is borrowing not just a song but a person. She focuses on different sides of Prince – sound, soul, and sexiness – and twists them to create a person more absurd than glamorous. Her makeover begins immediately. She dresses up Prince's funky dance tune in a new genre, the folk ballad. The transformation is an astounding one, for arguably there could not be two more disparate genres in popular music. The former switches on dancers with heavy rhythmic grooves created by an array of electronic instruments. The music connects with the corporeal, as do the lyrics, which usually stroke the basic topics of the body and sex. Recalling a back-seat encounter,

---

[42] Gary Indiana, "Interview with Sandra Bernhard," *Bomb* 24 (Summer 1988), 30.

"Little Red Corvette" is no exception. In the folk song, we hear little of either topic. Such songs seek emotional intimacy, as the lone singer tells us of his or her loves, heartbreaks, and aspirations, all of which are conveyed in an idiom with no trace of rhythmic bumps and grinds. Moreover, the emotional intimacy is enhanced by the use of acoustic instruments, there being no amplifiers or samplers between the singer and us.

What is surprising about her cover song is not so much the genre transformation itself but rather how well it works musically. Bernhard's covers have won us over more with their satiric than with their musical riches. With the performance of "Little Red Corvette," she offers us both. In her slow-tempo version of the song, Prince's melodic phrases, which Bernhard again keeps largely intact, emerge as limpid lines that glide over smooth melodic arcs, each landing creating a melancholic twinge. The new-found tenderness in the song is softened even more by Bernhard's plangent voice, which sensitively guides the original melody through its new folk-style surroundings.

Even with that tenderness, the song has a satirical edge. Like the other covers, it skewers aspects of American popular culture. Drawing upon a song by a black musician, it swaggers back into the field of racial appropriation. Full of funk rhythms and sensual falsetto yelps, Prince's song abounds with the corporeal energy and erotic sensation that white musicians have extracted from black styles. Bernhard, however, rejects these same qualities, taking everything else from the original. Leaving them behind, she separates herself from Madonna/Shoshana and other white stars by showing that she does not need such elements to give her work vitality and presence. Contrary to her earlier doubts, she is not a "phony." Quite the opposite: with her regained ability to transform and to satirize, her distinct presence emerges more and more clearly.

Bernhard has not completely sifted out the erotic elements from "Little Red Corvette." It would be almost impossible to do so. As she says in her tribute, Prince is above all "sexy," a quality intrinsic to both his music and his image. Drawing upon camp borrowing practices, she exteriorizes and mocks Prince's sexiness. The folk setting of "Little Red Corvette" provides the perfect means of doing so. It stills the rhythmic and corporeal currents of the song's eroticism and by doing so draws attention to its superficiality, especially the lyrics. In the original, the lyrics do little to draw attention to themselves; most listeners cannot remember more than the title phrase. If they would listen closely, they would hear the story of a young man seduced by a woman in her "little red corvette" and pushed to go "faster" than he would like to. The man, though, eventually hops into the driver seat and tells her that she has to "slow down" and that he will "tame" her "love machine" so that she can find "a love that's gonna last."

With a slow tempo and clear diction, Bernhard's performance brings out this vapid story. In that light, the cover song may seem to be nothing more than the cliché stunt of reading light pop lyrics with the starched elocution reserved for "poetry." Bernhard goes well beyond that old joke. She renders the tale of sexual prey turned romantic master into high melodrama, sent up with that characteristic mix of overdone singing and facial expressions which, in a typical Bernhard mix, commingle with the sensitive singing mentioned above. The young man's anxiety is exaggerated by pathetically faltering vocal phrases and his being "ill" conveyed through a wincing look of nausea. On the other side, the woman's taunt of "do you have enough gas" becomes an inflated and drawn-out phrase, capped off with the awkward two-syllable enunciation of the word "gas." Any traces of sexual tension and drama in the original song have been vaporized into melodramatic fumes.

Bernhard turns Prince's backseat love story not only into folk-song melodrama (yet another pairing of stylistic opposites) but also into a ballet. Throughout the performance, "Apollo," a male dancer wearing a loincloth and pretending to play a recorder, and three "hippie girls" dance behind her (the girls also sing back-up). As if the use of a folk style was not surprising enough, the dance is just dumbfounding. Who knows what it means, if anything at all? One thing that is clear is that the ballet is pure excess: a choreographed extravagance of tackiness, ludicrous failures, and incongruities. In other words, it is a *scène de camp*. With all the trappings of myth and ballet, the dance comes across as a high-art disaster, a sort of *Apollon musagète* meets *Hair*. "Little Red Corvette" is also thrown into the spectacle, creating even greater stylistic confusion. The ballet and the song appear to have no relationship with each other. Apollo rides the chariot of the sun not a Corvette. Yet Bernhard's scene suggests one connection. Here is another tale of sexual enthrallment as the noble Apollo (a stand-in or rival for the "purple paisley god"?) captivates the three girls and leads them around and eventually off the stage. Allegory has often drawn upon the tales of the Greek gods to throw light on general human truths, but, in Bernhard's performance, it – if the ballet is indeed an allegory – has gone astray and instead fallen into excess and frivolity.

Chained to the ballet, the song falls into a state of abjection. As it sinks, Bernhard rises out of her own depths, the anxieties about borrowing and creativity that plagued her at the opening of the scene. Camp has offered the means of escaping those doubts. By merely holding up "Little Red Corvette" to the audience, she has placed herself above the lightweight dance tune. Not content just to chuckle at it, Bernhard has transformed the song into some sort of stylistic monstrosity. That extreme transformation should dispel any doubts that she had about being a borrower. Far from being a "fraud," she has triumphed over the "purple paisley god," especially his vaunted sexual ego. The erotic vibrancy of his song has been muted and his tale of sexual mastery has become melodramatic fodder.[43] With the cover song, Bernhard has turned herself into a god. This absurd scene is a world that she has created, one in which she lords over both the "purple paisley god" and Apollo. As aesthetically blighted as it may be, it is very much a Bernhard world, full of people, styles, and perspectives that mean so much to her, including black musicians, black idioms, 1960s counterculture, a god of music, melodrama, and, above all, herself.

Creating a world is not enough of a triumph for Bernhard. She sets herself a new goal, a seemingly impossible one: to stand against Prince in his own world and without her powers as a borrower. After her cover performance of "Little Red Corvette," we hear a recording of the Prince original. How Bernhard responds to coming face to face with her source is even more shocking than the Apollo ballet. She drops the American flag wrapped around her and appears wearing only a Stars and Stripes g-string and pasties.[44] Dressed like a stripper, Bernhard begins to dance like one, or what amounts to her camp version of such a dance, with its awkward and literally cheeky moments (especially on the phrase "do you have enough gas"). With Bernhard dancing to someone else's performance and "stripped" of her ability to transform the music of the original song, the question arises whether or not she can hold the stage. Will she lose ground to Prince and become the dancing fool Apollo in his world?

The answer to that question depends on the answer to another: is stripping, to use two words applied to borrowing, an act of abjection or empowerment? It can be viewed either way. The woman who debases herself in front of lascivious men can also be the woman who breaks social constraints and flaunts her body and sexuality. The film shows us both sides. In an earlier scene, Shoshana does a brief striptease. As if it were not humiliating enough being a "fake," she further lowers herself as she mechanically takes off her clothes and hands a piece to a man in the audience, all of which is done to a bloated black-style rhythmic groove. Taking the abjection of striptease further, the scene shows how Madonna has tried desperately to enhance the corporeal basis of African-American styles through her appropriations, becoming in the process not an enhancement of but rather a cheap accessory to those

---

[43] It should also be noted that Bernhard assails Prince's sexual presence by other means in her performance. In particular, she sings only the first half of the song, leaving out that part in which the male character (Prince) "tames" the female "love machine."

[44] The outfit can be seen as a retort to the attempts to pass an amendment banning flag burning and desecration that were being made at that time. For a discussion of the flag and patriotic pasties and g-string as signs of "queer nationality," see Berlant and Freeman, "Queer nationality," 193–229.

idioms. With the Bernhard finale, striptease emerges as an act of sexual bravura, as the star displays her body and her self-confidence. Bernhard commands the stage, so much that Prince's song appears very much as background music, not as the imposing source for her borrowing. Taking the empowerment of striptease further, she resists becoming a subject in the "purple paisley god's" kingdom, instead making him part of her world. Moreover, the striptease affirms that Bernhard, unlike Madonna/Shoshana, does not depend on the erotic energy of black styles to create her own sexual displays. Quite the contrary, she uses her dancing to trump once again the sexual powers of Prince, her naked body drowning out his voice and music.

Proclaiming her triumph as a borrower, the striptease makes a fitting finale to the film. There is, however, one last scene. As the recording of "Little Red Corvette" fades away, Bernhard looks out at the empty Parisian Room, deserted by the clubgoers, who were most likely offended by either her crude dance or her self-absorption (the former being part of the latter). One person remains in the club: Roxanne, who writes on the tablecloth her lipstick curse "Fuck Sandra Bernhard." As mentioned earlier, the appearance of Roxanne and her curse are open to interpretation. One thing, though, is clear: we have abruptly returned to a scene of abjection. Bernhard has tumbled back into her depths, pleading for acceptance and once again being scorned by the audience, or what is left of it.

Those depths are not so menacing. Bernhard cushions her fall with camp. She is alone and wounded, but the whole scene, like others of abjection, is done as high melodrama. The fraught stare between her and Roxanne and the surging music accompanying it come right out of some old, hackneyed Hollywood film. So does Roxanne's theatrical departure. Only in such films do beautiful women make grand exits and disappear into an enveloping white light. But in those films, a black woman does not usually walk into that light after telling off a Jewish woman who may desire her and who has just danced to a song by a black performer, wearing nothing but a patriotic g-string. All of this after a funk song à la folk mythological allegorical ballet. Safe to say that only in a Bernhard film, one constantly at play with borrowing, do we ever get such a scene.

Conclusion

Topics for a good ending are hard to come by. So I felt quite fortunate that I walked into one. Hours of gnashing ideas of how to begin this section led me to abandon my writing and head to the Vancouver Art Gallery, which was putting on a show by the Scottish artist Douglas Gordon. Only a few rooms into the exhibition, I came across Gordon's best-known work: *24 Hour Psycho* (1993). This piece presents a complete screening of Hitchcock's film but now without sound and slowed down to a speed of two frames per minute instead of the usual twenty-four per second. At that pace, *Psycho* stretches across a day. I had heard of this work beforehand and dismissed it as a clever stunt. To my surprise, the piece clicked. I first watched it for around fifteen minutes and then returned for more viewings during my time in the gallery. With each encounter, I was caught up in the feeling of sluggish time and mesmerized by the many beautiful details – a close-up of Janet Leigh's gloves and purse, the coal black glasses of a policeman's stare – that have gone from fleeting shot to still life. Most of all, I was fascinated by how *24 Hour Psycho* relates to the practice of borrowing, particularly that of quotation.

That relationship, I realized, made the work an apposite choice with which to conclude this study. Gordon's piece takes many of the approaches discussed so far several steps further, so many steps that we arrive at an extreme. At that point, we can look back to see how much approaches to borrowing have changed over the twentieth century and sense how much further they may develop in the coming decades.

24 Hour Psycho represents what appears to be the endpoint for one borrowing practice discussed here – that is, the presentation of a whole or near-whole original in a new context. It is not the length by itself that distinguishes the work from Rochberg's Mozart, Berio's Mahler, or Oswald's Jackson, but rather the simplicity of the transformation. All Gordon does is change the speed of the film. He does not recolor the original and cut it off as Rochberg does, nor fill it with other borrowings as in *Sinfonia*, nor scramble it *à la* Oswald. Yet his one change creates a new experience of the original that is just as striking as the above transformations. The work that *24 Hour Psycho* has the most in common with is "DAB." Both draw upon originals that are themselves reproductions and change the source by manipulating the reproduction medium. Working from within, Gordon changes the speed, whereas

Oswald uses recording technology to undo the glue holding together the recorded parts in "Bad." In both works, the medium has been used to transform itself.

These large-scale borrowings have affinities with quotation. No matter how big, they, like a brief quotation, stand out as foreign elements placed within new surroundings. Moreover, composers often cut them off and/or mix them with foreign elements. *24 Hour Psycho* shuns such treatment. The work is the original in and by itself, running uninterrupted and neither surrounded nor infiltrated by outside materials. Nonetheless, Gordon still evokes quotation. Most viewers will only ever take in small excerpts from the original, as the small – say two to three minutes of Hitchcock – now veers to the long. Yet the long still comes across as a small part of a whole, the Hitchcock original. That relationship encourages us to make the comparison between the transformed excerpt and the original which is crucial to quotation. Here the halting scene relates not only to the corresponding moment in the original (if we can remember these usually passing moments) but also to the overall flow of the film itself. By forcing us to experience the film in small, altered, and seemingly extracted bits, Gordon pulls off a beguiling sleight of hand. He has the film quote itself. When borrowing is taken to such extremes, it turns in on itself, as the borrowed becomes the borrower.

Like many borrowing works, *24 Hour Psycho* also plays an intriguing game with the relationship between past, present, and future. According to Gordon, "the viewer is catapulted back into the past by his recollection of the original and at the same time he is drawn into the future by his expectation of an already familiar narrative... A slowly changing present forces itself in between."[1] That present proves viscous. It resists flow. The simplest movements unfurl statically. Facial expressions never settle, always staggered by the slow movement between frames. Stuck in this present, we, as Gordon points out, look back to the original we saw in the past and toward the future of the narrative that is being enacted in front of us. By separating the individual scene from the film through "quotation" and transformation, Gordon creates dimensions of time that either do not exist or have a different form in the original. *Psycho* has no past, in the sense that it does not look back to an earlier version of itself, but, in Gordon's transformation, it takes on a past, one as distant as 1960. Befitting a suspense film, Hitchcock's film has a narrative that drives us to some future point of resolution. Now, however, our sense of expectation has been so warped that we do not so much await the

---

[1] Quoted in Russell Ferguson, "Trust me," in Ferguson, *Douglas Gordon* (Cambridge, MA and London: MIT Press, 2001), 16.

climax of the film as the resolution of minutiae that occurs a few frames later. The future has been foreshortened.

Gordon's work may evoke facets of quotation but it is not a quotation. It belongs to a borrowing practice – the borrowing of whole or near-whole works – that is related to quotation but removed from it. The extreme length and simplicity of the transformation, in turn, separate *24 Hour Psycho* from that latter practice. Twice displaced, the work lies at the outer limits of quotation, and that point is where this study will end. To be more specific, we find ourselves far away from the conventional notion of quotation as a short excerpt cited and altered in a new setting. The last few chapters, particularly the discussions of Berio, Oswald, "culture jammers," and Bernhard, have ventured into that territory. However, none of those works, including *24 Hour Psycho*, has completely cut us off from quotation, for elements of that gesture still sound and appear in that distant realm.

The journey to the far reaches of quotation tracks one made during the course of the twentieth century. At the beginning of the century, quotation – of the short excerpt – was used more and more by composers. In particular, it served as a way of connecting to distant pasts and cultural realms. Those links were important, as modernist music had developed a broader chronological and cultural purview than that found in previous periods. The directness and specificity of quotation provided an effective means of making that connection. Ives, for instance, drew upon a variety of tunes to look back at nineteenth-century America, a sightline rare in American music of the time, which, like many growing traditions, was more aware of where it was going than where it had been. In *The Rite of Spring*, Stravinsky used quotation to evoke "primitive" Russia, a period that seemed not only chronologically but also culturally remote, or exotic, for most listeners and ballet-goers.[2]

By the end of the century, the specificity and directness of quotation had become less attractive to many musicians. The gesture, it should be emphasized, could still be used to point outside a work and did so in captivating ways. In his opera *Writing to Vermeer* (1999), Louis Andriessen colors the canvas of seventeenth-century Holland with fragments of Sweelinck. Jazz composer Jon Jang communes with Ellington about the struggle for civil freedoms in his *Tiananmen!* Suite (1993), which mingles phrases from "Come Sunday" with a Chinese folk song. These examples aside, borrowing in the late twentieth century became characterized by an increasing breadth. Bits of pre-existent works gave way to entire

---

[2] Stravinsky's neoclassical works offer a striking counterexample. In these pieces, the composer rarely quotes. Those works usually either recompose or arrange whole pieces (*Pulcinella*) or allude to past idioms (Octet and *Oedipus Rex*). Why Stravinsky would work with either whole blocks or stylistic traces and not actual fragments is an interesting question that could be pursued elsewhere.

or nearly entire pieces. Electronic composers reached out to the dimensions of sound and timbre. Oswald and Bernhard borrowed not so much melodies as people. Finally, the pinpoint references of quotation dilated to broad allusion, in many works so broad as to be open-ended. These works draw upon styles, sounds, or images to evoke an original that seems familiar but that does not exist. John Zorn's *Spillane* (1986), for instance, quick cuts between brief episodes in different, clearly marked styles to suggest the narrative of a detective film. Keeping with imaginary movies, Cindy Sherman's celebrated *Untitled Film Stills* series (begun in 1977) stages poses and looks that appear at first glance to come out of a Hollywood film. Closer scrutiny, though, reveals how slightly askew her staging is, making us see these familiar scenes in ways that comment on the representation of women in mainstream cinema.

Over the course of the century, the modes and scope of quotation may have changed but one thing remained the same: its role as a cultural agent. No matter the size or specificity of the borrowing, the gesture still played that role. From Ives's molding of Victorian childhood discourses to the Tape-beatles' "jamming" of the mass media, quotation remained culturally engaged. As the case studies presented here make clear, that engagement took many different forms. Although quotation continued to act as a cultural agent throughout the century the methods and focus of that role changed.

Just as the range of borrowing has broadened so has the cultural focus. The works of Bernhard and the "culture jammers" exemplify that change. Both express themselves and approach the world around them through borrowing. For them, it has become a worldview. Bernhard creates her own world through a string of cover songs. Borrowing is the foundation of her artistic self. She seemingly cannot refrain from it, for to do so would be to fall into muteness. The "jammers" approach quotation as a means of defining and "empowering" themselves. It is an act of resistance that must be constantly deployed to confront the mass media.

It is not surprising that both Bernhard and the "jammers" deal with elements taken from the media – popular songs, celebrity images, commercials, etc. That entity surrounds us, becoming our world in a way. It demands a borrowing strategy with breadth, one that can deal with the infinite variety of materials afloat in the media. That breadth also extends to the creative and cultural outlook of the artist. Once having engaged the media, most artists stay involved, as the media constantly offer something to respond to and transform. So involved can they become that borrowing forms the basis of their artistic self, their political *raison d'être*. Bernhard, for instance, has continually feasted upon popular culture elements in her subsequent performances, and the "jammers," needless to say, have dug themselves deep into the cultural trenches. For them and other artists, borrowing could be an activity that could go on and on, even lasting twenty-four hours a day.

That point has been reached. Gordon's work spans a day. It takes a Hollywood picture, the images of which (the shower scene, the foreboding house) have appeared non-stop in popular culture since the 1960s, and has the film go seemingly non-stop, making us see those images in new ways. Having watched *24 Hour Psycho* for forty-five or so minutes, I was left pondering what will happen to borrowing at the break of that "psycho" day. In other words, what's next?

APPENDIX 1. QUOTATIONS IN *RECITAL I (FOR CATHY)*

Track	Timing	Quotation
1	0:00	Monteverdi, *Lettere amorose*
2	0:00	Monteverdi, *Lamento della Ninfa*
4	1:02	Monteverdi, *Lettere amorose*
	1:25	Bach, "Ich nehme mein Leiden mit Freuden auf mich" from *Die Elenden sollen Essen* (BWV 75)
	1:37	Ibid.
	1:47	Liturgia Armena (as identified in score)
	2:03	Bach, "Ich nehme mein Leiden mit Freuden auf mich"
	2:42	Ravel, *Chanson épique* from *Don Quichotte à Dulcinée*
	2:57	Purcell, " Ye Gentle Spirits of the Air" from *The Fairy Queen*
	3:44	"Ich bin von Kopf bis Fuss auf Liebe eingestelt" (performed by Marlene Dietrich)
	4:22	Falla, "Polo" from *Siete canciones populares españolas*
	4:59	Poulenc, "Hôtel" from *Banalités*
	5:34	Wagner, "Träume" from *Wesendonck Lieder*
	5:49	Charpentier, "Quelle belle vie" from *Louise*
	6:10	Wolf, "Das verlassene Mägdlein"
	6:45	Milhaud, "La séparation" from *Chants populaires hébraïques*
	6:57	Purcell, "When I am Laid in Earth" from *Dido and Aeneas*
	7:22	Stravinsky, "At Home" from *Cat Cradle Songs*
	7:49	Massenet, "Adieu, notre petite table" from *Manon*
	8:28	Ernesto Berio, "Pioggerellina"
	8:48	Luciano Berio, *Epifanie*
5	0:00	Luciano Berio, "Avendo gran desio"
6	0:20	Bernstein, Lamentation from *Jeremiah*
	0:30	Schoenberg, "Den Wein, den man mit Augen trinkt" from *Pierrot lunaire*
	0:41	Thomas, Polonaise ("Je suis Titania") from *Mignon*
	0:46	Bizet, Recitative ("Je ne te parle pas") after *Seguidilla* from *Carmen*
	1:07	Unidentified
	1:24	Unidentified
	1:28	Ravel, "Placet futile" from *Trois poèmes de Stéphane Mallarmé*
	1:48	Schubert, "Der Tod und das Mädchen"

	2:01	Mussorgsky, *Song of the Flea*
	2:21	Paisiello, Unidentified
	2:57	Verdi, "Cortigiani, vil razza dannata" from *Rigoletto*
8	0:21	Mahler, "Oft denk ich, sie sind nur ausgegangen" from *Kindertotenlieder*
	0:47	Hahn, "L'heure exquise"
	1:21	Delibes, "Bell Song" from *Lakmé*
	1:29	Ibid.
	1:35	Rossini, "Non più mesta" from *La Cenerentola*
	1:44	Ibid.
	2:18	Donizetti, "Alfin son tua" from *Lucia di Lammermoor*
	2:40	Bizet, Card Scene from *Carmen*
	2:55	Meyerbeer, "Ombre légère qui suis mes pas" from *Dinorah*
	3:04	Donizetti, "O gioia che si sente" from *Lucia di Lammermoor*
	3:31	Schubert, "Der Jüngling an der Quelle"
	4:14	Prokofiev, "Fields of the Dead" from *Alexander Nevsky*
	5:03	Meyerbeer, "Ombre légère qui suis mes pas" from *Dinorah*
9	0:00	Luciano Berio, *Lied* (Libera Nos)

Timings taken from the recording by Cathy Berberian – BMG 09026 62540-2

APPENDIX 2: QUOTATIONS IN ROCHBERG'S *MUSIC FOR THE MAGIC THEATER*

FIRST MOVEMENT

fig. 1   Mahler, Symphony no. 9, mvt. 4, m. 13
2   Mahler, Symphony no. 9, mvt. 4, m. 14
4   Varèse, *Déserts*, m. 242
5   Mahler, Symphony no. 9, mvt. 1, m. 242*
6   Mahler, Symphony no. 9, mvt. 1, m. 3
7   Mahler, Symphony no. 9, mvt. 1, m. 4
12   Mozart, Divertimento no. 15, mvt. 1, mm. 2–3
13   Mozart, Divertimento no. 15, mvt. 1, mm. 9–23
20   Mozart, Divertimento no. 15, mvt. 1, mm. 60–66
23   Mahler, Symphony no. 9, mvt. 1, mm. 381–91
27   Mahler, Symphony no. 9, mvt. 4, m. 14

SECOND MOVEMENT

34   Near complete statement of mvt. 4 from Mozart,
                 Divertimento no. 15
51   Trumpet solo suggesting Miles Davis
52   Webern, Concerto for Nine Instruments, mm. 1–3
54   Stockhausen, *Zeitmasse*, m. 159 (flute part)
55   Stockhausen, *Zeitmasse*, m. 155 (bassoon part)
57   Mozart, Divertimento no. 15, mvt. 6, mm. 11–18

THIRD MOVEMENT

65   Rochberg, String Quartet no. 2, bottom of p. 5
66   Rochberg, String Quartet no. 2, top of p. 7
79   Beethoven, String Quartet no. 13, mvt. 5, mm. 40–45
89   Mozart, Divertimento no. 15, mvt. 4, mm. 50–51

* The next three sections (figs. 5–7) introduce motives from Mahler's Ninth Symphony that reappear throughout the work. Only the first appearance of each motive has been noted here.

SELECT BIBLIOGRAPHY

Adorno, Theodor W. *Philosophy of Modern Music.* Trans. Anne G. Mitchell and Wesley V. Blomster. New York: Seabury Press, 1973

Altmann, Peter. *Sinfonia von Luciano Berio: eine analytische Studie.* Vienna: Universal Edition, 1977

Bal, Mieke. *Quoting Caravaggio: Contemporary Art, Preposterous History.* Chicago and London: University of Chicago Press, 1999

Ballantine, Charles. *Music and its Social Meanings.* New York: Garden and Breach Science Publication, 1984

Berio, Luciano. "Meditation on a twelve-tone horse." *Christian Science Monitor,* 15 July 1968

Bicknell, Jeanette. "The problem of reference in musical quotation: a phenomenological approach." *The Journal of Aesthetics and Art Criticism* 59 (2001), 185–91

Breuer, Josef, and Sigmund Freud. *Studies on Hysteria.* Trans. and ed. James Strachey. The Standard Edition of the Complete Psychological Works of Sigmund Freud, vol. 2. London: Hogarth Press, 1955

Buchanan, Herbert H. "A key to Schoenberg's *Erwartung* (Op. 17)." *Journal of the American Musicological Society* 20 (1967), 434–49

Burkholder, J. Peter. "The uses of existing music: musical borrowing as a field." *Music Library Association Notes* 50 (1994), 851–70

All Made of Tunes: Charles Ives and the Uses of Musical Borrowing. New Haven and London: Yale University Press, 1995

Cartwright, Katharine. "Quotation and reference in jazz performance: Ella Fitzgerald's 'St. Louis Blues,' 1957–59." Ph.D. diss., City University of New York, 1998

Cleto, Fabio, ed. *Camp: Queer Aesthetics and the Performing Subject – a Reader.* Edinburgh: Edinburgh University Press, 1999

Cott, Jonathan. *Stockhausen: Conversations with the Composer.* New York: Simon and Schuster, 1973

Cutler, Chris. "Plunderphonia." *Musicworks* 60 (1994), 6–19

Dahlhaus, Carl. *Schoenberg and the New Music.* Trans. Derrick Puffett and Alfred Clayton. Cambridge: Cambridge University Press, 1987

Davies, Hugh. "A history of sampling." *Organized Sound* 1 (1996), 3–11

Dixon, Joy DeVee. *George Rochberg: a Bio-Bibliographic Guide to his Life and Works.* Stuyvesant, NY: Pendragon, 1992

Eco, Umberto. *Postscript to* The Name of the Rose. Trans. William Weaver. New York: Harcourt Brace Jovanovich, 1984

Travels in Hyperreality. Trans. William Weaver. New York: Harvest Books, 1986

Feder, Stuart. *Charles Ives "My Father's Song": a Psychoanalytical Biography*. New Haven: Yale University Press, 1992

Floyd, Samuel A., Jr. "Ring shout: literary studies, historical studies, and black music inquiry." *Black Music Research Journal* 11 (1991), 265–87

Foster, Hal, ed. *The Anti-Aesthetic*. Seattle: Bay Press, 1983

Foucault, Michel. *Madness and Civilization: a History of Insanity in the Age of Reason*. Trans. Richard Howard. New York: Vintage Books, 1988

Gabbard, Krin. "The quoter and his culture." In *Jazz in Mind: Essays on the History and Meanings of Jazz*, ed. Reginald T. Buckner and Steven Weitand, 92–111. Detroit: Wayne State University Press, 1991

Gates, Henry Louis, Jr. *The Signifying Monkey: a Theory of African-American Literary Criticism*. New York: Oxford University Press, 1988

Gervereau, Laurent. "Symbolic collapse: utopia challenged by its representations." In *Utopia: the Search for the Ideal Society in the Western World*, ed. Roland Schaer, Gregory Claeys, and Lyman Tower Sargent, 357–67. New York and Oxford: New York Public Library and Oxford University Press, 2000

Goodwin, Andrew. "Sample and hold: pop music in the digital age of reproduction." *Critical Quarterly* 30 (1988), 34–49

Gregory, Elizabeth. *Quotation and Modern American Poetry*. Houston: Rice University Press, 1996

Harrison, Lou. "On quotation." *Modern Music* 23 (1946), 166–69

Hartwell, Keith. "Postmodernism and art music." In *The Last Post: Music after Modernism*, ed. Simon Miller, 27–51. Manchester and New York: Manchester University Press, 1993

Harvey, Jonathan. *The Music of Stockhausen*. London: Faber & Faber, 1975

Hepokoski, James. "Temps perdu." *Musical Times* 135 (1994), 746–51

Hicks, Michael. "Text, music, and meaning in the third movement of Luciano Berio's *Sinfonia*." *Perspectives of New Music* 20 (1981–82), 199–224

"The new quotation: its origins and functions." DMA diss., University of Illinois, 1984

Holm-Hudson, Kevin. "Quotation and context: sampling and John Oswald's plunderphonics." *Leonardo Music Journal* 7 (1997), 17–25

Hopkins, Nicholas F. *Hymnen: Tractatus Musica Unita*. Feedback Papers 37. Cologne: Feedback Studio Verlag, 1991

Hurston, Zora Neale. "Spirituals and neo-spirituals." In *Negro: an Anthology*, ed. Nancy Cunard, 223–25. New York, 1934; abridged rpr. edn, New York: Frederick Ungar, 1970

Huyssen, Andreas. *After the Great Divide: Modernism, Mass Culture, Postmodernism*. Bloomington: Indiana University Press, 1986

Twilight Memories: Marking Time in a Culture of Amnesia. New York and London: Routledge, 1995

Igma, Norm. "Taking sampling 50 times beyond the expected: an interview with John Oswald." *Musicworks* 48 (1991), 16–21

Jameson, Fredric. *Postmodernism, or, The Cultural Logic of Late Capitalism*. Durham, NC: Duke University Press, 1991

Jankélévitch, Vladimir. *L'irréversible et la nostalgie*. Paris: Flammarion, 1974
Jencks, Charles. *What is Postmodernism?* New York and London: St. Martin's Press, 1986
Koestenbaum, Wayne. *Double Talk: the Erotics of Male Literary Collaboration*. New York and London: Routledge, 1989
  The Queen's Throat: Opera, Homosexuality, and the Mystery of Desire. New York: Poseidon Press, 1993
Kühn, Clemens. *Das Zitat in der Musik der Gegenwart – mit Ausblicken auf bildende Kunst und Literatur*. Hamburg: Verlag der Musikalienhandl, 1972
Lasn, Kalle. *Culture Jam: the Uncooling of America*™. New York: Eagle Brook, 1999
Lissa, Zofia. "Historical awareness of music and its role in present-day musical culture." *International Review of the Aesthetics and Sociology of Music* 4 (1973), 17–32
Lowenthal, David. *The Past is a Foreign Country*. Cambridge: Cambridge University Press, 1985
Maconie, Robin. *The Works of Karlheinz Stockhausen*. London: Oxford University Press, 1976
McClary, Susan. *Feminine Endings: Music, Gender, and Sexuality*. Minneapolis: University of Minnesota Press, 1991
McEvilley, Thomas. *The Exile's Return: toward a Redefinition of Painting in the Post-Modern Era*. Cambridge: Cambridge University Press, 1993
Monson, Ingrid. "Doubleness and jazz improvisation: irony, parody, and ethnomusicology." *Critical Inquiry* 20 (1994), 283–313
Negativland. www.negativland.com. Accessed 8 April 2002
Niedzviecki, Hal. *We Want Some Too: Underground Desire and the Reinvention of Mass Culture*. Toronto: Penguin, 2000
Osmond-Smith, David. *Playing on Words: a Guide to Luciano Berio's 'Sinfonia.'* London: Royal Musical Association, 1985
  Berio. Oxford and New York: Oxford University Press, 1991
Oswald, John. "Plunderphonics or, Audio piracy as a compositional prerogative." *Musicworks* 34 (1986), 5–8
  "Neither a borrower nor a sampler prosecute." *Keyboard* 14 (March 1988), 12–13
  "Bad relations: plunderography, pop, and weird in DAB." *Musicworks* 47 (1990), 9–10
Passler, Jann. "Postmodernism, narrativity, and the art of memory." *Contemporary Music Review* 7 (1993), 3–32
Pestalozza, Luigi. "Stockhausen und der musikalische Autoritarismus." *Schweizerische Musikzeitung* 116 (1976), 266–73
Pousseur, Henri. "Composition and utopia." *Interface* 12 (1983), 75–83
Rabinowitz, Peter J. "Fictional music: toward a theory of listening." In *Theories of Reading, Looking, and Listening*. Lewisburg, PA: Bucknell University Press, 1981
Robinson, Lisa. "Mahler and postmodern intertextuality." Ph.D. diss., Yale University, 1994
Rochberg, George. *The Aesthetics of Survival: a Composer's View of Twentieth-Century Music*. Ed. William Bolcom. Ann Arbor: University of Michigan Press, 1984

Schuller, Gunther. *Early Jazz: its Roots and Musical Development.* New York: Oxford University Press, 1968

Sonntag, Brunhilde. *Untersuchungen zur Collagetechnik in der Musik des 20. Jahrhunderts.* Regensburg: Bosse, 1977

Stewart, Susan. *On Longing: Narratives of the Miniature, the Gigantic, the Souvenir, the Collection.* Durham, NC, and London: Duke University Press, 1993

Stockhausen, Karlheinz. "Hymnen – Nationalhymnen (zur elektronischen Musik 1967)." In *Karlheinz Stockhausen*, ed. Rudolf Frisius, 273–80. Mainz: Schott, 1996

Straus, Joseph. *Remaking the Past: Musical Modernism and the Influence of the Tonal Tradition.* Cambridge, MA: Harvard University Press, 1990

Tape-beatles. pwp.detritus.net/. Accessed 8 April 2002

Théberge, Paul. "Random access: music, technology, postmodernism." In *The Last Post: Music after Modernism*, ed. Simon Miller, 150–82

Tomlinson, Gary. "Cultural dialogics of jazz: a white historian signifies." *Black Music Research Journal* 11 (1991), 229–64

Tucker, Mark. *Ellington: the Early Years.* Urbana: University of Illinois Press, 1991
(ed.) *The Duke Ellington Reader.* New York: Oxford University Press, 1993

Viens, Lisa. "Stratégies citationelles dans *Die Soldaten* de Bernd Alois Zimmermann." *Canadian University Music Review* 17 (1996), 1–19

Walser, Robert. "Out of notes: signification, interpretation, and the problem of Miles Davis." *Musical Quarterly* 77 (1993), 343–65

Watkins, Glenn. *Pyramids at the Louvre: Music, Culture, and Collage from Stravinsky to the Postmodernists.* Cambridge, MA: Harvard University Press, 1994

Welten, Ruud. "'I'm not ill, I'm nervous' – madness in the music of Sir Peter Maxwell Davies." *Tempo* 196 (April 1996), 21–24

Williams, Alan E. "Madness in the music theater works of Peter Maxwell Davies." *Perspectives of New Music* 38 (2000), 77–100

Wollen, Peter. "Ways of thinking about music video (and post-modernism)." *Critical Quarterly* 28 (1986), 167–70

Youens, Susan. "Memory, identity, and the uses of the past: Schubert and Luciano Berio's *Recital I (for Cathy)*." In *Franz Schubert – Der Fortschrittliche?*, ed. Erich Wolfgang Partsch, 231–47. Tutzing: Hans Schneider, 1989

INDEX